SHIFTING
SENTIMENT

SHIFTING SENTIMENT

PRESS OPINION IN IRELAND'S REVOLUTIONARY DECADE 1914–23

DERMOT MELEADY

EASTWOOD BOOKS

First published 2023 by Eastwood Books
Dublin, Ireland
www.eastwoodbooks.com
www.wordwellbooks.com

1

Eastwood Books is an imprint of the Wordwell Group.

The Wordwell Group is a member of Publishing Ireland,
the Irish Publishers' Association.

Eastwood Books
The Wordwell Group
Unit 9, 78 Furze Road
Sandyford
Dublin, Ireland

ISBN: 978-1-913934-34-7 (Paperback)
ISBN: 978-1-913934-53-8 (ebook)

British Library Cataloguing in Publication Data.
A catalogue record for this book is available from the National Library of
Ireland and the British Library.

Typesetting and design by the Wordwell Group
Copyediting by John Ryan
Printed in Ireland by Sprint Print, Dublin

ABBREVIATIONS

DMP	Dublin Metropolitan Police
GPO	General Post Office
IRA	Irish Republican Army
IRB	Irish Republican Brotherhood
RIC	Royal Irish Constabulary
RM	Resident Magistrate
UIL	United Irish League
UUC	Ulster Unionist Council
UVF	Ulster Volunteer Force
TD	Member of the Dáil

For my grandchildren (in descending order of age)
— Maila, Sahra, Esme, Jonah, Louisa and Layna

CONTENTS

ACKNOWLEDGMENTS

I owe a debt of gratitude to Michael Wheatley, author of *Nationalism and the Irish Party: Provincial Ireland 1910-1916* (Oxford, 2005) for his encouragement of this project, for much helpful advice on the extension of the original scope of the study and for generously sharing his detailed knowledge of Irish provincial newspapers, particularly those of the midlands and north-west.

The study benefited from conversations with Dr. Joseph Quinn, great-grandson of J.P. Farrell, founder and long-time editor of the *Longford Leader*, and with Felix Larkin, author of a study of the *Freeman's Journal* referenced in this book.

My thanks are also due to the directors, librarians and keepers of the National Library of Ireland for their curation of the large collection of microfilm copies of the newspapers studied here and their patient efforts in locating them as required.

LIST OF CHARTS
AND TABLES

Preface

CHRONOLOGY OF THE HOME RULE CAMPAIGN 1870–1914

1867   Failure of Fenian insurrection.

1868   Disestablishment of Church of Ireland by Gladstone's government.

1870   Foundation of Home Government Association by Isaac Butt.
            Land Act legislating for three Fs – fair rent, freedom of sale and fixity of tenure – enacted by Gladstone's government.

1871–72   Home Rule candidates win eight seats in Irish by-elections.

1874   Fifty-nine pro-Home Rule MPs elected in UK general election.

1879   Isaac Butt dies.

1880   Parnell is elected leader of Irish Parliamentary Party.

1881 The Great Land Act of Gladstone's government introduces land `periodic rent reviews and joint ownership of holdings.

1882 Murder of the Chief Secretary, Lord Cavendish, and the Under Secretary, Thomas Burke, in the Phoenix Park by the Invincibles.

1885 Ashbourne Land Purchase Act. Irish Party briefly allies with Tories.

1886 Gladstone introduces First Home Rule Bill. The bill is lost as the Liberal Party splits on the issue. Alliance of Tories and Liberal Unionists in power.

1887–89 Agrarian 'Plan of Campaign' is waged by members of Irish Party.

1890 O'Shea divorce case splits Irish Party; Parnell deposed as leader.

1891 Parnell dies; his followers, led by John Redmond, now a minority of the Irish representation at Westminster. The anti-Parnellite majority is led, first by Justin MacCarthy, then by John Dillon.

1892 General election brings Gladstonian Liberals back to power.

1893 Gladstone introduces Second Home Rule Bill. The bill passes the House of Commons but is vetoed by the House of Lords.

1895 General election restores Tories to power, beginning ten years of Conservative rule. The Parnell split continues in Ireland.

1900   Irish Party is reunited under John Redmond as leader with John Dillon as deputy leader.

1903   Wyndham Land Purchase Act is passed. Within twelve years it will revolutionise land ownership, allowing the transfer of over 60 per cent of agricultural land from landlords to tenants

1906   Liberal Party wins landslide in UK general election. Irish Home Rule is contained in its programme. Labourers Act passed.

1908   National University of Ireland is established by law. Redmond hails it as 'the first instalment of Home Rule'.

1909   The House of Lords vetoes the Liberals' radical Budget. Prime Minister Asquith announces intention of limiting or abolishing the veto. Redmond promises Irish support on condition that he place Home Rule at the top of his programme.

1911   Parliament Act, limiting the House of Lords power of veto, is passed. National Insurance Act also becomes law.

1912   Third Home Rule Bill is introduced. Irish Unionist Party led by Sir Edward Carson, in alliance with British Conservatives and Unionists, announces its opposition.

1913   Home Rule Bill passes its first and second circuits through the House of Commons. Ulster Volunteer Force founded and begins to arm. Irish National Volunteers founded. Redmond declares implacable opposition to partition.

1914   Asquith, with Redmond's reluctant acquiescence, proposes temporary partition scheme based on county plebiscites. Unionists reject it.

Ulster unionist gun running at Larne and other northern ports; membership of Irish National Volunteers mushrooms. Home Rule Bill passes third circuit in May despite arrangements for unionist Ulster not being settled. Buckingham Palace Conference fails to reach agreement.

Outbreak of Great War in August. Redmond promises Irish support for British war effort and later, after Home Rule Act is placed on the Statute Book, calls on Irishmen to form an 'Irish brigade' within the British army to fight for the Allies; recruiting campaign is launched.

Home Rule Act operation is suspended for minimum of twelve months and no later than the end of the war. Asquith declares there can be no coercion of Ulster into all-Ireland Home Rule and promises an Amending Act to make arrangements for unionist Ulster.

INTRODUCTION

This book is a study of the evolving editorial commentary of Irish provincial newspapers on the important political events in Ireland between the Home Rule crisis of 1914 and the Civil War of 1922–23. It is assumed throughout that this diverse commentary reflected equally diverse strands of Irish nationalist public opinion and, to a lesser extent, helped to shape them.

The importance of this subject arises from the role played by public opinion in the changes that revolutionised Irish politics in the short space of four years after 1914. Despite the Home Rule Act's having become law in that year, the Home Rule project later collapsed, bringing with it the demise of the Irish Parliamentary Party that had brought it to fruition and the electoral success of the separatist Sinn Féin movement in 1918. The thirty-month violent struggle that followed ended in a new Anglo-Irish Treaty and the establishment of the quasi-independent Irish Free State.

For a century, a single narrative has dominated the explanation of this radical transformation of nationalist public opinion. This is that the executions of the leaders of the Dublin insurrection of Easter week 1916 by the British authorities caused what has been called 'a revulsion of feeling' in the nationalist community that rapidly and severely damaged its support for the constitutional approach hitherto followed by its political leadership and paved the way for a retrospective sympathy with the rebellion and a mass conversion to the radical separatist politics of those who had staged it. The present study will test the strength of this narrative as an explanatory model. On the evidence presented, it will conclude that the transformation of nationalist feeling owed less to the executions than to factors latent in the pre-rebellion political situation, specifically to the unresolved contradiction between the all-Ireland terms of the Home Rule Act, placed on the Statute Book in 1914, and the demand of the Ulster unionist community to be excluded from those terms.

The assessment of public opinion in the age before radio, television and modern polling is an inexact science. Diaries and letters can offer glimpses into movements of popular sentiment among masses of people as they reacted to political events of their day. However, their value is limited by their often fragmentary and episodic nature and by the subjectivity of the writer. Although political speeches were commonly reported, they did not necessarily accurately reflect public opinion. The late-nineteenth century expansion of the franchise and the advent of the era of mass democracy provide better source material in the form of records of meetings of elected bodies that may be more sensitive indicators of public opinion than campaign rhetoric.

In Ireland, the development of mass literacy in English in the second half of the nineteenth century gave a new articulacy to popular sentiment, generating a mass following for nationalist movements. The proliferation of democratically elected bodies of local government brought about by the Local Government (Ireland) Act of 1898 allowed this sentiment to be expressed with greater force and focus than ever before, while the simultaneous burgeoning of the provincial press provided a sensitive barometer of its intensity. The study of editorial content in the provincial press of early twentieth-century Ireland is therefore one of the most useful means of access to the public opinion of the era.

Central to any study of newspapers as a barometer of public opinion is the question of whether editorial commentary leads such opinion or reflects it. Few newspaper editors regarded themselves as campaigners intent on bringing about major changes in popular sentiment. Most were not shaped in the mould of William Martin Murphy, the owner of the

Irish Daily Independent after 1900 (the *Irish Independent* from 1905) and their sister papers, dealt with here in Chapter 1. Murphy was consciously influenced by the achievement of the Harmsworth brothers in turning the British *Daily Mail* into a popular mass medium capable of exerting significant influence on public opinion and thus on the government of the day. Although Murphy's *Independent*, with its crusading editorial content, well-conceived business model and high circulation, was able to exert important influence over Irish opinion and a sizeable section of the provincial press, its authority was not limitless, and it is testimony to the independence of mind of many provincial editors that they could resist its persuasive powers.

More common were the papers, small in number, owned and run by members of political parties or movements, such as the *Westmeath Examiner* of J.P. Hayden and the *Longford Leader* of J.P. Farrell, both elected members of John Redmond's Irish Parliamentary Party (Farrell a more feisty and fractious follower of the Party than Hayden), or the *Mayo News* of P.J. Doris, a long-time Fenian and member of the Irish Republican Brotherhood. The fact that the Redmondite papers could outlive the Irish Party after 1918 suggests that they continued to represent a significant minority body of opinion or that their editorial commentary was tolerated to some extent by a readership that had turned against the message of the Party. However, in the case of the majority of provincial newspapers, the evidence indicates that they were anxious not to alienate their readerships and were prepared to adjust their editorial lines to majority sentiment in line with the often dramatic developments in political events. This was the case even when an abrupt *volte face* risked embarrassing self-contradictions, as with the shift in Thomas Chapman's *Westmeath Independent* from its 'absolute and unquestioned confidence' in Redmond's leadership in 1914 to its 'thrill of pride' at the Sinn Féin victory in the Roscommon by-election of early 1917, or the *Meath Chronicle's* vigorous republican castigation of dominion Home Rule in 1920 to be followed by its embrace of essentially the same settlement in the Treaty a little over a year later.

Previous studies of provincial press opinion on Irish political events have been limited in scope, both temporally and geographically. Owen Dudley Edwards' and Fergus Pyle's *1916: The Easter Rising* (London, 1968) included a survey of the reaction of three national and two provincial newspapers to the 1916 rebellion. J.J. Lee's *Ireland 1912–1985: Politics and Society* (Cambridge, 1989) sought to build upon this foundation by enlarging the sample to eleven newspapers. Michael Wheatley's *Nationalism and the Irish Party: Provincial Ireland 1910–1916* (Oxford, 2005) based much of its analysis of changing nationalist opinion on a study of twelve local newspapers in five north-western counties.

This book is the first to extend the scope of these earlier works, both in the size and geographical spread of the sample of papers studied and in the chronological length of the period covered. Beginning as a study of a relatively small number of provincial newspapers on the 1916 rebellion and the immediate aftermath, it was first enlarged to cover papers from all parts of nationalist Ireland. When it became clear that the responses of these papers could not be well understood without an examination of their stances in the pre-rebellion period, the study was then extended back in time to 1914, the closing stages of the Home Rule campaign and the onset of the Great War. Finally, the divisions emerging in the provincial press after the rebellion were followed forward in time to the ascendancy of Sinn Fein and the events terminating in the civil war.

A sample of forty-two provincial newspapers was chosen to represent a cross-section of editorial opinion in nationalist Ireland for the nine-year period from March 1914, when the Third Home Rule Bill entered its final circuit in the House of Commons, to May 1923 and the defeat of the republican forces in the Civil War. The sample consisted of two dailies, the *Cork Examiner* and the Belfast *Irish News,* together with forty weeklies or bi-weeklies: twelve from Leinster, fifteen from Munster, nine from Connacht and four from nationalist Ulster. The papers were chosen for their combination of circulation and geographical spread: most of them circulated not only in the counties of their titles but in the surrounding counties. Efforts were made to avoid distortion arising from duplication of editorial content in different newspapers under common ownership. Thus, for example, the *Roscommon Messenger*, a 'clone' of the *Westmeath Examiner* under the common ownership of J.P. Hayden, and the Midland Reporter, a clone of Jasper Tully's *Roscommon Herald*, were both excluded from the sample. Likewise omitted was the *Wicklow People*, a sister paper and partial duplicate of the *Wexford People* (see Table 1).

Apart from providing their readers with a miscellany of local news, many of these newspapers did consistent and sterling service to local democracy by reporting regularly on meetings of the county councils, rural and urban councils and boards of guardians in the areas of their circulation, which often covered not merely their own counties but parts of up to three or four neighbouring ones and their towns. Some were highly politicised and kept up a weekly criticism of British governments and an advocacy in the cause of Home Rule or, later, of independence. A significant number, however, exhibited a slumbering political consciousness that sprang into life only at times of very acute political crisis; for weeks at a time their editorials would concern only matters of local agriculture, trade or other non-political concerns.

Some favoured long-winded and rambling editorials that aped the portentous 'high' style used by the *Freeman's Journal* in the 1880s but appeared old-fashioned by the late years of the Great War; others expressed their views bluntly in one or two brief and simply written paragraphs. A few, like the *Tuam Herald*, repeatedly carried moderately judged editorials in clear and measured prose that would have done justice to any national paper of record.

This study does not attempt to measure unionist opinion at local level; it is concerned solely with the debate within nationalism. A recent study by John Horgan of the reporting of the 1916 rebellion by more than thirty local newspapers, spanning both Ulster communities, goes some way to fill the deficit.[1]

The events covered in this survey include the first partition proposals of early 1914, the outbreak of the Great War, the signing into law of the Home Rule Act, the rebellion of 1916, the decline of the Irish

Parliamentary Party and its demise at the 1918 general election, the escalation of revolutionary violence in 1919–21, the onset of partition with the establishment of the Northern Ireland parliament under the 1920 Government of Ireland Act, the negotiation of the Anglo-Irish Treaty and the outbreak and conduct of the Civil War in 1922–23.

The book will reveal an evolution of public opinion from a condition of near-consensus at the start of the period, through a turbulent phase of several years of disunity and divergence, to a renewed state of near-consensus at its end. However, as the following chapters will show, the causes of this evolution turn out to be much more complex than those envisaged in the dominant narrative.

Table 1. Irish provincial newspapers sampled (N=42)

Leinster (pop. exc. Dublin 684,848)	**Munster** (pop. inc. Cork 1,035,495)
Carlow Nationalist	*Cork Examiner* (daily)
Drogheda Argus	*Cork Free Press*
Dundalk Democrat	*Clare Champion*
Kilkenny People	*Clonmel Nationalist*
Leinster Leader	*The Kerryman*
Longford Leader	*Kerry Sentinel*
Meath Chronicle	*Killarney Echo & S. Kerry Chronicle*
Midland Tribune (Birr)	*Limerick Echo*
King's County Independent	*Limerick Leader*
Westmeath Independent	*Munster Express* (Waterford)
Westmeath Examiner	*Munster News*
Wexford People	*Nenagh Guardian*
	Southern Star
	Tipperary People
	Tipperary Star
	Waterford News
(12)	(16)
Connacht (pop. 610,984)	**Ulster (nationalist)** (c. 400,000)
Ballina Herald	*Anglo-Celt (Cavan)*
Connacht Tribune	*Irish News & Belfast*
Connacht Telegraph	*Morning News* (daily, Belfast)
Galway Observer	*Derry People & Donegal News* (Omagh)
Mayo News	*Derry Journal* (Derry)
Roscommon Herald	*Donegal Vindicator* (Ballyshannon)
Roscommon Journal & Western Reporter	
Sligo Champion	
Tuam Herald	
(9)	(5)

Chapter 1

THE WAR OF THE
NEWSPAPERS: THE DUBLIN
NATIONALIST DAILIES

For most of the decade covered by this book, as for most of the quarter of a century that preceded it, the two leading nationalist daily newspapers published in Dublin were not merely rivals but were locked in mutual antagonism. The quarrel between the *Freeman's Journal* and the *Irish Independent* was of a different nature than the ideological rift that separated both of them from the principal organ of opposition to Home Rule, the unionist daily *The Irish Times*. Both papers supported and campaigned for Irish Home Rule. When the Great War came, both supported the British war effort against the Central Powers, at the start when it was popular in Ireland as at the end when it had become significantly less so. When the Home Rule Act was put on the Statute Book in September 1914, both supported the call from the Irish Parliamentary Party leader, John Redmond, for Irishmen to enlist in the British army.

The *Freeman* was the older of the two, founded in 1763, its front-page logo showing the sun rising incongruously in the north-west over the old houses of parliament in College Green with the banner 'Ireland a Nation' underneath. The enduring feud between the two papers had its origins in the Parnell split of the early 1890s. The *Freeman*, under its proprietor Edmund Dwyer Gray MP, had evolved from opposition to Parnell's leadership of the Irish Parliamentary Party in 1880 to full-blooded backing for the first Home Rule Bill and the Land League and National League agrarian agitations of that decade. Gray died in 1888. In the Party split precipitated in late 1890 by the divorce scandal arising from Parnell's long-running affair with Katherine O'Shea, the paper at first stood by Parnell. However, threatened by falling circulation as a new anti-Parnellite newspaper, the *National Press*,[1] gained popularity and Parnell's support collapsed in Ireland, Gray's widow replaced the pro-Parnell board in September 1891 and the paper immediately declared against the former leader, having merged with the *National Press*. Just before his death the following month, Parnell set in motion a plan to found a new daily newspaper supportive of the political stand he had taken during the split. The first issue of the *Irish Daily Independent* appeared at the end of 1891.

For the remainder of the 1890s, the Irish Party was split between the majority anti-Parnellite faction, whose most prominent members were T.M. Healy, John Dillon and William O'Brien, and the minority Parnellites led by John Redmond. The two factions carried on a war of words against each other from public platforms across Ireland, from their seats at Westminster and from their respective newspapers, and fielded candidates against each other at the general elections of 1892 and 1895. Seats were won by the two groups in a rough ratio of 8:1, though the ratio of votes cast was closer to 4:1. The anti-Parnellite *Freeman* (with its sister papers the *Evening Telegraph* and the *Weekly Freeman*) poured scorn on the policies and characters of Redmond and his fellow-Parnellites while the *Independent*, controlled by Redmond as the chairman of the Independent Newspapers company (which also published the *Evening Herald* and the *Weekly Independent*) returned the invective. The former portrayed the Parnellites as disruptors of the effort to win a new Home Rule Bill in alliance with the British Liberal Party; the latter excoriated the anti-Parnellites for perceived failure to maintain an independent Irish policy at Westminster and for excessively close ties to the Liberals. When this split in the Irish Party was healed in early 1900 with the election of Redmond as leader and Dillon as his deputy, this phase of the newspaper feud came to an end.[2]

However, a second divide had opened up within the anti-Parnellite camp, one that would prove to be bitterer and more lasting than the original split. The later stages of the newspaper feud can only be understood with reference to the complex dynamics of the political and personal relationships between the four protagonists[3] Redmond, Dillon, O'Brien and Healy, with a fifth, the businessman William Martin Murphy, also playing a central role.

The anti-Parnellite leaders were divided from the beginning as to the appropriate way to deal with the Parnellite minority. Healy stood for a policy of political extermination and tried to carry this into effect with a rhetoric that combined forensic dissection of policy argument with vulgar abuse and character assassination. Dillon and O'Brien favoured a more restrained approach that tried to focus on policy and avoid personalities, although the bitterness surrounding the events of Parnell's tragic last year made it difficult to disentangle them. The divergent approaches found expression in a struggle for power on the board of the merged *Freeman-National Press* in 1892. Although Healy at first had a strong editorial influence over the *Freeman*, he failed to have his nominee, Murphy, a kinsman and member of the 'Bantry band' (a group of prominent nationalist politicians who had originated in that part of west Cork), elected to the board. The paper instead came under the management of Thomas Sexton, an Irish Party MP (he would retire from politics in 1896), an acknowledged expert on financial matters and an ally of Dillon. Within a few years more, Murphy had been heavily defeated in a by-election in Kerry and Healy had been marginalised further, being voted off the council of the Party's national organisation and the committee of the Party itself. Healy's defeat was sealed by the election of Dillon as leader of the anti-Parnellites in 1896. Dillon now found himself leading a majority faction that contained a sizeable dissident minority led by Healy. The latter sometimes echoed the criticisms leveled by the Parnellites at, for example, the parliamentary alliance between the anti-Parnellites and the British Liberal Party (the continuation of the relationship first forged between Parnell and prime minister William Gladstone that had brought in the first Home Rule bill in 1886) What Healy's biographer, the historian Frank Callanan, has called 'a settled loathing' came to characterise the relations between the two men and the one permanent feature amid the shifting relationships of the other protagonists.[3]

As Party reunification came nearer, Redmond's relations with Healy were paradoxically warmer than those with Dillon and O'Brien. When it arrived in 1900, it was a merger of three, not two, factions. However, as Redmond settled into the leadership role, he gradually won the allegiance of Dillon and O'Brien. Healy, in contrast, kept up a barrage of attacks on the latter two and soon found himself isolated in spite of Redmond's best efforts to keep the peace between all sides. At the December 1900 convention, Healy was expelled from the reunited Party on a motion of O'Brien's, with Redmond voting against. In line with the warming relations between Redmond on the one hand and Dillon and O'Brien on the other, the *Freeman* gave restrained support to the new Party leader.

In the late 1890s, the *Irish Daily Independent* was suffering a gradual fall in circulation and facing increasing financial distress. With the end of the Parnell split, Redmond looked for a buyer who could restore the paper to health. He approached William Martin Murphy, whose business experience to date included tramways and hotels but not newspapers, and persuaded him to take it in hand. Under the new management, the *Independent* took a line broadly supportive of the reunited Party albeit critical of what it saw as dictatorial tendencies of Dillon and O'Brien, and sympathetic to Healy. By 1905, Murphy had decided to do his utmost to turn it into an organ both popular and influential, emulating what Lord Northcliffe (the Dubliner Alfred Harmsworth) had done in Britain with the *Daily Mail*, and re-launched it as the *Irish Independent* with a modernised printing press, clearer typeface, generous use of photographs and priced at a halfpenny, half the price of the *Freeman*.

In the meantime, a fresh rift had opened within the Party. Redmond and O'Brien worked closely together in convening a land conference in which they met as representatives of tenant farmers with landlord representatives in late 1902. The conference drew up a scheme of Treasury financing to accelerate the purchase of their holdings by tenant farmers. Chief Secretary George Wyndham based his epoch-making Land Purchase Bill of the following year on the conference report and Redmond and O'Brien again co-operated in getting it through parliament. The Land Act, together with a successor Act in 1909, would be instrumental in having ownership of more than 60 per cent of agricultural land transferred to the tenants by 1915. However, a strong body of opposition to the Act emerged within the Party, led by Dillon with the support of the veteran agrarian activist Michael Davitt. This current of opinion received the vigorous backing of the *Freeman*, with Thomas Sexton launching a sustained editorial campaign hostile to the Act. The argument in essence was that the Act, especially its bonus provision to encourage estate sales, was too generous to the landlords and set a purchase price standard far in excess of that embodied in any previous purchase legislation. For several years afterwards, the paper carried daily the text of the 'Limerick Resolution' (passed at a United Irish League meeting in that city in late 1903) asserting that 'Ashbourne prices' (those set by Lord Ashbourne's land purchase Act of 1885, which, according to Redmond, had offered insufficient incentive to landlords to sell) should be the unchanging standard for all land purchase deals.

The method by which the land legislation had been obtained – conference rather than confrontation – encouraged O'Brien and, to a lesser extent Redmond, to see it as a model for the resolution of other Irish social problems and controversies and even, in time, of the differences between unionists and nationalists over Irish self-government. The doctrine of 'conciliation' became a fixed element of O'Brien's and Redmond's thinking. Dillon, for his part, advising tenants to hesitate before entering bargains with landlords, stated that he had no faith in the conciliation policy. Since the Party had voted to approve the terms

of the Act as passed, O'Brien viewed the criticism of it, not as a difference of opinion but as an undermining of Party policy and discipline.
He urged Redmond to face the challenge head on. The more pragmatic
Redmond, however, aware that his support base within the Party was
much smaller than Dillon's, declined to do as O'Brien demanded, reck-
oning that Dillon could not do much in practice to damage the working
of the Act and, above all, dreading a return of the horrors of the 1890s
split. An infuriated O'Brien resigned from the Party in late 1903, joining
Healy in the wilderness.

As Redmond moved to hold the Party together, playing down his
differences with Dillon over the Land Act while making several unsuccessful attempts to persuade O'Brien to rejoin, the *Freeman* became the
Party's loyal mouthpiece. The paper would maintain this role for the
next two decades, through the Party's electoral demise in 1918, and afterwards, in defence of the Party's legacy, until its own demise in 1924.
Responding to nationalist public demand, Redmond made one more
determined effort to bring both Healy and O'Brien back into the Party.
The rifts were patched up in early 1908 but the healing was short-lived.
Healy continued to speak and vote in parliament with cavalier disregard for Party policy and had become alienated once again within nine
months. In O'Brien's case, the peace lasted a little longer, but was broken
in spectacular fashion during a debate on the Land Act at the 'Baton
Convention' of February 1909 in Dublin (so called because the crowded
Mansion House meeting was attended by baton-wielding 'enforcers'
brought from Belfast by Joe Devlin, the dominant figure of the Party in
Ulster, to quell potential disruption by followers of O'Brien). O'Brien's
hurried exit sealed for good the rupture between the Party of Redmond
and Dillon on the one hand, and the mavericks Healy and O'Brien on
the other. Remarkably, and in defiance of all expectations, the latter two,
mortal enemies only a few years previously, had begun a slow process of
rapprochement, brought together now by a shared hatred of Dillon and
contempt for Redmond, whom they viewed as his catspaw.

O'Brien soon founded his own party, the All For Ireland League, and contested the two general elections of 1910, winning seven seats each time to the Irish Party's 74 seats. In terms of parliamentary seats, the divide was not very different from the Parnell split of the 1890s. However, being localised mostly in the west Cork constituencies, it was easier to ignore. Healy did not join the All For Ireland League but retained his North Louth seat as an independent nationalist. The O'Brien–Healy alliance increasingly received the editorial support of Murphy's *Irish Independent* as it unfolded a comprehensive critique of the Irish Party, one perceived by the *Freeman* and other Party supporters as a campaign of wanton disruption. The chief points of attack at first were its alleged weakness in failing to pressurise its Liberal allies to bring in the promised (third) Home Rule Bill, and its perceived acquiescence in the taxation measures introduced by Lloyd George as Chancellor of the Exchequer to fund his radical social programme of old age pensions and national insurance. Some of the criticism was constructive, as with its monitoring of the poor attendance of some party MPs at crucial votes on the 1909 Finance Bill, and it acknowledged Redmond's efforts to win exemptions from land taxes, whiskey tax and other impositions.

However, the paper showed its opportunistic side just when Redmond at last found himself with the balance of power and the leverage he needed with the Liberal government for Home Rule. Both general elections of 1910 left the Conservatives and Liberals with an equal number of seats. Liberal Prime Minister Asquith needed the support of the Irish Party to bring in the legislation necessary to curb the power of the House of Lords, which had used its veto to stop the radical Budget of 1909. Redmond needed the removal of the veto in order to clear the path for a Home Rule Bill. When compromising tendencies in the British parties threatened to remove his leverage, Redmond demanded that the anti-veto legislation be given priority before he would vote for the Budget. The *Independent* first criticised Redmond for tardiness in confronting Asquith, then, when the former had stood his ground, condoned the

Healy-O'Brien accusation that he had backed the government into a corner on the Budget.

It was at this time that the two newspapers, the *Freeman* and the *Independent*, escalated their attacks on each other directly in polemical and often acrimonious editorials, the rancour fuelled by the emotional energy of the old Murphy-Dillon feud. However, the capacity of the *Freeman* to defend Redmond was limited by its weakness as it suffered increasingly from the competition of its rival; its circulation fell to half that of the latter even as its price remained at double. Under Sexton's chairmanship, priority was given to maintaining dividends rather than to investment. Falling profits in 1909 and 1910 and a collapse in the company's share values prompted shareholders to demand an inquiry into its management. Sexton was forced to resign in 1912, and Redmond tried to stem the decline by nominating new members to the board and arranging for the injection of subsidies from the Party's coffers.

By the time the Home Rule Bill was introduced in 1912, the whole question of Irish–British financial relations had become a live political issue. The *Independent* had staked out a position within the constitutional nationalist movement as the leading advocate of fiscal autonomy (full control of customs and excise), which it set as the benchmark by which it intended to judge the bill. The paper's stance on this issue gave it a policy in common with the extra-constitutional Sinn Féin ("Ourselves") party (founded in 1905 by Arthur Griffith, a group with tiny electoral support in 1912 but whose founder's writings on all aspects of the campaign for Irish self-government were widely read and respected). For the Irish Party to accept anything less, wrote the *Independent*, would be to accept 'Home Rule in name only'. In January it set out a demand for effective colonial (dominion) Home Rule: We insist upon full legislative and fiscal autonomy, subject to Imperial control over the Army and Navy, and the exclusion of matters appertaining to the Crown and treaties with foreign States. This is, we take it, the Irishman's conception of Home Rule. Nothing less can be regarded as a satisfaction of the national aspiration.

When the bill appeared in April with financial terms that fell short on customs powers for the Home Rule parliament, the reactions of the two Dublin dailies were predictable. The *Freeman* called it 'the greatest, boldest and most generous of the three' Home Rule bills. The *Independent* was editorially lukewarm: '… it gives three quarters of what we expected, and probably not so large a share of what we demanded … It may fairly be described as a moderate measure.' However, the nationalist public at home and abroad overwhelmingly approved the bill and there was little overt criticism of the financial provisions. It seemed as if the paper was ahead of nationalist opinion on this issue for the time being.

The power of the Lords to veto Home Rule had been removed in 1911. In its place was a requirement that the bill must be passed through the House of Commons in three successive parliamentary sessions before becoming law. The bill faced vigorous opposition from Irish and British Unionists in the sessions of 1912 and 1913, including extra-parliamentary threats of unconstitutional resistance and violence. By early 1914, as the third session began, it was clear that these threats applied no longer to Home Rule for nationalist Ireland as a whole but to any attempt to impose it on the unwilling Ulster unionist community. In March 1914, Asquith, with the reluctant acquiescence of Redmond, announced a scheme of temporary partition based on plebiscite majorities in Ulster counties (see Chapter 2). The rejection of the scheme as inadequate by Carson and the Ulster Unionist Party (who demanded the permanent bloc exclusion of six counties) did not prevent the *Independent* from accusing the government and the Irish Party of bending to Orange threats and blackmail. The *Freeman* hit back in defence of the Party, while no less critical of the Ulster Unionists. Through the tumultuous events of March to May – the Curragh crisis, the gunrunning of the Ulster Volunteers, the meteoric rise of the Irish National Volunteers (founded in Dublin in November 1913, hereinafter referred to as 'the Volunteers') – the war of the newspapers simmered. The Home Rule Bill passed its final stages on 25 May, with the curious feature that the question of its applicability to all parts of the island was still a matter of uncertainty and disagreement. The uncertainty was corralled into a separate amending bill, to be introduced in the next session before Home Rule came into operation. By late July, the combination of political deadlock and the mass mobilisation of two opposed sets of armed and arming Volunteers had brought tensions in Ireland to a point where civil war was predicted. While the *Freeman* hewed close to Redmond's policy of trying to defuse tension, the *Independent* was adamant in asserting that nationalist Ireland would not tolerate any more concessions to unionism.

The momentous events of early August 1914 temporarily united the two antagonists (and the country's unionist organs) in common outrage at the Kaiser's invasion of Catholic Belgium and common welcome for Redmond's declaration of Irish support for the British war effort. The tense wait of seven weeks before the Home Rule Bill became law on 18 September did not dent either paper's enthusiasm for the Allied cause or their endorsement of Redmond's call for Irishmen to join the British forces to go 'wherever the firing line extends'. The *Independent* began its practice of publishing photographs of Irish officers who featured in its lengthening casualty lists. However, given Asquith's assurance in parliament that the coercion of Ulster was 'absolutely unthinkable', the king's signing of the Act evoked different reactions. While the *Freeman* greeted 'Ireland's Day of Triumph', the *Independent* reminded readers that the Act's suspension for a minimum of one year (or the duration of the war at latest) was not the only obstacle in the path of its implementation: 'when the Amending Bill comes to be considered, Sir Edward Carson, instead of modifying, will harden his demand ... now we are told that an Act passed by the Imperial Parliament can come into force only in compliance with the vetoing power of sixteen Ulster members.'

In August 1914, the *Independent* claimed that its sales averaged 102,083 copies per day, almost double those of the previous August, giving it a circulation seven times that of the *Freeman*. In 1915, with the introduction of enemies of Home Rule into the Cabinet for the first time in nine years as Asquith formed a coalition government to run the war, the paper used its powerful position to open a new and more virulent round in its campaign against Redmond and the Irish Party. In more than twenty editorials over four months, it returned repeatedly to its twin themes of the deficiencies of the Home Rule Act – its 'profoundly disappointing financial provisions' and the danger posed by the amending bill – and the ineptitude of the Irish Party leadership, which it held responsible for the former. 'We do not suggest that the Liberals should have been thrown out,' it wrote, 'but we do suggest that the policy of weakly climbing down on all occasions when much was at stake … has had disastrous results'. The criticism was overwhelmingly destructive, based in part on a refusal to recognise political realities at Westminster, in part on a failure to give credit where it was due and in part on outright untruths. A favourite target was Dillon, who above all others was blamed for silencing dissenting voices and imposing a stifling conformism on political life, especially through the Party's system of selecting election candidates. There was a serious point here, but much of the blame lay with the constitution of the party organisation, the United Irish League, written in 1900 by William O'Brien. There can be little doubt that, as the first anniversary of the suspended Home Rule Act came around with no sign of a ceasefire in sight (see Chapter 3), the paper did much to increase nationalist disenchantment with the war it supported and to stoke unease for the future of the legislation for Irish self-government that lay on the Statute Book.

Despite these sustained attacks from the most powerful media organ in the country, and its own internal weaknesses resulting from the decay of its organisation in the country, the Irish Party continued to win by-elections. The limits of the *Independent*'s influence were seen in its failure to win extensive support for its campaign against the government's war taxation measures, and incidentally against the Irish Party, in the early months of 1916 (see Chapter 3).

The fires of the insurrection of 1916 inflicted unequal damage on the two papers. The *Independent*'s premises emerged unscathed, allowing it to join with *The Irish Times* in calling for 'the worst of the ringleaders' to be 'dealt with as they deserve'. The *Freeman* did not have a similar opportunity to voice its feelings, having lost its Prince's St. premises next to the General Post Office (GPO) along with its machinery and account books (leaving it unable to follow-up debts worth £18,000), and was off the streets for almost two weeks. This was a source of great anxiety to Redmond and Dillon as they watched their newspaper languish with a daily circulation of 20,000 at most against the *Independent*'s 120,000. Dillon wrote to Redmond, 'Murphy now thinks he at last has the *Freeman*, and the Irish Party, by the throat, and that he has not the slightest notion of proposing or accepting any terms which will not leave him in practical control … if Murphy and Healy control the National Press in Dublin there will be an end of the Party, the movement, and of your leadership.'

Redmond wished to find a sympathetic donor willing to invest in the paper, and to re-launch it at half its previous price. However, Dillon felt that investment would be sinking money in a bottomless pit without a change in editorial policy to a stronger anti-government stance in the post-rebellion atmosphere. Their party colleague, T.P. O'Connor MP, canvassed in London for such a person, and found one in Sir Alexander Maguire, the Liverpool match manufacturer. Loans raised by Maguire and a large donation to Redmond from Lord Pirrie, the Ulster Liberal peer and chairman of Harland and Wolff, enabled the paper to stay in business pending the government's payment of compensation for the rebellion damage, and to reorganise itself with new machinery in new premises.

With the launch of Lloyd George's attempt at a Home Rule settlement in June 1916 through the immediate implementation of the 1914 Act with the provisional exclusion of a six-county Ulster bloc (see Chapter 4), the *Independent*'s anti-partition crusade went into overdrive. Outdoing its campaign of the previous year, it carried no fewer than thirty-eight anti-partition editorials in the months of June and July under such headings as 'The Perdition Policy', 'The Mutilation Scheme' and 'Away with Exclusion'. At a representative conference of six-county nationalists, Redmond, with the indispensable aid of Devlin, won a majority of 475 to 265 votes in favour of the proposal. The *Independent* refused to accept the verdict, alleging the meeting had been packed with Party supporters, and that Redmond's threat to resign unless the motion were carried was a 'Pistol to the Heads of Delegates'. When the entire initiative collapsed in late July over the issue of the permanence of the Ulster exclusion provision, the paper called for Redmond's head. Its headline of 27 July ran: 'Ireland's Joy at Fate of Partition Plot – Mr Redmond To Blame – His Deception His Own Work'. The difference between the two papers now turned on the issue of where the blame lay. For the *Freeman*, Asquith was guilty of bad faith towards Redmond; the *Independent* indicted the latter as the author of his own misfortune for entertaining the scheme at all. Redmond's predicament was that he had accepted the principle of six-county bloc partition without having anything to show for his concession.

With the spectre of partition now the most burning issue in Irish politics, the Irish Party's authority began to crumble among a sizeable portion of the electorate. The result was evident in 1917, when it lost all four of that year's by-elections to a resurrected and burgeoning Sinn Féin movement now committed to the political legacy of the insurrectionists of 1916. By the end of the year the latter had become a well-organised cohesive political party under the leadership of Éamon de Valera with Arthur Griffith as deputy leader, and with a nationwide network of clubs and membership similar to that once enjoyed by the United Irish League. Redmond died, a broken man, in March 1918. The *Freeman* blamed the Party's eclipse on British government treachery and the sabotage of Irish wreckers. The *Independent* hailed the new forces and kept up the attacks on the Home Rule Act throughout as it gloated on the Irish Party's woes. The pattern was repeated in 1918 when the paper's determination to hammer into the ground a party that appeared bound for extinction at the polls may seem excessive in retrospect. A possible explanation is that the new leader was John Dillon.

The result of the December 1918 general election eliminated the Irish Party from the politics of nationalist Ireland (see Chapter 5). Without its support the *Freeman* could not continue as before, and it was sold the following October to a new owner, Martin Fitzgerald, a Dublin merchant, who received financial assistance from R. Hamilton Edwards, an English former employee of the Northcliffe press. The election result, along with the death of Murphy in June 1919, also finally took the heat out of the quarrel of the two nationalist dailies. With the British government refusing to recognise the mandate obtained by Sinn Féin at the election and maturing its own plans for a fourth Home Rule Bill that would create two devolved parliaments in a partitioned Ireland (see Chapter 7), the two papers followed broadly similar editorial lines critical of government policies. And as the violence of the armed wing of the independence movement escalated throughout 1919 and 1920, both were equally vocal in their denunciations. Each suffered punishment from the targets of their criticism, the *Freeman* through official suppression and the jailing of its proprietor and editor, the *Independent* through a destructive raid by armed IRA men (see Chapter 6).

Both papers were enthusiastic in their welcome for the terms of the Anglo-Irish Treaty and for its ratification by the Third Dáil, and later vociferously urged the new Provisional Government to impose law and order during the turbulent events of the first half of 1922 that led to the outbreak of the Civil War. In retaliation, the *Freeman* was attacked again, its printing presses smashed by a 200-strong gang of anti-Treaty IRA. From the same source came an order to Fitzgerald to leave Ireland on pain of death, a threat he ignored, having published a facsimile copy of it. A threat of a different kind to the paper's existence came in 1924 when an unsuccessful business venture by Edwards led to his absconding, leaving crippling debts. The paper's last issue appeared in December 1924, after which it was incorporated into the *Irish Independent*.[4] In a formal sense, if no other, Dillon's nightmare of 1916 had come true.

The long-running newspaper war between the *Freeman* and the *Independent* may be seen as a classic exemplar of what Sigmund Freud called 'the narcissism of small differences'.[5] Both papers at every stage of their existence were undeviating in their support of the politics of constitutional nationalism. Until the immediately post-1916 period, both stood for the attainment of devolved Irish self-government within the United Kingdom; by the time of the 1918 general election, both had taken up the demand for a dominion form of Home Rule. Both equally failed to understand Ulster unionism, and were equally vehement in their rejection of the partition option. And, although, in both cases, their preferred options for an Irish settlement were at all times to be achieved through non-violent means – though both were adept at resurrecting the rhetoric of safely dead revolutionary heroes – the pressure they exerted on British governments to ignore the wishes of Ulster unionists and enforce an all-Ireland settlement had the potential, if acted upon, to bring on serious inter-communal strife if not outright war. Finally, during the violent thirty months of the War of Independence, both papers combined vigorous criticism of the government with an eagerness to embrace all chances for peace, and were in the front line of those welcoming the truce and the Anglo-Irish negotiations and calling for the ratification of the Treaty.

It is indisputable that the *Irish Independent* became the most powerful newspaper organ of the revolutionary period. Its influence, and that of the failed politician whose business acumen elevated it to that dominant position, have endured. The British *Star* newspaper declared in 1914: 'Next to the Kaiser, Lord Northcliffe has done more than any living man to bring about the war'.[6] Adapting the judgment to the Irish context, it could be argued with equal reason that, next to Edward Carson, William Martin Murphy did more than any man in Ireland to bring about the fall of John Redmond and the collapse of the Irish Party.

A postscript lying slightly outside the time span of this book reveals much about the ideology of the amalgamated *Irish Independent-Freeman's Journal*. For a newspaper that had done more than any other to prepare the way for the rise to power of Sinn Féin and the coming of the Free State, it showed little appetite for commemorating the tenth anniversaries in 1926 of the seminal revolutionary events. This was in line with the attitude of the Free State authorities themselves, whose official commemorations were the lowest of low-key. There was no official commemoration of the rebellion, either at Easter itself or three weeks later on its date anniversary. Instead a mass and brief military ceremony were held at Arbour Hill cemetery in May on one execution anniversary. Only one relative of an executed leader was present as volleys of shots were fired over the graves. Elsewhere, privately organised republican processions took place across the country.

The *Irish Independent* carried no news reports, editorial comment or photographs of commemorations on any of these dates, apart from a very brief report of local republican gatherings at cemeteries in Cork, Clare and Roscommon. Its editorial concerns lay elsewhere.

On Easter Monday (5 April 1926) its main editorial was an account of the compensation claims issue facing the Free State government – compensation for damage to property during the war of independence period January 1919 to July 1921 (not including the burning of 199 large country houses during the civil war). A total of 18,000 such claims had been judged valid. On the principle that the British government accepted liability for damage done by its forces and the Free State for damage done by the IRA in that period, the state had already paid out £8.87 million on these claims to the end of 1925 with another £2.17 million estimated for the current year (equivalent to £545 million and £134 million respectively in 2020 values). Under the London agreement of 1925, the Free State had also agreed that Irish taxpayers would pay the remainder in annual instalments of £250,000 (£15.38 million in 2020 values) for 60 years.

The crippling effect of these payouts on the finances of the fledgling Irish state may be gauged by the fact that Ernest Blythe, the Free State finance minister, had managed to save the state a mere £350,000 when, to his everlasting notoriety, he had been forced in 1923 to cut one shilling (10 per cent) from the old age pension payment of 10 shillings.

The *Independent* had been a stern critic of the radical high-spending policies of Lloyd George, preaching that pensions and national insurance were luxuries that Ireland could not afford. In 1912-13 it had denounced Dublin Corporation plans to build a new art gallery, to be designed by Edwin Lutyens and spanning the Liffey, to house the modern art collection which Sir Hugh Lane wished to bequeath to the city.[7] In the 1920s it seemed to add revolutions to the list of things the country could not afford. No wonder its editorials throughout the 1920s kept a close eye on government spending and rang with constant calls for financial retrenchment.

Chapter 2

THE FIRST PARTITION PROPOSALS, THE HOME RULE ACT AND THE GREAT WAR, 1914

A. THE GOVERNMENT'S PROPOSAL OF TEMPORARY PARTITION, 9 MARCH 1914

When Asquith opened the debate on the Second Reading of the Home Rule Bill's third and last circuit of the House on 9 March 1914, he introduced his concession to Ulster with the words:

> ... On the one hand, if Home Rule as embodied in this bill is carried now, there is ... in Ulster the prospect of acute dissension and even of civil strife. On the other hand, if at this stage, Home Rule were to be shipwrecked, or permanently mutilated, or indefinitely postponed, there is in Ireland, as a whole, at least an equally formidable outlook.

Under his scheme, the parliamentary electors of any Ulster county (with the cities of Belfast and Derry to be treated as separate counties for the purpose) could vote by county plebiscite to opt out of the operation of Home Rule for six years, after which time it would automatically 'come in' unless the imperial parliament decided otherwise. The scheme implied the temporary exclusion of four counties, Antrim, Down, Armagh and Londonderry, along with Belfast, but offered the possibility of exclusion becoming permanent should the Unionists win either of the next two general elections.

Announcing his Party's acquiescence in the government's offer, Redmond said that they had gone to 'the very extremest limits of concession'. He asked the House to recognise the great sacrifice they were asking their nationalist countrymen to make. If the proposals were rejected, nationalists could not accept them either, and the duty of the House would then be to place the bill on the Statute Book without delay. Carson admitted that the acknowledgement of the principle of exclusion was an advance, but said that the time limit made acceptance impossible. Ulster wanted this question 'settled now and for ever. We do not want sentence of death with a stay of execution for six years,' he declared.

Provincial press reaction to the government's proposals were critical in varying degrees but did not generate a crisis for Redmond's leadership. Of thirty-seven papers that commented, twenty-nine (78 per cent) were willing to accept the proposals with reluctance (made up of nine expressing unquestioned support for Redmond and twenty expressing opposition but willingness to accept the leader's judgement) while eight (22 per cent) rejected them (six adding veiled criticism, and two condemnation, of the Party leadership, including the *sui generis* response of William O'Brien's *Cork Free Press* (14 March) which called them 'a fantastic caricature of Home Rule').

The *Dundalk Democrat* (14 March) typified sentiment in the first group by stating that there was no enthusiasm for the proposals in any quarter. For nationalists, they were 'frankly objectionable on many grounds, practical as well as sentimental'. But it would not join with William O'Brien and T.M. Healy in their frenzied denunciation of Asquith and the Liberals as betrayers of Ireland. The partition offer had been dictated by strong pressures, as indicated in the King's Speech at the opening of parliament. Its most satisfactory aspect was the prime minister's declaration that if the Ulster Unionist Party refused it he would pass the Home Rule Bill in its original form (this condition had been insisted upon by Redmond); in the light of this the declarations of prominent Unionists that they would not accept it might be 'the best thing that could happen'. The worst possible outcome was that four counties plus the city of Belfast might exempt themselves from Home Rule. However, given the large pro-Home Rule minorities in counties Armagh and Derry, only two counties might be excluded. And, in any case, the exclusion was only for six years.

Opinion in the rest of the first group ranged from the *Connacht Tribune* (14 March), which thought that Redmond's was 'the wise and the only course' and the *Longford Leader* (14 March) which expressed disappointment at the proposals, though 'the Irish Party must be the judges', to the *Limerick Echo* (10 March), which felt that 'that great loyalty to the Irish leader which has been his happy fortune during his occupancy of the position will, without doubt, bear due weight in the country in calm consideration of the probable effects which the proposed partition of the country will have on the future of an Irish Parliament', and the *Southern Star* (14 March) which declared that, although the Irish people could never submit to permanent partition, Ireland wanted peace.

Interestingly, two neighbouring midland newspapers which would end up on opposing sides in the coming years were at one for now in their ringing declarations of loyalty to the Party leadership. The *Westmeath Examiner* (Mullingar), a paper owned by John C. Hayden MP, a Party colleague and personal friend of Redmond, stated (14 March) that the Party had the 'sympathy, confidence and support' of all nationalists; the *Westmeath Independent* (Athlone) went further in declaring (14 March) its 'absolute and unquestioned confidence in the Leader who in many anxious years has served [the country] so well'. Another paper that would end up in the anti-Party camp in the future, the *Leinster Leader* (14 March), lauded the 'skill, ability and faithfulness to principle which has marked Mr John Redmond's leadership all through this great and momentous crisis' and tried to explain the leader's policy. 'While holding out for the maintenance of the nation intact under the Irish Parliament,' it wrote, 'Mr Redmond has repeatedly declared that there is no length to which he would not go … in order to win the consent of Ulster … By waiving [sic] the principle of exclusion, Mr Redmond and the Irish Party have, in our opinion, more than redeemed their pledges to win a settlement by consent if that were possible'.

The pessimistic second group included the *Munster News* (Limerick), which claimed (11 March) that 'Carson's game of bluff' had succeeded, and the *Roscommon Herald* (14 March) which saw the proposals as a 'sop' to Carson and claimed that Redmond had been 'wire-pulled' by Lloyd George, rumoured to be the progenitor in the Cabinet of the temporary partition plan. For the *Waterford News* (13 March) 'we think the majority of the Irish people would prefer to go into the wilderness again rather than to submit to the partition of Ireland in any shape or for any period'. Stronger criticism was voiced (14 March) in *The Kerryman* (Tralee). In an editorial titled 'Disappointment!', the paper asserted that the prime minister's pronouncement would cause 'the most intensively bitter disappointment to every Irish nationalist'. It had never anticipated that the government's concessions to the 'Ulster bluff' would take the shape of the disintegration of Ireland, despite 'the soothing assurances of the Nationalist leaders that it was unthinkable and impossible'. Now the 'dismemberment of Ireland' had been decided on by the Cabinet and assented to by the Irish leaders, the probable result being 'to create two warring factions in the country'.

If *The Kerryman*'s comments stopped just short of overt criticism of the party leadership, those of the *Mayo News* (Westport), a paper owned and edited by the Westport Irish Republican Brotherhood (IRB) figure P.J. Doris, crossed the boundary. The Nationalist leaders had assented to these proposals without consultation with the people of Ireland, and the great danger for Ireland was that the Orangemen might assent to them too. 'There was punishment for the mutilation of animals and human beings', but 'today in Ireland we are asked to be patient and passive while a party of men styling themselves the national leaders of the country are participating … in the shredding and tearing to pieces of a land … [resulting in] the disruption and virtual annihilation of a whole nation' (21 March)

It should be mentioned that both of the latter papers already had a low opinion of the Home Rule legislation before the partition proposals and were thus predisposed to criticise the Party leadership. For *The Kerryman* (30 May) the concession to Unionists 'promised to render a Bill, not too good or generous in its original shape, still more worthless'; for the *Mayo News* (30 May) the bill was 'a very poor measure'.

Implicit in the commentary of almost all of the newspapers, in varying degrees of strength, was the demand that the opposition of unionist Ulster to Home Rule should be overridden and the province forced to accept the governance of an all-Ireland parliament. The *Sligo Champion* (14 March) spoke for most when it wrote that unionist pronouncements against the partition proposals mistook the attitude of the government and the Irish Party, who would be quite happy if they were rejected. The government's duty would then be clear, though the paper did not spell it out.

Two other papers were more explicit. The *Galway Observer* (14 March) wrote that Asquith's motivation was his fear that he would otherwise face civil war in Ulster, but 'he may be safer to face civil war in three or four counties now than have to face it in three or four provinces hereafter'. The *Midland Tribune* (21 March) quoted John Dillon in calling the exclusion of Ulster a 'bitter draught' which nationalists would nevertheless swallow for the sake of peace. 'But if Ulster persists, strong measures should be adopted; in fact, a sample of their own Coercive Measures …'

Since Ulster nationalists were the most likely to be affected directly by the partition proposals, it may be worthwhile to look at the responses of the five papers from that province. The *Anglo-Celt* (Cavan) confined itself (14 March) to sectarian abuse: the ancestors of the Ulster unionist leaders had come to the country as 'the scum of England, the veriest dregs of society, the lowest of the low', and if they would not compromise, they would be the ones to suffer. For the thrice-weekly *Derry Journal* (11 March), everything would turn on whether this was truly the last word of the government as it was for the Irish Party. The latter must now say to the government: 'Thus far and no further'. The sacrifice from the nationalist point of view was 'a bitter one': 'over a large and important area, at all events, it would bring Nationalist and Catholic Ulster under a rehabilitated domination that for generations it has striven – and with some measure of success – to break down. It is a poor reward for a heroic and most unselfish struggle in its share … of the battling for Irish national rights'.

Two other Ulster papers engaged in denial. In the view of the *Derry People & Donegal News* (Omagh) (14 March) Carson could not be sure that any county, or even Belfast, would vote itself out of Home Rule. Ulster unionists did not want and would not vote 'to be cut off politically, socially, commercially, economically and financially from a self-governed Ireland'. For the *Donegal Vindicator* (Ballyshannon) (13 March), 'the Carson brigade know that not a single county in Ireland could be induced to contract out for a year, six years or permanently. Belfast would reject it with scorn … To contract out would spell financial ruin'. The most moderate response came from the Belfast *Irish News* (10 March), a paper that had often championed the cause of the Irish Party and its local leader, Joseph Devlin MP. It did not fear 'the civil war that no sane man believes in'. But for the sake of peace the proposals had 'been accepted – reluctantly and painfully, but sincerely – by Irish nationalists in the spirit of Mr. Redmond's admirable and truly patriotic speech. We have gone very far indeed; we cannot afford to go a step further'.

At the other end of the island, certain papers reflected the political (and sometimes physical) warfare waged between the followers of the Irish Party and those of the dissident group of Home Rule MPs, the All For Ireland League, led by William O'Brien, which held seven seats in Cork city and county, and its ally T.M. Healy, also a Cork MP (see

Chapter 1). For O'Brien, his policy of "Conference, Conciliation and Consent" offered a pathway to peace, brotherhood and amity between fellow-Irishmen while the current Redmond-Dillon policy, and especially its northern manifestation as led by Devlin, was 'sectarian' and a sure path to violent conflict.

In early 1914, O'Brien had advocated various types of concession to north-east Ulster to win its consent, including a right of veto for Ulster MPs over legislation of the Dublin parliament, over-representation for Ulster in the Irish House of Commons (60 out of 164 MPs) and the right to appoint its own court judges, magistrates and education inspectors. (However, the one concession he would not countenance under any circumstances was the exclusion of any part of Ulster from Home Rule.) In the winter 1913-14 private conversations with Asquith, Redmond had expressed himself willing to consider similar concessions to those of O'Brien, and even a Home-Rule-within-Home-Rule scheme whereby Ulster would have local autonomy within an all-Ireland parliament.

That O'Brien and Redmond could entertain such proposals, even when they entailed a departure from strict democratic principles, was a sign of their anxiety to assuage unionist opposition to their plans, something they understood as emanating from a populous Ulster community with an internal life of its own and a different conception of its place on the island, and in the United Kingdom, from that of most Irish nationalists – a composite that would now be termed a different 'identity'. However, most of their followers, and their press organs, knowing little of that community, perceived it through a series of stereotypes: in the political sense as a mere coterie of bigoted ultra-Tory reactionaries whose chief *raison d'être* was the frustration of the hopes and dreams of nationalism. To contemplate such a fifth column enjoying undemocratic privileges within an Irish parliament was no more attractive to nationalist editors than to accept a territorial separation of part of the province from the rest of Ireland.

In any case, neither Redmond nor O'Brien could point to evidence that any of these measures interested Ulster unionists sufficiently to make them reconsider their fundamental opposition to Home Rule. It was these realities that had helped persuade Redmond to acquiesce in Asquith's tactical offer of (temporary) exclusion.

O'Brien's paper the *Cork Free Press* (14 March) greeted Asquith's speech as 'a proposal to cut off for six years from the rest of Ireland four counties, which are perhaps the wealthiest but are certainly the most populous … the mutilation and dissection of the corpse of Ireland, so hateful and revolting to nationalists'. Austen Chamberlain's theory of 'two peoples, two nations' was anathema to nationalists. 'If it is accepted the basic reason for Home Rule is gone. It is because Mr Redmond has accepted it that he deserves to be driven out of Ireland as an open and avowed traitor to the Irish cause.'

The pro-Party daily *Cork Examiner* (10 March), the morning after Asquith's speech, hit back at O'Brien and Healy, writing that the proposals were based on the assumption that peace had to be reached through compromise. But although they represented the limit of concession that nationalist Ireland could accept, 'they do not at all approach the grovelling and abject proposition that has been made by Mr O'Brien, and approved by Mr Healy, that ten Orangemen should have a suspensory veto on all the legislation of the Home Rule Parliament'. The *Clare Champion* (14 March) weighed in on the same side, claiming that the saddest aspect of the affair was that the proposals had been made the basis for a 'rancorous and unjust attack on the Irish Party' by O'Brien, who only a few weeks ago was calling for 'sweeping concessions to Ulster' but was 'now shrieking that the same Orange pets of his have got too much' while the 'cynical Mr Tim Healy makes bitter and envenomed attack on Mr John Redmond, and all for love of Dark Rosaleen [poetic name for Ireland]'.

The problem for Redmond in answering O'Brien's charges was that, a mere five months earlier, he had used almost identical language to denounce a suggestion by Winston Churchill, in a speech at Dundee, that the exclusion of part of Ulster might pave the way to an agreed settlement. 'Irish nationalists can never be assenting parties to the mutilation of the Irish nation,' he had declared at a huge rally at Limerick on 12 October 1913 alongside sixteen other party MPs on the platform, 'the two-nation theory is to us an abomination and a blasphemy'. In the years to come, these words of his would be quoted against him often by his political enemies as he struggled and failed to find an accommodation with Ulster unionism.

O'Brien and Healy had a powerful ally in Dublin. The *Irish Independent* (see Chapter 1) was the property of the businessman William Martin Murphy, whose origins lay in the same region of south-west Cork as T.M. Healy, to whom he was related by marriage. The paper had been a trenchant critic of the Party's alliance with the British Liberals for at least six years, at first refusing to believe that the latter would fulfil its promise to introduce a Home Rule Bill, later a relentless critic of the bill's deficiencies and the Party's alleged weakness in not demanding a stronger measure, particularly in its fiscal and financial terms. Conversely, it tended to give favourable coverage to the All For Ireland League.

While the *Freeman's Journal* passed off the six-year exclusion as merely a 'transitional period' to all-Ireland Home Rule, the *Independent* wrote that 'more than a sacrifice has been demanded from the Irish people … We are to have a Parliament in Dublin, but it will not be a Parliament of the nation'. The day after Asquith's speech, it installed on its editorial page a box containing the 'mutilation' reference from Redmond's Limerick speech. For the next four years it would keep that quotation in the eye of the nationalist public.

B. THE PASSING OF THE HOME RULE BILL AND THE BUCKINGHAM PALACE CONFERENCE, MAY–JULY 1914

The months of March and April saw dramatic events that strengthened the Ulster unionist position. In mid-March, responding to increased activity by the Ulster Volunteer Force (UVF), the government prepared for precautionary troop movements to Ulster. Sixty army officers stationed at the

Curragh, under the impression that they were about to be ordered to take part in 'active military operations against Ulster', declared themselves, in what has since been termed the 'Curragh mutiny', as preferring dismissal to accepting such orders. In the ensuing political sensation, the Secretary of State for War, Col. J.E.B. Seely, was forced to resign, Asquith himself taking over the office. But although the prime minister repudiated an unauthorised assurance to army officers that the government did not intend to crush political opposition to Home Rule, the episode effectively removed the government's capacity to impose it by military force on unionist Ulster. In late April, at Larne and two other northern ports, the Ulster Volunteers smuggled ashore and efficiently distributed across the province 35,000 German rifles and tons of ammunition.

Between these two events, the debate on the Home Rule Bill resumed on 31 March. No progress was made towards agreement; in fact, Carson's demand now included not only the abolition of the six-year time limit but the exclusion of a bloc of counties – the 'clean cut' – rather than county plebiscites. He and Redmond accused each other of offering nothing new; Redmond said that the government must now 'proceed calmly with the Bill'. In early May, Asquith affirmed his intention to do this. However, he had also agreed, under pressure from the king, to re-open his conversations with Bonar Law and Carson; at this meeting he agreed to incorporate any changes to the Home Rule Bill in a separate amending bill, to become law ideally on the same day as the original bill. This disquieting (for nationalists) development led Redmond to voice criticism that threatened a break with the Liberals, since an amending bill introduced in the absence of agreement left the way open for further concessions to Ulster. He warned Asquith that if that bill were to contain anything more than the 9 March proposals, he would be forced to make a public protest immediately.

Meanwhile, the long journey of the original Home Rule Bill through parliament ended with the passage of its final Third Reading on 25 May by a majority of seventy-seven votes. Nationalists were now faced with the strange reality of the bill whose triumphant passing into law they had anxiously awaited through three parliamentary sessions, yet whose full implementation must to some degree be affected by another bill whose provisions were not yet agreed and might never be. For much of the nationalist press, the cognitive dissonance could not be absorbed. Of thirty-nine newspapers commenting, 26 (67 per cent) expressed unqualified rejoicing and paid tribute to Redmond's leadership. The *Connaught Telegraph* (30 May) wrote that the 'infamous Union' was no more and 'nationalist Ireland went mad with delight … on the night the Bill was passed the hill-tops of Ireland were a veritable chain of fire'; the *Longford Leader* (30 May) compared it to the deliverance of the Jewish people from Babylonian captivity while the *Westmeath Independent* (30 May) borrowed from the New Testament for its editorial title: 'It is consummated'. The *Cork Examiner* (26 May) expressed 'jubilation and gratitude for the glorious victory which has been won by the Irish Leader and his faithful colleagues of the Irish Parliamentary Party … every patriotic heart in Ireland will throb with joy at the glad news'. For the *Limerick Leader* (27 May) the bill 'may now be regarded as the law of the land'. The Irish Leader 'deserves the everlasting gratitude of his race … a great man with greatness unmistakeable … no Irish Leader ever had a more trying task to face than he had to encounter during the past few years … his superb statesmanship, his keen and far-seeing intellect and his indomitable patience and perseverance'.

A few of these papers, though aware of the amending bill, were not worried by it; the *Wexford People* (27 May) for example, trusted the Irish Party to deal with it. However, another thirteen papers saw it as cause for concern. The *Kilkenny People* and the *Leinster Leader* (both 30 May) found it an overhanging or disturbing factor that marred their celebrations and meant the struggle was not yet over. 'The prospect would be altogether bright if the shadow of the Amending Bill were not hanging over,' wrote the first paper, '… patriotic Irishmen, unionist no less than nationalist, loathe the very idea of partitioning Ireland and stereotyping racial and religious divisions.' The *Tipperary Star* praised Redmond who 'with head as cool as snow-capped Galteemore… went on his well-considered way, boldly and confidently', until the bill was through the Commons. But 'when the Amending Bill comes up our leaders should see to it that too much is not conceded to Ulster, and that that there is no partition of Ireland. They are the only dangers now, but they are grave ones.' For the *Mayo News* (30 May) the amending bill meant that the Home Rule Bill, already a 'very poor measure', would not become law: 'The result is announced as a great National victory ... What a gullible people we are!'

The *Roscommon Herald* (30 May), a paper owned and edited by the idiosyncratic Jasper Tully, a former Land League activist, anti-Parnellite MP and gadfly member of Redmond's reunited Irish Party from 1900 to 1906, felt it had the remedy. The hope of the Tories had been anti-Home Rule rebellion in Ulster, but the rise of the Irish National Volunteers (their numbers now mushrooming in the wake of the Curragh and Larne affairs) had changed all that; their proficiency in drill now equalled that of the best of Carson's men, and all they lacked was arms. In language of recklessness tempered only by impracticability, it claimed that 'three hundred thousand young nationalists' could put an end to Ulster's opposition: 'With them in action, it is beyond the power of Carson or any of his intriguers, in Parliament or out of it, to mutilate Ireland'.

As promised, the amending bill, containing the March proposals, was introduced in the House of Lords on 23 June. However, in the committee stage, the Lords' amendments remoulded it into what was essentially a new measure: the permanent exclusion of all nine Ulster counties *en bloc*. Despite Liberal objections, it passed all stages by mid-July and was sent to the Commons. By this time, tensions had risen to high levels in both communities. Carson announced that an Ulster 'provisional government' was ready to take over the province as soon as the Home Rule Bill became law. Ulster Volunteers were marching with rifles and bayonets in Belfast. The membership of the Irish National Volunteers was reported to have risen to 250,000 and efforts were being directed to procuring weapons.

The deadlock was now acute. The earlier recognition of the principle of partition made it impossible for the government to withdraw the amending bill; on the other hand, if Asquith presented the Lords' reconstructed version of it to the Commons, the Irish Party would have to vote against it, making a general election inevitable. Behind the scenes, negotiations took place with Asquith and between the two sides using intermediaries, with attention fixed on whether compromise could be reached on the territorial boundaries of the excluded area. These talks failed to bring agreement.

Deciding to invoke the king's help, Asquith suggested a conference between the parties at Buckingham Palace, to which the king readily agreed. Thus, in response to royal invitation, Redmond, Dillon, Asquith and Lloyd George met with Carson, Captain James Craig, Bonar Law and Lord Lansdowne at the palace on Tuesday 21 July. The king began by expressing his feelings of attachment to Ireland and her people, and his deep misgivings about the slide towards an 'appeal to force' there. It was unthinkable that his Irish subjects should be brought to the brink of fratricidal strife on 'issues apparently so capable of adjustment'. Praying God's help on their deliberations, he concluded: 'Your responsibilities are indeed great. The time is short …'

Three days of talks failed to break the deadlock. The Unionists refused to discuss Redmond's county option proposal, while he and Dillon refused to discuss either the exclusion of the whole of Ulster (something Carson claimed would lead to the earliest possible unification of the island) or the exclusion of six counties to vote as a single bloc. Other options, such as dividing the province according to parliamentary constituency boundaries, or according to Poor Law Union boundaries, were rejected by one side or the other as impractical, the worst sticking point being the division of County Tyrone, a county with a small nationalist majority.

The announcement of the breakdown of the conference on 24 July came after most weekly newspapers had gone to press and in any case the participants had agreed to preserve confidentiality as to what had transpired. The *Cork Free Press* (25 July) pursued William O'Brien's individual line that, while north and south needed to be reconciled, territorial compromise was exactly the wrong way to go about it. Under the heading 'The Boundary Commission Collapses', it recorded its 'joy and pleasure' at the failure, and deployed the kind of hyperbolic rhetoric at which O'Brien excelled: 'To reconcile Irishmen they called a conference to divide Irishmen. To make Ireland a Nation they called a conference to devise means to rob her of her Nationhood'.

However, most of the papers took their cue from the British Liberal and Labour press, which in the absence of detailed insight, were highly critical of what they saw as 'the King's intervention'. Of the twenty-two papers commenting, twenty-one (95 per cent) were negative to some extent, with five seeing the conference as another Tory attempt to scupper Home Rule. The *Longford Leader* (25 July) denounced 'this most outrageous interference of the King, the most revolutionary thing since Cromwell ordered the members out of the House of Commons'. A consoling feature was that 'the young men of Ireland had sprung to their feet manfully'. However, it was careful to add, 'we are not advocates of war and above all civil war'. The *Galway Observer* (25 July) could not see what the Irish leaders could possibly be asked for except more concessions. The *Carlow Nationalist* (25 July) assured its readers that Mr Redmond, like every Irish Party MP, 'loathes the very idea of the conference' and was attending only by express command of the King'. In more conciliatory tones, the *Tuam Herald* (25 July) called the king's action 'a most important and unusual proceeding, without precedent or parallel in past history … perilously near being an encroachment on constitutional government', and while animated by 'the best possible intentions towards Ireland', it was an innovation which might prove dangerous for British politics.

The *Derry People & Donegal News* (25 July) drew the conclusion that 'the March proposals were altogether too generous an offer' by nationalist Ireland; the offer had 'proved abortive' and only intensified 'Carsonite truculence'. Nationalists had hoped Home Rule was safe, but, it asked, 'are we to get a mutilated Bill and is our country to enter on a new era surrounded with the barbed wire of sectarian and political passion?' 'The Conference must fail,' it added, unaware that this had already happened.

Several papers objected to the king's reference, in his opening message, to the risk of civil war in Ireland. The *Dundalk Democrat* (25 July) wrote that the wording of the king's message to the conference had 'aroused the deepest indignation in Ireland'. In saying that 'the cry of civil war' was on the lips of most responsible and sober-minded people, the king 'takes the Carsonites at their own value … [and gives] a most undeserved character for sobriety of thought to men who are nothing better than turbulent mischief-makers and self-declared rebels'. The *Westmeath Examiner* (25 July) saw the conference as an attempt by 'Unionist wire-pullers' to circumvent the abolition of the Lords' veto: 'The House of Lords has failed but its spokesmen think they can drag the King into the political controversy of the day'. At the opening of the conference he had gone 'far beyond his province' by using the Tory language of civil war. In an editorial titled 'The King's Interference', the *Connacht Tribune* (25 July) claimed that 'George V has been loading the dice unfairly against Ireland', and his talk of civil war showed the source of his inspiration. If the conference failed, 'the prestige of the Throne will be shaken'.

None of the newspapers, even those few enthusiastically promoting armed confrontation between the nationalist Volunteers and their unionist counterparts, showed any inclination to consider whether it might be unfair to blame the king for adverting to a real threat of civil war. The conspiracy-minded *Roscommon Herald* (25 July) had its own version of scapegoating the king: the conference was part of a devious plan to enable the Liberals 'to get out of their Home Rule promises, while inducing the people at the same time to believe that they are thoroughgoing Home Rulers'. The game was to keep the Irish Party on side while allowing the blame to fall on the king – 'an elaborate game of fooling the Irish public'. But as long as the Volunteers held the field, the partition plot would not succeed.

In the two weeks following the breakdown of the Buckingham Palace Conference, events in Ireland and abroad unfolded with dizzying rapidity. Privately, Asquith told Redmond and Dillon that he must proceed with the amending bill, and would have to remove the six-year time limit. Redmond, who had made no territorial concessions to Carson at Buckingham Palace, but assuming that the end of the parliamentary session was only days away, and with it the royal assent for the original Home Rule Bill, secretly prepared a grand speech of conciliation to be delivered in the moment of victory. In a major departure from his March policy, this carefully argued speech would give way on the time limit while insisting on the county option (a measure that would have resulted in the indefinite partition of four Ulster counties plus Belfast.) The message of the speech to Ulster unionists was to be "stay out as long as you like, come in when you are ready". The speech was scheduled for the Second Reading debate on the amending bill, originally set for 28 July.[1] However, in the meantime, a tragic development had intervened at home.

On Sunday 26 July, a group of nationalist individuals had landed a cargo of 1,100 rifles and ammunition, intended for the Irish National Volunteers, at Howth, twelve miles from Dublin, from a private yacht. A party of 700 Volunteers were at the port to unload it. On the way back to the city, the Volunteers were confronted, first by a force of police, then by troops called out by Assistant Commissioner Harrel of the Dublin Metropolitan Police (DMP). A company of the King's Own Scottish Borderers blocked the road and demanded the surrender of the arms. This being refused, scuffles followed and the Volunteers escaped with most of the consignment. Returning to the city centre, the soldiers were pelted by a crowd with stones and other missiles. At Bachelor's Walk, without waiting for orders, they fired on the crowd, killing three and injuring thirty-eight with bullet and bayonet.

Apart from the killings themselves, fierce indignation was caused in nationalist Ireland at the partiality of the Dublin Castle authorities. The previous day, an infantry brigade of 5,000 Ulster Volunteers had marched through Belfast fully armed and with four machine guns. In the House, Redmond voiced his anger, demanding an adjournment and a full judicial and military inquiry. The affair caused a predictable explosion of outrage from all twenty-two of the provincial papers that commented. More papers (eight) were inclined to blame Dublin Castle rule than British rule per se (two) for the killings, while many more vented unfocused anger. For the *Sligo Champion* (1 August), 'an end must be made, once and for all, of Castle rule in Ireland'. It was 'an unparalleled act of savagery' (*Leinster Leader*, 1 August), 'one of the blackest chapters of British rule' (*Donegal Vindicator*, 31 July); it showed that there was 'one law for Ulster, a different one for the rest' (*Wexford People*, 29 July. Among the milder reactions, the *Cork Examiner* (27 July) expressed 'no little astonishment and consternation', the *Westmeath Examiner* (1 August) blamed 'the evil disposition of Castle officialdom' and the *Munster News* (29 July) praised Redmond's 'powerful indictment' in the Commons.

C. THE OUTBREAK OF THE GREAT WAR, AUGUST 1914

Because of the Bachelor's Walk killings, the debate on the amending bill was postponed from 28 to 30 July. Nothing was publicly known about any impending further concession to Ulster unionists, although the *Irish Independent* seemed to have got wind of it when it wrote gloomily on 31 July that 'the time limit has probably gone'. Neither had the newspapers given much attention, until the last days of July, to the diplomatic manoeuvres set in motion in the chancelleries of Europe by the assassination of the Austrian Archduke Ferdinand at Sarajevo on 28 June.

The Irish debate rescheduled for 30 July, and with it Redmond's planned set piece speech of conciliation, never took place; the Cabinet by then was focused on the interplay of European alliances and on whether Britain should involve itself in a European war. The Unionist leaders suggested that the amending bill be postponed indefinitely in the interests of British national unity; Asquith and Redmond agreed. The Ulster deadlock remained unresolved, and an impending clash between Ireland's two communities was averted by the cataclysmic outbreak of the Great War.

In the Irish nationalist press, hardly had the furore over the Bachelor's Walk killings died down than papers were faced, not only with the unanticipated outbreak of European war, but with the response of Redmond to that outbreak, a response articulated without any prior consultation with the Party's grass-roots supporters or with most of his colleagues. On 3 August, Foreign Secretary Sir Edward Grey declared in the House that a violation of Belgium's neutrality by Germany would make British intervention unavoidable. Redmond reacted with an impromptu speech in which he spoke of past conflicts with nationalist Ireland and Great Britain on opposite sides. However, the situation was now very different in the light of Home Rule:

> *what has occurred in recent years has altered the situation completely … today I honestly believe that the democracy of Ireland will turn with the utmost anxiety and sympathy to this country in every trial and every danger that may overtake it … Today there are in Ireland two large bodies of Volunteers … I say to the Government that they may tomorrow withdraw every one of their troops from Ireland. I say that the coast of Ireland will be defended from foreign invasion by her armed sons, and for this purpose armed Nationalist Catholics in the South will be only too glad to join arms with the armed Protestant Ulstermen in the North.*

The response of the newspapers was overwhelmingly positive. Thirty papers commented, of which twenty-seven (90 per cent) supported or praised Redmond's stance. The *Connacht Tribune* (8 August) so scathing of the 'infamy of ascendancy rule' only a week before, wrote, 'In this moment of crisis, Mr Redmond has once more spoken for our own land words of wisdom and justice … History knows no such parallel of national generosity and political sagacity and courage'. The *Connacht Telegraph* wrote that Redmond's statement had created 'a splendid impression in England' and all Ireland was 'united as never before', a point of view shared with the *Ballina Herald* (13 August) which wrote that 'a solid phalanx, a united front, is presented to the foe common to us all'. For the *Tuam Herald* (8 August) his 'manly and magnanimous declaration' showed 'the instincts of a statesman. He accurately gauged and faithfully represented Irish nationalist opinion'. The *Clonmel Nationalist* (5 August) praised 'the masterly tactics of the Irish Leader' and his 'consummate tact and statesmanship to offer the Volunteers to protect Ireland'.

The *Munster Express* (8 August) asked, 'Who would have expected … that what cannot be denied as the traditional attitude of Ireland towards England should be completely transformed by the historic speech of Mr Redmond?' The *Dundalk Democrat* (8 August) hailed Redmond's 'splendid day's work for Ireland'. The *Longford Leader* (8 August) thought that the statement, 'has done more to promote the hopes of Ireland than a thousand public meetings or years of political agitation … We do not want to exchange British rule, bad as it has often proved in the past, for German rule, which is, as anyone who ever went to that country knows, the most autocratic, bureaucratic and tyrannical in the world'.

The Kerryman, still angry at the events of Bachelor's Walk, quoted on 1 August the old Fenian maxim: 'England's difficulty is Ireland's opportunity … we trust the Irish Party will make the most of the advantage which fate has given them'. A week later, after Redmond's statement, it wrote that there was 'not a man in the country who would not support England in the struggle now on'. The *Roscommon Herald* made a similar (though short-lived) about-turn, from describing Serbia on 1 August as 'one of the most contemptible nations on God's earth' and Austria 'a great Catholic country', to finding a week later (8 August) that the Kaiser's 'success spells Europe under the jackboot of the Prussian dragoon'. Under the title 'A Titanic Struggle – Bravo England!' the *Westmeath Independent* (8 August) wrote, 'in the emergency of epoch-making happenings, the Leader of the Irish people lifted the weighty responsibilities of Britain in great part from her shoulders with the magnificent proposition that England might withdraw her troops from Ireland'. Even the hostile *Cork Free Press* (4 August) wrote of 'Mr Redmond's extraordinary offer'; he had been 'wise in his generation for once … the House would have been content with a promise of neutrality. This offer of help was an unexpected piece of generosity …'

Some papers were somewhat more detached. The *Midland Tribune* (8 August) felt that it should be insisted upon that the Home Rule Bill be placed on the Statute Book. In the meantime, the people should stay cool and await events. The *Leinster Leader* (8 August) was similarly concerned at the delay in finalising Home Rule, though it conceded that Redmond had been 'magnanimous' in offering Ireland's support to the British. The *Mayo News* (8 August) carried an editorial titled 'War! War! War!' but took no stance on the issues involved and ignored Redmond's speech. The *Killarney Echo* (8 August) took a pacifist and neutralist approach in an editorial titled 'The Beating of the Wings of the Angel of Death': There is no glory in the clash of arms under existing conditions. If the awful struggle continues the price for the men engaged in it will be a heavy one … Behind them there will be left humble homes with women and children desolate, starving and, perhaps, famine stricken. Even the descendants yet to come will have to drink the cup of sorrow to the dregs if the mad monster of War is fully unloosed among the nations …

The *Derry Journal* (5 August) had no words of praise for Redmond's statement but devoted a long editorial to criticism of war fever and jingoism, followed by a sour tirade at Ulster unionists:

> *There was one note lacking in the memorable accord of Imperial patriotism: 'Ulster', the Ulster of the self-assertive monopolists of loyalty in Ireland was dumb. One would have thought, so pretentious had been the 'Ulster' posing as warden of all that is worth conserving and protecting in the British connection, that Commander Carson and his aides-de-camp, Captain Craig and associated heroes of hypothetical achievement, would have been in the frontal line … but … the 'dour determined men of Ulster' were voiceless, and deliberately so. 'Ulster' of course will fight, but for what? The Empire? No; but for their 'Covenant' …*

D. THE SIGNING OF HOME RULE INTO LAW, SEPTEMBER 1914

The good feeling between Irish nationalists and southern unionists produced by Redmond's Commons speech was not replicated in his relationship with the Ulster Unionist Party in parliament. Apart from lobbying to have the Volunteers enrolled by the War Office as a home defence force, his chief concern was to have the Home Rule Bill signed into law as quickly as possible. In normal times, this would have happened in early August when parliament was prorogued for the autumn recess. But Redmond's urgency brought him into direct conflict with Bonar Law and Carson, who had expected that their willingness to suspend discussion of the amending bill in wartime should be reciprocated by a suspension of further progress of the Home Rule Bill itself, something completely unacceptable to Redmond.

When Asquith appeared to dither between the two sides, Redmond told him that if he allowed himself to be bullied by the Unionist leaders, 'a position of the most serious difficulty' would arise for the Irish Party, with 'the most unfortunate and disastrous results in Ireland … It would make it quite impossible for me to go to Ireland, as I desire to do, and to transform into action the spirit of my speech the other day'. They must not lose the 'greatest opportunity that ever occurred in the history of Ireland to win the Irish people to loyalty to the Empire'.

With two adjournments totaling three weeks in August and September, and with nationalist opinion at home in a state of growing impatience, Redmond anxiously lobbied Asquith. Finally, on 15 September, Asquith announced that the Home Rule Bill would be placed on the Statute Book that week. It would be accompanied by a suspensory bill to postpone its operation for a minimum of twelve months and until no later than the end of the war. Defending the government's decision, he spoke of the effects on Irish opinion around the world should the bill's signing be postponed indefinitely as the unionists wanted: it would be 'an unspeakable calamity'. But he also had an assurance for unionists: 'the employment of force, any kind of force, for what you call the coercion of Ulster, is an absolutely unthinkable thing'. Accordingly, before Home Rule came into operation, the amending bill would be re-introduced to allow the Act to be modified 'with general consent'. And in the climate created by 'this great patriotic spirit of union', he believed that it might have a better chance of winning such consent. Voicing his sense of betrayal, Bonar Law led Tory and Unionist MPs in a walkout from the House.

The king signed the Home Rule Bill and the suspensory bill into law on Friday 18 September, bringing the forty-year constitutional nationalist campaign to an end. Redmond had already responded to Asquith's speech in terms that went beyond his words of 3 August:

> [Ireland] will feel that the British democracy has kept faith with her … I have publicly promised, not only for myself, but in the name of my country, that when the rights of Ireland were admitted by the democracy of England, that Ireland would become the strongest arm in the defence of the Empire. The test has come sooner than I, or anyone, expected … I say for myself, that I would feel myself personally dishonoured if I did not say to my fellow countrymen, as I will say from the public platform when I go back to Ireland, that it is their duty, and should be their honour, to take their place in the firing-line in this contest …

Accepting the pledge on the amending bill, he believed and hoped that it might lead to a bill 'very different from that about which we have been quarreling in the past'. The two things he cared most about were, firstly, that self-government should extend to all of Ireland, and secondly, 'that no coercion shall be applied to any single county in Ireland to force them against their will to come into the Irish Government'. These goals were at that moment incompatible. But would they still be so after a few more months?

> *No, Sir, I do not believe they will. During that interval, Catholic Nationalist and Protestant Unionist Irishmen from the north of Ireland will be fighting*

side by side on the battlefields on the Continent, and shedding their blood
side by side; and at home in Ireland, Catholic Nationalists and Protestant
Ulstermen will, I hope and believe, be found drilling shoulder to shoulder
for the defence of the shores of their own country … I do not think I am too
sanguine when I express my belief that, when the time has arrived for the
Government to introduce their Amending Bill, we may have been able by this
process in Ireland to come to an agreement amongst ourselves …

The main points of this speech were contained in a manifesto issued by Redmond the day before the royal assent. Declaring that a new era had opened between Ireland and Britain, it claimed that Ireland would be 'false to her history, and to every consideration of honour, good faith and self-interest, did she not willingly bear her share in its burdens and its sacrifices'. It ended with the hope that, since Irish soldiers of both traditions were going to fight and die side by side, 'their union in the field may lead to a union in their home, and that their blood may be the seal that will bring all Ireland together in one nation'. The following Sunday, driving to his Wicklow home, he gave a brief impromptu speech to a company of Volunteers lined up for drill practice at Woodenbridge, County Wicklow. Here he made explicit what he had urged in his manifesto – that Irishmen should voluntarily enlist in the British armed forces: 'Their duty was two-fold: to go on drilling, and then to 'account yourselves as men, not only in Ireland itself, but wherever the firing-line extends, in defence of right, of freedom and of religion in this war'. It would be 'a disgrace forever to Ireland, and a reproach to her manhood' if young Irishmen were to stay at home to defend the island's shores from an unlikely invasion.

In the euphoria produced by the final victory of Home Rule, all commentators noticed the wartime suspension but not so many the second obstacle to an implementation of the bill (now act) as it had been passed back in May: the promise that the amending bill must pass first, ensuring that ultimately the writ of the Home Rule parliament would not run in all thirty-two counties of the island. The two national dailies took different approaches. The pro-Party *Freeman,* not anxious to dwell on negatives, greeted 'Ireland's Day of Triumph' when the country had taken her 'place of sisterhood in the Empire, endowed with equal rights and privileges, and free to achieve her own destiny'. The *Independent*, however, considered the second obstacle and spelled out the implications: 'We are told that an Act passed by the Imperial Parliament can come into force only in compliance with the vetoing power of sixteen Ulster members'.

The division of opinion in the provincial press followed roughly the same proportions as in May. Of thirty-seven papers commenting on the Home Rule enactment, twenty-five (67.6 per cent) celebrated the triumph or heaped paeans of praise on Redmond's leadership, and refused to be worried by the amending bill. Reaction to the recruiting manifesto was somewhat less enthusiastic. Twenty-eight papers commented, of which seventeen (61 per cent) were in support, with eleven (39 per cent) negative, non-committal or neutralist. It should be added that, although all the papers occasionally or frequently carried editorials on non-political matters in times of quiet, for a paper that usually commented on political affairs to ignore such a historic turning point as the successful end of the forty-year Home Rule struggle or Redmond's recruiting call for the war seemed like the making of a statement in itself. For example, the *Midland Tribune*, one of five papers that did not comment on the first, on 12 September had demanded the urgent signing of the Home Rule Act into law but snubbed the actual event with editorials on tillage and rent reduction on 19 and 26 September respectively. Perhaps even more pointed was the failure of fourteen papers, one-third of the total sample, to register any response to the recruiting call. If most of these non-responses are interpreted as silent rejection, combining them with the negative, non-committal or neutralist comments of those that did respond yields an overall less-than-positive response of 50-60 per cent to Redmond's call.

The *Clare Champion* (19 September) celebrated 'a day of thanksgiving for the whole Irish race. Ireland will take her place in the Empire ...' The *Limerick Leader* (16 September) hailed 'the crowning vindication of Mr Redmond's policy' and felt that one year was not too long to wait.

The *Dundalk Democrat* (19 September) rejoiced that 'the long and anxious period of waiting is over'. Home Rule was now law, and there was nobody who would resent the suspension of its operation until the end of the war. As for the amending bill, 'its scope and its fate we may leave to the future. There is no need to trouble about it now'. The *Tuam Herald* (19 September) likewise thought that not much would be lost by the suspensory period. It saw the royal assent as putting 'the crown on the work of the Irish Party backed by the Irish people and led by the greatest Parliamentarian Ireland ever produced'.

The Woodenbridge policy enunciated by Redmond, based more on hope than on realism, that the war would resolve the amending bill issue by dissolving the differences between Irishmen at the Front, found its echo in several of the papers. The *Connacht Tribune* (19 September) shared his aspiration for 'the union of all Irishmen in a common affliction'. The *Sligo Champion* reckoned that 'the war will swallow up the small issues' and bring unity. 'The fact that Home Rule is on the Statute Book,' it added hopefully, 'must needs have a great influence on the character and fate of [the amending bill] … We have probably heard the last of exclusion'. The *Connaught Telegraph* (19 September) considered that 'the dream of Irishmen has been realised'; although 'we cannot claim that it is a perfect measure, nevertheless it concedes the main demand'. On the exclusion of Ulster: 'there will be no exclusion of a permanent character. If Ulster wants exclusion, she will get it for a definite period, but we believe the industrious people of Ulster will not be so foolish as to cut off their connection with the rest of Ireland'. It was probable that no amending bill would ever be introduced. The relentlessly optimistic *Donegal Vindicator* (18 September) was certain that 'the Home Rule Bill we have received is only an instalment' (it had earlier called it 'painfully defective in its financial clauses'), 'but it is a substantial one, and from it will emerge a greater as soon as Ulster realises itself and takes its stand with the rest of Ireland … we have no fear of the promised Amending Bill'. In like vein, the *Derry People & Donegal News* (26 September) wrote that although more would be heard of exclusion, 'we should not be surprised to learn in the near future that, such silly utterances notwithstanding, the policy of partitioning Ireland is dead and buried'.

Among the more critical organs, the *Leinster Leader* (19 September) opined that although 18 September was an historic date and 'the consummation of the triumph of the cause', there had been a lack of enthusiasm because 'the Government's shifty postponements and delays have not only tried the patience of the people of this country, but their vacillation and hesitation in ratifying the will of Parliament have robbed their policy of much of the limited value it contained … [The Act is not] a really valuable one or worthy of the dignity of a treaty of peace. The Volunteer force must be maintained and strengthened'. The *Carlow Nationalist* (19 September) criticised 'the period of unnecessary suspense which annoyed the public mind', adding that, although Redmond's speech had been 'manly and truly statesmanlike', 'given the truculence and abuse indulged in by the Unionists of the Government and the Irish leaders, we confess that we look forward with some misgivings to the end of the suspensory period'. The *Clonmel Nationalist* (19 September), on the other hand, felt that Irish nationalists would not be 'disposed to criticise without measure the delay in putting the bill on the Statute Book. They will remember that if Mr Redmond and his colleagues had difficulties to surmount, Mr Asquith's task was anything but easy. He did his best for Ireland, and his best is the Home Rule Act'.

Mayo News (19 September) thought that, notwithstanding the placing of the Act on the Statute Book, 'our people should adopt Asquith's motto "Wait and See"'. If it were to become law in its present form, it might with time be made the basis for a fully fledged parliament for Ireland. But that would not happen; it would be amended if the Liberals were still in power after the war, or worse if the Tories won the post-war election. The *Meath Chronicle* (19 September), which had hailed Redmond's 3 August 'historic utterance', had since hardened its tone: 'The pitiable fact remains that Ireland is to have an Act of Parliament dignified with the name of Home Rule, but of unknown extent, at some future date. She will get something, somehow, some time'. For the *Tipperary*

Star (19 September) 'the actual measure is nothing to crow over, but the enforced recognition of the principle it involves is a great deal gained. However, if Carson and Co. had their way, 'the Amending Bill will be an Amputating Bill or rather a Beheading Bill'; it was for the majority of the Nation, it added bullishly, to 'squelch this, not by lung power but by force of arms, if needs be'. Carson and his friends 'will come round to right reason only when we compel their respect'.

Responding to Redmond's manifesto, the *Ballina Herald* (1 October) was unrestrained in its support: 'It has been stated in some papers that Ireland's response to Lord Kitchener's appeal is not as it should be, and be that reproach justified or not up to the present, we are convinced that Mr Redmond and his party having now promised to actively interest themselves in the matter [of recruiting], that the martial spirit, for which the Irish people are so famous, will find vent, and that every available young man will go to do his duty by his country and the Empire'. The *Dundalk Democrat* (26 September) suggested, now that the Irish had the right to govern themselves, that nationalists needed to revise their outlook regarding Great Britain and international relations. It would be hard for 'some Irishmen of the old school' to do this. The *Tuam Herald* (3 October) wrote: 'We are now at the parting of the ways in nationalist politics and it behoves us to face the changed political situation like sensible men'. Enthusiastically backing the call for an 'Irish brigade', it added that it would be treachery for Ireland to withhold aid to 'the cause the Irish people have at heart – independence within the Empire and under it'. In the view of the *Drogheda Argus* (26 September), 'one question must be asked and answered. What are we going to do? But a few years ago we sympathised with the gallant little Boers because they sought to guard the independence of their nation. We upheld the weak as against the strong. We opposed aggression then, and we must oppose aggression now'.

In a full-blooded endorsement of the manifesto under the title 'The Call to Arms', the *Westmeath Independent* (19 September) wrote, 'Ireland, won to the Empire, by the restoration of National Freedom, is asked to spring to arms to defend the Empire, of which she is an integral part, is asked to defend the liberty and freedom of other small nations like our own. If we should fail to do that, if the German barbarian over-reached us, and by force of arms succeeded in his diabolical plans ... let there be no mistake about it, we in this country would sooner or later ... have handed out to us the outrages, shootings, incendiarism, revolting crimes against wives and daughters, which have stamped with the likeness of Hell the trail of the German in Belgium and France'. It wholeheartedly approved of Redmond's call for a distinctively 'Irish brigade':

> As it is there are forty thousand Irish troops at the front, and no one can deny the splendour of their services. But their magnificent self-sacrifice, while it sheds lustre and undying honour on British arms, is largely lost to Ireland as a distinctive effort. These men are spread over all arms of the British Service as well as the purely local Irish regiments. They have performed prodigies of valour ... We want now, if possible, an exclusively Irish brigade to reinforce them. Every claim that appeals to the human heart urges the formation of that brigade. National sentiment, patriotism, sympathy with the sufferings of others, a sense of our own self-preservation ...

There must be no prevarication (26 September):

> Any apathy there was must be replaced by enthusiasm; the Irishman on the farm or in the workshop, in business or commercial employment, everyone of them who can be spared – Catholic, Protestant, Dissenter, Orange and Green, they must all answer the call of their political leaders, they must all give of their best to this titanic fight! We have the assurance of the greatest soldier of our day, Lord Kitchener – our own countryman – with another five hundred thousand soldiers capable of taking the field next year, the infamous German can be beaten to the dirt ... Are we Irishmen, hailed by every country as the fighting race, not to do our part? The mention of such a thing is unthinkable. It would be a disgrace to our new-found freedom; it would beggar us in the eyes of the world as men of principle and of honour ... Away with such nightmare fancies ...

The *Donegal Vindicator* (25 September) while supportive of the manifesto, sounded an ambivalent note: 'The Irish Nation will respond [to Redmond's call] and it will have the approval of its sons scattered all over the world, scattered by the rapacious foe for which it is now asked to shed its blood … we must be able to broaden our outlook or it will be impossible to reconcile the position taken up by John Redmond with pure Irish patriotism'. The *Southern Star* (19 September) hailing 'the Irish Party and its distinguished Leader, Mr John Redmond, [due] to whose undoubted genius, patriotism and valour, Ireland has at last broken the chains which enthralled her and taken her place among the nations of the earth,' was ardent in its wish that 'even at the cost of many more thousands of lives the War Lord [Kaiser Wilhelm] must be put down'. However, the paper astutely stopped short of suggesting that Irishmen's lives should be risked in this procedure. The *Tipperary Star* (3 October) referred to Redmond's 'unpleasant appeal' but placed the blame for it on Carson, whose 'boasts are unquestionably the cause that has driven Mr Redmond' into making it.

The *Kerryman* (19 September) was non-committal: 'At last the Home Rule Bill is at safe anchorage … King Carson is raging … Mr John E Redmond has also issued a manifesto, which, to put it mildly, is strongly imperialistic'. He had appealed to the men of Ireland to fight on the side of England, but how far his influence would weigh with his fellow countrymen, 'time will tell'. The *Roscommon Herald,* interpreted (19 September) the manifesto as Redmond's part of the bargain involving 'Asquith's latest dodge about Home Rule', the elements of which were 'passing Home Rule, suspension, an Amending Bill to satisfy Carson and no coercion of Ulster … This shuffle means 100,000 nationalist recruits – farmers' and labourers' sons to go to France to be shot to pieces by German shells'. The London papers were calling on the Irish MPs 'to earn their £400 a year by becoming recruiting sergeants for the English army'. On 3 October, Tully took aim at what he saw as double standards regarding the chief focus of Irish war enthusiasm. Only four years earlier, Belgium had been excoriated by many, led by the Archbishop of Canterbury, for its behaviour in the Congo. England had 'got up the usual atrocities agitation'. One Irish MP, the independent Home Ruler John McKean, had stood up for fair play for Belgium but was 'hounded down' by the Party's John O'Connor MP as 'Congo Jack'. 'Now,' wrote Tully, 'we are all to go out and get shot to death in France for the sake of Catholic Belgium'.

The *Leinster Leader* (26 September) also objected to the recruiting call: 'Ireland is to be exploited and stumped for recruits for service… as the price for this belated and bound-down Act'. It would be time enough to consider the needs of the Empire when Ireland had a surplus, but it hoped that recruiting would go ahead for the National Volunteers for the defence of the country. The *Midland Tribune* (3 October) was frankly opposed: 'Carson and Co. continue their opposition to Home Rule. An Amending Bill is to be passed. We have nothing to be grateful to England for what she has given with one hand and taken back with the other'. Ireland should stay neutral. A national convention should decide whether Ireland's representatives were to become recruiting sergeants.

The above findings are summarised in Chart 1.

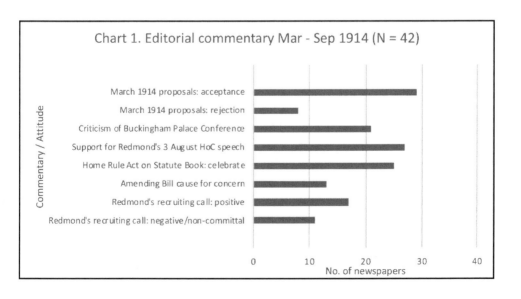

Chart 1. Editorial commentary Mar - Sep 1914 (N = 42)

E. THE SPLIT IN THE VOLUNTEERS, SEPTEMBER–OCTOBER 1914

In June, Redmond had used his political authority to force the Volunteers' founding body, the 'provisional committee', to co-opt nominees of his own to ensure a measure of democratic control over the movement. Agreement had been reached only after a prolonged tussle with Eoin MacNeill, the Volunteers' chief of staff. In September, Redmond's manifesto and Woodenbridge speech were not long in producing a reaction within the movement.

On 25 September, a statement signed by MacNeill and nineteen others of the original provisional committee of the Volunteers declared Redmond's twenty-five nominees expelled from the committee. The signatories included at least five members of the Supreme Council of the secret Irish Republican Brotherhood (IRB, commonly known as 'the Fenians'). The statement accused Redmond of having 'consented to a dismemberment of Ireland, which could be made permanent by the same agencies that forced him to accept it as temporary'. He had now 'announced for the Irish Volunteers a policy and programme fundamentally at variance with their own … [and] declared it to be the duty of the Irish Volunteers to take foreign service under a government which is not Irish'; he had done this without consulting the committee, the Volunteer membership or the people of Ireland.

The signatories pledged themselves 'to oppose any diminution of the measure of Irish self-government which now exists as a Statute on paper, and which would not now have reached that stage but for the Irish Volunteers. This was in line with the ostensible *raison d'être* of the Volunteers, whose founding manifesto declared them to be 'defensive and protective' and would not contemplate either aggression or domination. However, the public was not informed, and neither MacNeill, the non-IRB members of the committee or the rank and file of the Volunteers were aware, that the executive of the IRB Supreme Council had already met in a room in Dublin on 9 September – nine days before the Home Rule Act had gone on the Statute Book – to decide on a course of action that consigned the prospect of Home Rule, and any conceivable outcome of the legislation, to irrelevance. Their decision was that the period of the war would not be allowed to pass without a separatist armed insurrection at home.

Throughout October, meetings of local Volunteer companies took place all over the country. The overwhelming majority voted support of Redmond's position and opposition to that of the MacNeillites. By late October it was estimated that a total of 158,360 members (henceforth to be called the 'National Volunteers') supported Redmond as against 12,306 (to be called the 'Irish Volunteers') for the minority manifesto. In Dublin City and county, however, the division was more even: 4,850 for Redmond and 1,900 against; in two inner-city battalions, the dissidents were in the majority. As time passed, the Irish Volunteers in Dublin city would ally themselves with the eighty-strong Citizen Army founded by the socialist James Connolly.

Provincial press commentary largely followed the lines of the Volunteer vote. Thirty-one newspapers commented on the issue of the Volunteer split, of which twenty-three supported the Redmond policy, five were neutral or emphasised the need for unity and three, either through news coverage or by direct comment, indicated support for the dissidents.

The *Limerick Leader* reported on a manifesto issued by local Volunteers under the headline 'Limerick Volunteers/Behind Redmond and Party/Will Not Be Led By Sinn Féiners'. In the paper's opinion, the Sinn Féin minority on the provisional committee 'excited mingled feelings of pity and contempt ... [they] have made consummate fools of themselves ... the obvious absurdity of a minority expelling a majority with bell, book and candle ... [is] only a fit subject for laughter' (21, 28 September). The Belfast *Irish News* (23 September) called the dissidents 'a useless, worthless, practically unknown little coterie of seasoned mischief-makers ensconced in Dublin, and largely, if not mainly, composed of persons who have some means and a vast amount of leisure for the task of working harm'. The *Cork Examiner* (26 September) headlined its news of the controversy 'The Sinn Féin Soreheads/Confidence in Party'; its editorial criticised the 'few dissentients [and their] puerile efforts to create dissension and to blacken their country's good name'. 'Miniature Napoleons, mostly unknown' and 'a band of Sinn Féin nincompoops and egotists' were the judgments of the *Longford Leader and Drogheda Argus* (both 3 October) respectively. The *Connacht Tribune* (26 September) called their action 'inopportune' and 'uncalled for' and attacked the manifesto of 'Mr John MacNeill and his nineteen practically unknown followers' and 'their naive ingenuity [sic] and almost unparalleled impudence'. The 'little clique of mischief-makers … will fail in Dublin as they will fail in Galway'. The *Longford Leader* (26 September) wrote that 'the Sinn Féin element, small though it be, has again raised its war cry at a time above all others when it can do most harm to the hopes of Ireland'. The *Wexford People* (26 September) called the controversy 'just a hint regarding what some young Irishmen are unfortunately doing at present – what will result in thwarting the efforts of the Irish Party to have the Amending Bill an improving Bill instead of a Bill in favour of the Orangemen's claims'. Under the heading 'Promoting Discord', it assailed 'the ill-timed and ill-advised manifesto by the Sinn Féin section of the provisional committee'; the aim of those malcontents was 'to discredit the Irish Party and cause mischief'. For the *Clonmel Nationalist*, it was bad enough to have to deal with 'vindictive Carsonites', but the 'audacious attempt of a minority on the provisional committee to disrupt the National Volunteers and flout the Irish Leader and the Irish Party' was 'a most treacherous movement'. Epithets such as 'obscure', 'contemptible', 'coterie', 'clique', 'factionist', 'malcontents', 'cranks' and 'mischief-makers' abounded in the editorial matter of this majority group of papers.

The *Sligo Champion* (3 October) had no harsh words for the dissidents, but reckoned that the question of control of the Volunteers was simple. Pending the establishment of a Home Rule government, this should rest with the Leader and the Party that had placed Home Rule on the Statute Book, enjoyed the confidence of the overwhelming majority of the people of Ireland and were 'the nearest thing to a government we have'. For the *Meath Chronicle* (3 October), the rupture was 'nothing short of a calamity'. It tried to understand the views of both sides, but concluded that 'the broad fact remains that the Volunteers were intended for home purposes' and not for service abroad. The *Tipperary Star* (3 October) was more circumspect, saying 'If we can't agree, let's agree to differ … let the Volunteers who are panting for the front go'.

Other papers, perhaps reluctant to comment directly, indicated their stance by the news they chose to report. The *Roscommon Journal* had already commented sceptically on the royal assent and Redmond's manifesto. It is difficult to know whether the paper was communicating a message of neutrality or a more subtle one of opposition when, under the startling headline 'Irish National Volunteers/Meeting in Roscommon/Mr Heverin and the Sinn Féiners/"The Man Who Would Die Happy"/"If He Got Three Shots at John Redmond"', it reported (3 October) a meeting held in Roscommon town to organise the county's Volunteers into battalions. The meeting had adopted a resolution protesting against the action of the minority of the provisional committee and expressing 'implicit confidence' in Redmond and his able colleagues. The proposer of the resolution was reported as saying, 'A great many of them knew the class of fellows that were working this game against the Irish Party … A good many of them are hobnobbing between themselves and trying to buttonhole persons around it'. An exchange followed:

> *Chairman – Well, gentlemen, I was never more ashamed than I was this morning in Roscommon. I was talking to a certain person belonging to the town and he said he would die happy if he got three shots at 'Johneen' Redmond …*
> *Mr Johnston – You will get black sheep in every flock.*
> *Chairman – We won't go one step outside John Redmond and the Irish Party.*
> *Mr Donnelly – I think the whole country will stand by John Redmond.*

The *Mayo News* did not comment on the Volunteer split but reported (26 September) on a Westport meeting of dissident Volunteers addressed by local Commandant Joe McBride in terms close to the views of the paper – neutralist on the war and critical of the Home Rule Act. In subsequent weeks it reported on Redmond's flying of the Union Jack (alongside the green Irish flag and the Stars and Stripes) at his Aughavanagh home, and carried an editorial titled 'Irish–American Opinion of Mr John Redmond as Recruiting Sergeant'. Claiming to have received many letters from Irish–American subscribers, it alleged, 'They all bear the same spirit of unmeasured condemnation of Mr Redmond's action'.

The *Killarney Echo* (3 October) also dwelt on the flying of the Union Jack at Aughavanagh. Recalling the nineteenth century patriot Thomas Davis who had told how 'our fathers rose in fierce array to proudly set the Irish Green above the English Red', it noted the defiance shown in recent speeches by Unionist leaders who had reassured their followers that Home Rule would never become a reality in Ulster:

> *The trio of sedition mongers are, no doubt, led on to the use of their wild words by the promise of the prime minister that when the war is over no force will be used to make Ireland a nation by establishing Home Rule in Ulster. In the hurly-burly of it all Irish Nationalists are invited to give up the healthy hopes by which their sinking hearts were fed in dark and evil days. It is hard to do it, hard to be asked to do it, and harder still to know what to do. It is, indeed, a time to search men's souls in a supreme way. Poor Ireland, with the Union Jack floating proudly in the breeze at Aughavanagh, and the burning words of Thomas Davis thrilling its real soul, even yet finds herself faced with a mighty problem from within while seriously disturbed by a monster problem from without.*

The Volunteer split was the catalyst for *The Kerryman* to signal a further and daring move from its denigration of the Home Rule Act to something not yet seen in the mainstream of the provincial press – open criticism of the Irish Party leadership. In an editorial on 3 October, it ignored the Belgian–French Allied dimension fuelling Irish war enthusiasm and attacked the leadership's appeal to the young men of Ireland 'to rush to support of the Empire … to spill their blood, cheerfully and copiously in the attempt to maintain England's supremacy'. It accompanied this with an article under the headline, 'Home Rule Act: Straight Talk by a Priest: "Mr Redmond Degrading Himself"', a report of a meeting of the executive of the West Limerick United Irish League (UIL, the national organisation of the Irish Party). Reverend John Fitzgerald was reported to have said that there was 'nothing to be enthusiastic about in the Home Rule Act. Ireland's battle was far from being won, for it was quite possible that the Act as it stands might not be worth the paper on which it is written. He never got such a surprise in his life as when he read Mr Redmond's recent manifesto. He never believed that Mr Redmond, or any member of the Irish Party, would so degrade himself as to become a recruiting sergeant for the English Government'.

Chapter 3

THE RECRUITING CAMPAIGN, THE COALITION GOVERNMENT AND HOPES FOR HOME RULE, 1915– APRIL 1916

A. THE NATIONAL VOLUNTEER REVIEW, APRIL 1915

Following the Volunteer split, nationalist politics entered a period of quiescence, at least on the surface. Redmond and other party MPs launched an intensive campaign of weekly recruiting rallies and inspected musters of the National Volunteers in every Irish province. After one of these meetings, the *Kilkenny People* (24 October) called Redmond's reception 'probably the most remarkable and striking display of popular enthusiasm ever witnessed in this city'. At the same time Redmond sought to encourage enlistment by privately lobbying the Cabinet to have the National Volunteers officially recognised as a home defence force and to ensure that an Irish division within the British army would have a distinctive national character, just as the Thirty-Sixth (Ulster) Division embodied the identity of Protestant Ulster. Meanwhile, the dissident

Irish Volunteer faction went its own way, recruiting, drilling, arming and conducting propaganda through its own paper, *The Irish Volunteer,* while its IRB manipulators secretly prepared for revolution. Although most papers cleaved to the majority opinion, few if any were inclined to criticise or engage in debate with the minority body. An exception was the *Tuam Herald*, which on 3 April 1915 hit out at the critics of the Party's policy. The views of the Irish Volunteer minority should be respected, it wrote, but 'it is an act of insufferable intolerance for those who are confessedly in a minority in a country to arrogate to themselves the right to interfere with a majority in the exercise of its privileges'. If the British Navy were not so well protecting our coasts and the French, Belgian and British armies keeping the Germans at bay, 'Ireland would be another Belgium today'.

Public attention was overwhelmingly concentrated on the progress of the war, which replaced national politics in the editorial commentary of many newspapers, especially when it became clear in early 1915 that the war was likely to last longer than originally imagined. While recruitment was slower than in the first months of the war, it proceeded at a steady pace despite news of the April disasters at Gallipoli and the long lists of casualties that soon began to appear in the papers. (The *Carlow Nationalist* (29 May) was untypical of the provincial press in commenting on the heavy losses suffered by families in the Kildare and Dublin areas as a result of the casualties sustained by the Dublin Fusiliers at Gallipoli, while continuing to urge young men to join up). However, a rift opened between Redmond and his deputy, John Dillon, who became convinced that the Woodenbridge speech had been an error of judgment that might discredit the party and told his leader that he would take no further part in recruiting. By the end of 1915, 28,000 of the National Volunteers and 40,000 others had enlisted. Among those were Redmond's brother Willie, his son William Archer Redmond and others close to him including Stephen Gwynn MP and the ex-MP Tom Kettle, all of whom would soon be on active service.

The first major event of 1915 that attracted the attention of most provincial papers was the review of 27,000 National Volunteers held in Dublin's Phoenix Park on Easter Sunday, 4 April, followed by a Volunteer convention the following day. Of a total of twenty-nine newspapers that commented, twenty-three (79 per cent) were positive.

The dominant theme of the commentary was the demonstration itself and what it signified. The *Nenagh Guardian* (10 April) headlined its report: 'Historic Review of National Volunteers/Magnificent Display in Dublin/Witnessed by 100,000 People/Over 25,000 Volunteers on Parade'. The *Limerick Leader* (7 April) called it 'a striking manifestation of the strength and virility of Irish nationalism … by far the most inspiring and historic spectacle seen in the metropolis since the memorable days of the immortal Henry Grattan'. The *Donegal Vindicator* (9 April) reported that 'never within living memory has Dublin witnessed such a gathering of Irish manhood'. The *Derry Journal* (5 April), in a reference to Redmond's difficulties in having the National Volunteers officially enrolled as a home defence force, reckoned that the 'historic day in Dublin' would 'probably' cause the War Office to wake from its 'unresponsive and Sphinx-like attitude'. The *Westmeath Independent* (10 April) gave its 'most enthusiastic approval and commendation' to the display, though it noted that not all recruits were of the same standard: the 3,000 Tipperary men taking part were 'fine soldiers in the making', while many from the west and the midlands were 'mere striplings and elderly men'. (Enlistment rates were particularly strong in the south-eastern counties of Tipperary, Kilkenny, Waterford and Wexford, the recruiting ground of the Royal Irish Regiment.) The *Longford Leader* (10 April) carried a report on the 'splendid turn-out' from Longford alongside a speech by its proprietor–editor, J.P. Farrell MP, warning young nationalists not to be misled by Sinn Féin. An extra dimension was added to this story by the paper's cross-Shannon rival, Tully's *Roscommon Herald*, which claimed that Farrell, at a recent UIL meeting, had contradicted a story afloat in County Longford that the Volunteer parade had been organised by the Irish Party 'to strap men into the British army, and if he thought it were such a thing, he for one would not have hand, act or part in the parade'. The *Irish News* (5 April) wrote that 'not since the unveiling of the Parnell monument [in 1911] has there been such remarkable enthusiasm ... Sunday, April 4th, will be remembered as an epochal date in our country's story ... a superb spectacle of Irish manhood and resolve'. The *Clonmel Nationalist* (7 April) outdid all others in enthusing that 'Ireland has been thrilled from the centre to the sea by the glorious success of the great Volunteer Review ... The Irish heart throbs with new life ... [since] the wonderful triumphs won under able leadership by constitutional methods against almost insuperable odds ... we share in upholding the Empire, of which we are now willing partners'.

The nationalist–unionist harmony that had enjoyed a brief midsummer flowering in the wake of Redmond's 3 August 1914 speech soon dissipated as the review brought the issue of recruiting into the realm of controversy. Unionist papers criticised allegedly slow nationalist rates of enlistment; nationalist organs responded in kind. The *Dundalk Democrat* (10 April) was sensitive to unionist criticism of the review. The *Irish Times* had found fault with the soldierly deficiencies of the Volunteers on display and also with the slowness in the completion of the Sixteenth (Irish) Division (founded the previous September and engaged in training its three brigades of recruits at Tipperary town, Fermoy and Buttevant). The *Democrat* asked why the paper did not find similar fault with the Ulster Volunteers and their delay in filling up the Ulster Division. The *Tuam Herald* (10 April) developed the theme. Unionist papers had asked why these 25,000 fine fellows were not at the Front. 'We can reply by asking why are not the 30,000 Ulstermen who were supposed to be fit for action last year, who were then, on paper, so formidable that they made the German Empire believe in their boasts ... why are not they, these seasoned warriors, in the post of danger? ... Either they are willing or they are not. Surely, it is time to end this sham, if it be a sham'. The *Connacht Tribune* (10 April) joined the fray with a bitter attack on Carson and his 'bigoted Orange rabble', acidly observing that 'it seems a larger number of Carsonites are still north of the Boyne than in the trenches of

Flanders'. The *Anglo-Celt* (3 April) also took a swipe at recruiting levels in Ulster, asserting that nationalist enlistment would be greatly boosted if it were announced that the Ulster Division would be going to the Front with the 'Irish Brigade'. Cleverly combining sectarian prejudice with plausible deniability, it claimed that 'the prevailing idea from one end of the island to the other is, that the Ulster Volunteers will never be asked to fight,' adding that while it did not believe a word of it, the belief was 'firmly fixed in the minds of the populace'.

A third question raised by the review was the question of what the purpose of the Volunteers should be in the new conditions of the war with Home Rule the law of the land. The Home Rule Act precluded an Irish government from having a permanent defence force at its disposal. When Redmond had called on Asquith's government to enrol and equip the Volunteers as a home defence force for the duration of the war, he was already stretching this provision to its limit. When he called on Irishmen to join a fighting 'Irish brigade' in the British army, he was laying the groundwork for a future native standing army, as he recognised at his recruiting rally in Wexford in October 1914 when he spoke in just such terms. The difficulties that beset him in realising both of these goals in late 1914 related to the reservations in British official and army circles arising from an awareness of the limitations imposed by the Act. In early 1915 he was told by his colleague T.P. O'Connor, who had interviewed Kitchener, that the War Office was wary of the creation of a second armed force in Ireland, which, given the existence of the Ulster Volunteers, could 'lead directly to civil war and perhaps to revolution'. Kitchener had referred, O'Connor wrote, to 'revolutionary forces in Ireland which you could not control and of whose existence perhaps you were not even cognisant'. Some newspapers seemed to understand these difficulties; most, however, were not inclined to pay much heed to them.

The *Westmeath Examiner* (10 April) wrote that the National Volunteers did not 'want to attack anyone, even those whose stances they find abhorrent'; they were 'really a constitutional party in military form' and a defensive force. For the *Sligo Champion* (3 April), the force 'contemplate[s] neither aggression nor domination. Their duties are defensive and protective … in defence of British law'. Other papers were less demure. The *Leinster Leader* (10 April) agreed that as long as the Volunteers kept their objects in view – to be ready for any emergency in defence of their country and the rights and privileges of the Irish people – 'it is, in our opinion, immaterial who directs or controls their organisation'. The *Southern Star* and the *Connacht Tribune* (both 10 April) both referred to 'Ireland's National Army' while the *Cork Examiner* (5 April) saw in the National Volunteers 'a native army prepared to defend her liberties so dearly won, and equally ready to repel the foreign invader'.

Of those papers that had indicated disagreement with the recruiting policy, all ignored the event altogether and substituted material that made it easier to vent their opinions. The *Meath Chronicle* (10, 17 April), pro-war albeit with misgivings on the deployment of the Volunteers, concentrated on the progress of the war. The *Killarney Echo* (22 May) gave notice of a forthcoming review of Kerry Irish Volunteers in May by Eoin MacNeill and reminded its readers that the latter 'has declared his reasons against any division of the Irish Nation, and, though a follower of Mr John Redmond's, he parted company with him when he considered his policy and the action of the Irish Party nominees on the governing body of the Volunteer organisation endangered the principles which the Volunteers were established to uphold'. The *Mayo News* (3 April) substituted a letter from the maverick Irish Party MP for West Clare Arthur Lynch expressing vehement opposition to the prospect of partition and recalling his parliamentary question to the prime minister: 'Are we fighting for Ireland a Nation or for three-quarters of Ireland a province?' The *Kerryman* seemed keen to provoke a response from the authorities when on 9 January it published war communiqués from the Berlin chancellery on its front page (the equivalent action by a German paper would have caused its immediate closure and the execution of the editor).

William O'Brien's *Cork Free Press* (3, 5 April) was also critical of the Review, but from a strongly pro-recruiting standpoint, calling it 'an exhibition of National Foolery'. Taking a view diametrically opposite to that of every other nationalist organ, it headlined its report 'Ireland's National Disgrace/Reviewing the Stay-At-Homes'. This was denigratory invective of the type *The Irish Times* and the Ulster unionist press had been serving up for the previous six months. Claiming that only 10,800 Volunteers 'could be lured to turn up', it wrote 'an intended demonstration of the unheard-of mightiness of Ireland's armed strength turned out to be a demonstration of the sensational feebleness of Redmondism'.

B. THE FORMATION OF THE COALITION GOVERNMENT, MAY 1915

In the spring of 1915, Asquith's Liberal government came under sustained criticism in the press, particularly in the papers of the Northcliffe empire, *The Times* and the *Daily Mail*, for its conduct of the war. The failure to make a decisive breakthrough on the Western Front and the realisation that the war would last far longer than originally predicted, together with the fresh news of the Royal Navy's failure at the Dardanelles, all contributed to this pressure. The inter-party truce instituted in August began to fall apart and political controversy revived. The inability of the War Office to account for the shortage of artillery shells focused criticism on the Munitions Department. Reports that excessive drinking among munitions workers in parts of Britain was lowering productivity led the Chancellor of the Exchequer, Lloyd George, to introduce legislation in late April to double the duty on whiskey and place a surtax on certain beers. Since the whiskey provision involved a major blow to an important Irish industry, Redmond had no option but to oppose it. Backed by two large protest meetings in Dublin, the Irish Party abstained in the votes on the bill, ensuring its defeat. The munitions crisis was left unresolved. It was the first break in the alliance between Asquith's Liberals and the Irish Party on a national issue since the general elections of 1910. The political crisis was intensified by the resignation on 15 May of the

First Sea Lord, Admiral Fisher. By then it was clear that the first landings of ground troops on the Gallipoli peninsula on 25 April had gone disastrously wrong. Asquith decided to ask for Conservative co-operation in running the war. The formal announcement that steps were being taken to form a coalition government was made by Asquith on 19 May.

The advent of the coalition government, with its invitation to some of the bitterest former opponents of Home Rule to join the Cabinet, caused profound unease across nationalist Ireland, despite the prime minister's assurance that the change did not go beyond the purpose of the better prosecution of the war. For the provincial press, it was the biggest political story of 1915. In the last two weeks of May and into early June, the commentary focused on its three dimensions: the implications for the future of the suspended Home Rule Act; the entry to the Cabinet of F.E. Smith and Sir Edward Carson, the latter as attorney general, and the offer of the lord chancellorship to James H. Campbell, MP for Trinity College Dublin, a strong Irish unionist who had talked of civil war in 1914; and the question of whether Redmond was right to have rejected Asquith's counter-balancing offer of a seat in the Cabinet.

Redmond had decided to follow the long-standing principle of the Irish Parliamentary Party that Home Rule MPs should maintain independence by refusing paid employment of any kind under a British government. However, in doing so, he deprived himself of all power to influence events even as Irish opinion tended to hold him responsible for the government's mistakes. Of thirty papers that commented editorially, overlapping groups of fifteen expressed misgivings and unease at the implications for Home Rule, sixteen condemned the Unionist appointments, sixteen felt that Redmond was right to refuse the Cabinet post offer while eight thought he should have accepted, five were non-committal on the issue, and five felt that Home Rule was either dead or would be long delayed. Only one paper directly criticised the Irish Party or its leader.

The mildest initial response came from the *Sligo Champion* (22 May), which wrote that the change had been not wholly unexpected. There were 'compelling reasons for the adoption of a Coalition Cabinet [following] … a vile campaign against leading Liberal Ministers in a section of the Tory press'. But there was 'no necessity for alarm'. The presence of Redmond in the Cabinet (as it recommended and as the English press unanimously desired) 'would be a guarantee to the Irish people that in regard to the application of any measures which the new Government may consider necessary there would be no discrimination against any section of the community'. Two weeks later, after the announcement of the Carson and Smith appointments, its tone had changed. Under the title 'Gratuitous Insult', it wondered if these appointments meant that the 'purpose of the war' was the sole reason for the formation of the coalition. Recalling Carson's threat in 1912 to 'break every law that was possible', it found it 'beyond comprehension' that he was now to be entrusted with the chief administration of the law'. 'It would strain the party truce to breaking point. Apart from hindering recruiting and placing a new weapon in the hands of the anti-Redmond factionists, it would make Irishmen almost repent of the loyalty they have hitherto shown', it wrote. The *Longford Leader* (22 May) was less certain about the effects of the change but agreed regarding the presence of Redmond in the Cabinet. Before learning of the Unionist appointments, it called Asquith's action 'a cowardly abdication of the functions of Chief Minister of the Crown' in the face of malignant attacks in the press. 'We have no way of knowing,' it wrote, 'how this will affect the Home Rule Act on the Statute Book … once more Ireland is faced with the prospect of bitter disappointment at the last moment … If this [is] to be a national government representing all parties, nationalist Ireland ought to be represented in it. But we are sure Ireland will promptly follow whatever course [Redmond] advises with his wisdom and sagacity'. A week later, it claimed that the appointments had caused 'the utmost consternation in Ireland' and the offer to Redmond was 'little short of an insult' if it meant his sitting alongside such colleagues. But it had all aroused a 'new spirit of national resistance' as the Party had called on the people to resume nationalist activities and reorganise the branches of the UIL.

The *Clare Champion* (22 May) found Asquith's assurance 'satisfactory as far as it goes' but 'in this case, as in all others, the Irish people will be guided entirely by the advice and counsel of Mr John E. Redmond. In him they have, and must have, implicit and absolute confidence and trust. In obedience to his word, thousands of Irishmen have given up their lives on the battlefields'. As to whether Redmond should accept the offered seat in the Cabinet, it wrote, 'In view of the fact that Home Rule is on the Statute Book, and considering the very peculiar circumstances which have arisen, we think the acceptance of office by Mr Redmond would neither violate principle nor tradition, but, that it would very materially strengthen the position of Mr Redmond'. The *Tuam Herald* (29 May) agreed that, although the Party had taken all considerations and arguments into account regarding the offer of the Cabinet seat, it believed 'that a mistake was made on this occasion and that an opportunity of in some degree controlling the policy of the new Cabinet, so far as Ireland was concerned, was lost'. The inclusion of Carson had 'entirely altered the situation' and made Redmond's presence in the Cabinet absolutely necessary for the protection of nationalist interests.

The *Galway Observer* (22 May) was brusquely pragmatic on the issue: 'We do not pretend to judge whether it is best for the country for Mr Redmond to be in or outside the new Cabinet, except to give an opinion on the broad principle that, where Ireland is concerned, if he joins he will be in a much better position to influence the Government than if he was out of it. We thought the tradition that no Irish nationalist member should take office in an English ministry till Home Rule was obtained was done away with by this time, especially since whole batches of nationalists have taken positions under the Government in every department of State'. The *Waterford News* (21 May) regretted that Redmond had declined the post: he would be 'the right man in the right place as Chief Secretary for Ireland'. The war had created revolutionary conditions, and at such a time to hold that he should not break with tradition 'smacks of the academic'. But the *Kilkenny People* (22 May) thought otherwise. Adapting Mordaunt's poem, it wrote 'Even a crowded hour of glorious life would be a poor recompense for an old age spent on a political St Helena'. The *Dundalk Democrat* (29 May) defended Redmond's decision though it admitted that many nationalists thought 'he might have joined with profit to this country and without loss of political prestige'. In any case, there would be no change in Ireland's attitude to the war, to Ireland's place in the empire or to the fight for small nations.

The *Westmeath Independent* (22 May) equivocated, saying 'the exceptional circumstances of the case would, of course, justify a departure from the rule' but his acceptance of such an appointment 'would not popularly appeal to his countrymen, who think an informal alliance with the Liberals is far enough'. The *Limerick Leader* (26 May) had no doubts: all nationalists would 'heartily concur with Mr Redmond in refusing to enter the Coalition Cabinet'. True, Home Rule was on the Statute Book, but 'until such time as the Amending Measure is disposed of and our native legislature is at work for the whole of Ireland, there can be no acceptance by our Parliamentary representatives of offices of emolument or patronage under an English Parliament'. *The Wexford People* (22 May) wrote that the main question for all Irishmen was how the new government might affect Ireland: 'We are concerned for the speedy and successful termination of the war, but we have been so long struggling for Home Rule that it is natural we should be fearful lest such changes might injuriously affect the completion of that measure'. On the Unionist Cabinet appointments, it took its lead (as did many of the Irish papers) from the English Liberal *Daily Chronicle*, which called Carson's inclusion 'wholly deplorable upon three grounds'. The *Carlow Nationalist* (22 May) was similarly 'certain that a coalition Ministry – unless certain guarantees are given – will be regarded with misgivings here in Ireland … we must only anticipate that this latest arrangement has been arrived at after due consideration of what its consequences will mean to the cause of Irish nationality'. Both of these papers were non-committal on whether Redmond should accept office, happy to accept whatever he decided.

Commenting on Asquith's statement that the change in government was intended solely for war purposes and would have no effect on other matters, the *Irish News* (20 May) declared that, while it would take the words of English party leaders at face value, it must assert very clearly and emphatically 'that there will be no alteration in the vital principles of Irish Nationality, no change in the measure of the national demand which has been acceded to and which is on the Statute Book, and no variation in the methods of independent political organisation and parliamentary effort by which the Irish cause was carried on from the beginning of the constitutional movement'. The Carson appointment, it wrote moderately, 'is not likely to ease the situation or to lend authority to the new Government in the eyes either of those whom he has taught to defy authority or of the others, the bulk of the Irish people, over whom it is proposed to place him as one of their virtual rulers'.

The other Ulster papers were unsparing in their attacks on Carson and the other Unionist appointees. The *Anglo-Celt* (29 May) claimed that Asquith had submitted to Lord Northcliffe's cry to bring Unionists into the Cabinet, but it was nonsense to say that they would work for a common purpose; before nine months had elapsed there would be another, more serious, crisis. The *Derry Journal* (21 May) exclaimed: 'Here we have the amazing spectacle of the disaffected barrister who a year ago was openly threatening to lead hordes of his supporters against the Crown and who has since declared the threat holds good, getting the position of Attorney General in the Government'. For the *Derry People & Donegal News* (29 May), the selection of Carson for that office 'surpasses the limit of political cynicism'. The *Donegal Vindicator* (28 May) went furthest, blaming Carson for the war itself: 'Sir Edward Carson caused the war more than any one man alive, not excepting the Kaiser. Germany believed a civil war was coming in Ireland, otherwise it would not have gone to war,' it wrote. This 'jury bluffer of palpable mediocrity … would be serving a term in jail in any law-respecting country' and his appointment was 'a gross and unpardonable insult to Ireland'. So long as the Unionists remained in the Cabinet, 'we, at least, will not urge one Irishman to join the colours'. Redmond had been right to refuse office: 'In a Cabinet which included Carson, he would be held back by the responsibilities of office. Pray Heaven that outside of it he may more clearly recognise the dangers that beset the future of the country'.

The gloomiest prognostications for Home Rule came, predictably, from the small group of anti-Party papers. The *Tipperary Star* (22 May) in an editorial devoted mainly to factual reportage, was convinced that 'the long war and the long war Cabinet' meant that 'only one thing is certain, that it will be many a day before Home Rule will be a fact … in the sweet by and by'. Withholding judgment itself, it averred that the new government would have 'a very sinister effect some think'. For the *Roscommon Herald* (22 May), the governmental change 'buries for good and all Mr Redmond's Home Rule Bill. From the first that was only a champion hoax, and it comes to an end now like a stupid practical joke that was meant to fool the Irish people for a season'. The other big change was the 'certainty that conscription in one shape or another will be put into force'. In true Tully style, it claimed to know the real reason for Redmond's rejection of the Cabinet offer – he knew he would have to 'face Ireland' as a conscriptionist at the next general election. (Redmond had been consistent from the beginning in publicly and privately opposing Irish conscription.) The *Roscommon Journal* (29 May) likewise felt that, with 'Carson now on top', the Home Rule Act was 'as dead as Brian Boru'. With greater gravitas of tone, the *Leinster Leader* (29 May) agreed. It approved 'the dignified attitude of the Irish Party and its leader' in rejecting the offer of a Cabinet seat, and felt that the country would re-echo the endorsement of it by his followers. However, noting that the Party had decided to support 'the new regime', it stressed that the Liberal government had ceased to exist. 'The prospect of the Home Rule Act ever coming to life seems, therefore, a remote one' – it would disappear into the limbo of defunct Liberal legislation. But Home Rule had been 'exploited and served its purpose' to have Ireland shoulder some of the burden of the war.

The *Kerryman* (29 May) asked how Home Rule would stand when some of 'the most inveterate Unionists' were playing a big part in the government of Ireland': 'We believe that our chances of getting Home Rule now are not very rosy, despite the oft- and much-advertised fact that it has been placed on the Statute Book'. The *Mayo News* (29 May) wrote that there would be no advantage now in repeating the worthless boast, 'I told you so'. Irish parliamentarians had been over-trustful of the Whigs, and the announcement of the names to be included 'justifies all our misgivings'. The *Killarney Echo (29 May)* under the title 'What Will Poor Ireland Do?', wrote that the transformation would cause 'consternation in the minds of all thinking Irishmen'. 'For nine years the Liberal Government have been weaving a tangled web over the eyes of the Irish people. During the process we have been told many stories of the fine things we would see later on when our vision was restored, but the most substantial results we now find are increased Budget Taxes, Insurance Acts, and other charges of a similar character ... Imagine a Coalition Government with Sir Edward Carson and Mr. Smith in it having in their hands the fate and future of Ireland!' Articulating what seemed like the rudiments of a Sinn Féin policy it was yet hesitant to name, the paper went on:

> The situation demands the serious and careful consideration of the Irish people. They should begin to think out for themselves what policy is likely to be effective in placing an Irish Government in actual control of every inch of Irish soil. Hope deferred, alas too often, has made our hearts sick ... We must cling now more than ever to the old hope for Irish Nationality, and in doing so to make it clear that it will endure as long as the British Empire and outlive the powers of the Coalition Government.

C. UNITED IRISH LEAGUE REORGANISATION AND THE ANNIVERSARY OF THE WAR, MAY–AUGUST 1915

A strong private protest from Redmond at length induced Asquith to withdraw Campbell's appointment and find a less controversial Unionist for the post of attorney general. The storm over the coalition gradually subsided over the summer. However, because Redmond kept his lobbying of Asquith secret for the sake of the party truce, his victory on the appointments issue did not win him the plaudits he might have expected. His standing was further undermined by the unrelenting campaign waged against the Irish Party and its leadership by the *Irish Independent* (see Chapter 1). Although the *Independent* was a constitutionalist organ, its campaign, in view of its huge circulation and an efficient distribution system that ensured its penetration into every hamlet in the country, very likely did more than any Sinn Féin or separatist paper to unsettle the rank and file, undermine the leadership's authority and damage wider public confidence in the Irish Party.

The National Volunteers organisation, with little to do in the becalmed political atmosphere, had also fallen into a state of disrepair by summer 1915, many of its most highly motivated members, along with its trainers and drill instructors, having already enlisted for the Front. The general demoralisation was reflected in recruiting figures, which fell from more than 6,000 per month up to mid-June to a third of that rate by early autumn. The decay of the UIL organisation, largely the result of complacency now that the Home Rule struggle appeared to be over, was apparent in a series of by-elections in which local disputes marred the process of candidate selection. In by-elections at Tullamore in December 1914 and in Dublin College Green in June 1915, unofficial candidates professing loyalty to Redmond stood against officially selected ones and, in the first case, won the seat despite a plea from Redmond. In a third election, in Tipperary North, there were not enough branches to hold a convention and three candidates, all Redmondites, canvassed the voters, the victory going to the son of the deceased former MP.

Redmond and Dillon drew the lesson that the decline of the UIL organisation must be arrested. Between July and November, more than twenty county conventions of the UIL were held, many attended by Redmond, Dillon or Devlin. Calls were made for coherence and discipline as being more necessary than ever in the interval before the implementation of Home Rule. Altogether, sixteen of the newspapers in this sample supported the Party's cry for improved discipline and organisation. The *Limerick Leader* (26 July) hailed the large UIL convention at the Theatre Royal on 21 July addressed by Dillon, whose warning of the threat of conscription was warmly received. It drew the lesson from the advent of the coalition that the ranks must be preserved 'unbroken, with unity and discipline unimpaired'. The *Sligo Champion*'s editorial (24 July) on this meeting relayed Redmond's emphasis on the need for optimism and his call to 'put every county in a proper state of defence ... perfect the existing organisation and stand ready for any emergency that may arise'; they must also keep the convention system for as long as they needed to elect members to sit in the imperial parliament. Responding to the growing frequency of attacks on the Party coming from both constitutional and separatist sources, it endorsed his allegation that 'the Sinn Féiners and factionists were a greater menace to Irish liberty than were the traditional enemies of the country'; they tried to belittle the efforts of the Irish Party, attacked the measure of self-government achieved and now, inconsistently, blamed the Party for the delay in the operation of the Act.

One of the largest conventions, in Thurles on 3 August, received massive coverage over six news columns of the *Tipperary Star* (7August) alongside an editorial on the fall of Warsaw. The *Dundalk Democrat* (7 August) under the title 'Magnificent Tipperary' claimed that the 'splendid Thurles convention' showed that 'the great bulk of intelligent Irish public opinion is behind Mr Redmond'. However, the *Kilkenny People* (7 August) wrote that the speeches of Redmond and Dillon indicated that they did not regard the Home Rule battle as finally won, and that the 'Ulster difficulty' seemed the main reason for the welcome call for reorganisation. In a note of criticism new for this paper, it added that their acceptance of the exclusion proposals [of March 1914] had been 'a hideous blunder'. The *Midland Tribune* (31 July) described the 'splendid reception for Redmond and Dillon' – 'the manhood of Tipperary was there'. Other papers – the *Carlow Nationalist* (7 August) and the *Limerick Leader* (4 August) – carried favourable editorials alongside coverage of the speeches, while still others, including the *Tipperary People*, the *Clare Champion*, the *Nenagh Guardian* and the *Clonmel Nationalist* made do with extensive news reporting.

A small number of papers had become so intensely focused on the war that they showed little interest in domestic politics. On the first anniversary of the war, the *Limerick Echo* (3 August) wrote: 'We do not want a policy of peace with the Huns. Rather do we want – and must secure – a practicable and lasting peace, which will be sought for to the bitter end'. This appeared the day before the Bishop of Limerick, Dr O'Dwyer, issued a public letter to Redmond endorsing Pope Benedict's recent appeal for a peace conference and begging him to throw his influence on the side of peace, an appeal that received a curt reply that 'to the best of my judgment, the course of action you suggest would not be calculated to promote the cause of peace'. The *Ballina Herald* (5 August) marked a year of war in language indistinguishable from that of any British newspaper, writing of 'our war' and 'our Empire'.

Around this time, in the summer of 1915, a new note of critical commentary – more a questioning than an expression of disloyalty – began to appear in a small number of papers and in public bodies that had previously been unquestioningly loyal to Redmond and the Party. The combination of unease over the prolongation of the war, impatience at the consequent delay of Home Rule, forebodings over the amending bill, grief at escalating casualty figures and fear of possible conscription lifted the taboo that had once kept criticism of Party policies to a minimum. The new commentary, often couched in a plea for greater freedom of thought or in criticism of the dominance of the Irish Party narrative, reflected the influence of the *Irish Independent* in the provinces. An example was the *Drogheda Argus*, which wrote cryptically on 31 July that 'Some of the people who are now allowed to think for themselves – and they are becoming ominously few in Ireland – are wondering why the Home Rule Act was not put in force in due course when the King put his signature to it … But we dare not tell the truth! … Ireland is certainly a wonderful country at the present time. If you tell the truth about the war you are dubbed by the man in the street a "pro-German", and if you tell him that you are a better Home Ruler than he is you are called a Sinn Féiner'. Other papers such as the *Killarney Echo* would not have been insulted to be called 'Sinn Féiner' and by this time had more in common with the seditious sheets that circulated in spite of the censorship constraints of the Defence of the Realm Act, especially in the cities where the Irish Volunteer faction was relatively strong and growing stronger.

The increasing audacity of the separatist elements was underlined in mid-July when thirty-nine members of the Dublin Corporation, among them a group of Sinn Féin councillors seeking to discomfit the Irish Party and others acting apparently in good faith, requisitioned a special meeting to consider a resolution demanding of the government that the Home Rule Act be put into operation for all of Ireland on 17 September, the anniversary of its signing. Embarrassment to the Irish Party was deflected when an amendment expressing confidence in it to 'select the best and speediest means' for bringing it into operation was passed by thirty votes to twenty-two. The *King's County Independent* (24 July) rejoiced that the Sinn Féin element had been 'hoist with their own petard'. The *Connaught Telegraph* (7 August) commented that the 'grotesque spectacle' of 'a certain class of Irishman' passing resolutions calling for the putting of the Home Rule Act into operation was a source of amusement to those who knew the "sinister game" of those who had done all in their power to thwart the progress of the Bill and embarrass the [Irish] Party; they were the same ones who desired the success of 'the barbarous enemy we have drawn the sword against'. The *Wexford People* (31 July) felt that 'the aim and object, it would be thought, of people who are really anxious for the success of the Home Rule cause would be to smoothen the path of the Irish Party and to remove the difficulties that beset it as far as possible. There are certain parties, however, who never did a day's work for Home Rule, but who on the contrary lose no opportunity of spreading distrust of the Irish Party'.

Another paper opposing the radical elements was the *Munster News*. Its editorial of 28 July dealt with the address of the president of the Gaelic League, Dr Douglas Hyde, to the Oireachtas, the annual festival of 'Irish

Ireland', being held in Dundalk. The president had referred to the growing attempts to politicise the Gaelic League. 'For some past,' wrote the
paper:

> [A]*n insidious attempt has been made to identify the Language Movement
> with the Sinn Féin party in Ireland. One important branch of the* [Gaelic]
> *League turned itself into a political platform for John* [Eoin] *MacNeill not
> many months ago. The outcry raised in the country against the outrageous
> action of this Dublin branch produced a wholesome effect ... Notwithstanding
> this, however, the attempts have been continued in a hundred little ways to
> make the Gaelic League a subservient body to what has been misnamed the
> 'extreme party'. For instance, the MacNeill Volunteers have been invited to
> attend Feiseanna, while the National Volunteers, who represent the views of
> the Irish people, have been cold-shouldered ... if this strange policy is still
> pursued, and if it succeeds to any considerable extent the Gaelic League will
> be wrecked, and perhaps the last hope of saving the Irish language will be lost.*

'We are glad, therefore, that Dr Hyde made the position of the Gaelic
League clear on this point,' the editorial concluded, quoting the president's warning that as long as he had charge of the movement he would
never allow 'the pure ideal of the Irish Language' to be 'trailed in the
dust or in the mire' of any political faction or party. (The attempts to
politicise the Gaelic League continued, however, forcing Hyde to resign
in September.)

D. THE O'DONOVAN ROSSA FUNERAL, 1 AUGUST 1915

A secondary purpose of Redmond in his speeches at the Thurles and
(later) Waterford conventions was to confront the latest and most explicit
challenge to his authority from the radical minority he had yet encoun-
tered. At Thurles, he was presented with an address of welcome signed
by the chairmen of all thirty-two elected public bodies in Tipperary, and

replied that 'this really is a parliament of Tipperary. The whole people of Tipperary are here, and they are here by popular suffrage ... I will speak to you as the elected representatives of this great historic county of Tipperary'.

The challenge took the form of a brilliantly orchestrated piece of separatist propaganda centred on the funeral of the veteran Fenian Jeremiah O'Donovan Rossa who had died in New York at the age of eighty-three. The pioneer of the 'dynamite policy' (the contemporary term for terrorist bombing) and a highly divisive figure even within IRB circles in the 1880s, Rossa had last visited Ireland in 1904, and on a previous tour in 1894 had bitterly recounted his prison experiences and denounced the leaders of the (then) split constitutional movement. The IRB arranged with Clan-na-Gael, its American wing, to have the body transported to Dublin for burial. On previous experience of such events, Irish Party leaders anticipated that the funeral would be turned into a 'physical force demonstration' but saw no way of taking it out of the hands of the IRB. Rossa's remains, arriving in Dublin on 27 July, were taken to St. Mary's Pro-Cathedral for a memorial service; the coffin then lay in state for three days in City Hall. On Sunday, 1 August, an immense crowd followed the funeral to Glasnevin Cemetery. Every step was carefully choreographed. At the graveside, armed members of the Irish Volunteers fired volleys of shots and sounded the Last Post.

The climactic moment came with a passionate and highly politicised eulogy delivered at the grave by Patrick Pearse, a member of the secret seven-man IRB 'Military Council', then engaged in preparing for insurrection. Known from his published works to believe that the mandate for political action should derive from the 'dead generations' of past revolutionaries rather than from democratic majorities, and scathing in his views of those who had led Ireland for the previous twenty-five years, Pearse now claimed to be speaking on behalf of 'a new generation that has been re-baptised in the Fenian faith'. Calling on 'God, who ripens in the hearts of young men the seeds sown by the young men of a former generation', he attacked the entire Home Rule settlement:

*They think that they have pacified Ireland. They think that they have pur-
chased half of us and intimidated the other half. They think that they have
foreseen everything, think that they have provided against everything; but
the fools, the fools, the fools! – they have left us our Fenian dead, and while
Ireland holds these graves, Ireland unfree shall never be at peace.*

The *Irish Independent* set the template for an acceptable constitutionalist response to the event, noting that while 'other methods than those
favoured by O'Donovan Rossa have accomplished much of what he had
hoped to achieve', all could recognise the sterling patriotism of the man'.
However, given the tendency of even the most respectable organs to
romanticise 'physical force' figures of the past once they were safely dead,
and given the extensive advance publicity, with seventeen special trains
laid on from all parts of the island, it is perhaps surprising that seventeen
(40 per cent) of this sample of forty-two provincial papers ignored the
proceedings altogether. Of the twenty-five papers that commented editorially, overlapping groups of twenty-one described it in terms ranging
from perfunctory to reverential, fourteen mentioned without criticism
the presence of the Irish Volunteers, nine referred to the Pearse oration,
with five quoting it in full and two in precis, while seven reported on the
firing party and the volleys.

In advance publicity, the *Connacht Tribune* (31 July) and *Westmeath
Independent* had urged all nationalists to attend, the latter seeing it
as proof 'that Irish Nationality still stands undisturbed and uncon-
founded by temporary happenings … part of the nation's glorious
past'. At one end of the spectrum of coverage of the funeral stood the
Connaught Telegraph's curt three-line news report (7 August) and the
Kerry Sentinel's brief paragraph (4 August) with the rider, 'the policy in
which O'Donovan Rossa was such a prominent figure is not one that will
appeal to Irishmen of the present day'. At the other end was the blanket
coverage of the *Killarney Echo* (7 August) with its detailed report of the
funeral, accompanying reports of separate commemorations at Tralee
and Killarney and the full text of Pearse's panegyric on its front page.

In between these extremes, it was notable that many papers which, ten months earlier, had been highly critical of the breakaway movement of Irish Volunteers, now seemed relaxed at the spectacle of 'all sections of Nationalists united' (the *Irish News*) or shared the naïvete of the *Drogheda Argus* (7 August) when it wrote, 'Nothing could have been finer than the appearance and equipment of the National Volunteers and the Irish Volunteers … A splendid oration was delivered over the grave of the dead patriot by Mr Pearse, BL, who said that Irishmen would continue the programme of O'Donovan Rossa where he left off'. Some papers noted that the Irish Volunteer contingent was armed while that of the National Volunteers was not, but for the *Irish News*, the difference did not seem to matter: it described the concluding part of the theatrics as 'unique in the history of interments in Glasnevin Cemetery. A firing party of the Volunteers formed up, and at the word of command, given by Captain James O'Sullivan, fired three volleys over the grave … a touching tribute to the labours and suffering of a gallant soldier of Ireland'. The *Leinster Leader* (7 August) applauded the 'magnificent display' of the Irish Volunteers. In an editorial titled 'All Ireland United by the Bier of Rossa', the *Connacht Tribune* (7 August) respectfully gave the names of Irish Volunteer officers and their role in marshaling the crowds, but made no reference to the firing party or to Pearse's oration.

Some Redmondite papers appeared set on enfolding the dissident demonstration in a loving embrace tight enough to smother it. The *Wexford People* (4 August) opined that in his youth, Rossa had 'loved Ireland perhaps not wisely but too well', and claimed that in later life he had joined the UIL of America and 'thrown in his lot' with the Irish Party (this had been first reported in the British press but strenuously denied by his widow). 'A certain group,' it added, 'thought to exploit the dead patriot's funeral last Sunday to their own advantage, but all sections of Irish nationalists attended to honour the man'. The *Westmeath Examiner* (7 August) welcomed the fact that 'the concourse comprehended every section of nationalist thought and patriotic activity'. The *Cork Examiner* (2 August) gave the funeral two columns of news reporting with photographs of 'the distinguished and patriotic Irishman' and of the cortege, together with a long historical account of the Fenians and a reminder that Rossa's policy 'is not one that will appeal to Irishmen of the present day'. The *Clonmel Nationalist* (4 August) extolled Rossa's 'hallowed memory' and told his life story in glowing purple phrases, ending with 'his advancing years were gladdened by the dawn of better and brighter days for the land he loved and dared so much for'. None of these four papers made any mention of the Irish Volunteers, the firing party or Pearse's panegyric.

The ominous pageantry of the Rossa funeral marked the reawakening of a buried atavism in the public space of nationalist Ireland. Fifty-four years earlier, the Fenians had brought home the body of the Young Ireland rebel Terence Bellew MacManus from San Francisco and given it a massive funeral at Glasnevin. More recently there had been another huge nationalist outpouring of grief at the burial of the constitutionalist Parnell. Neither had been attended with graveside volleys or the withering and threatening scorn for constitutional politics displayed in Pearse's rhetoric, both of which would have been unthinkable only a few years earlier. Only in the militarist atmosphere of total European war could such a demonstration have been even conceivable. The newspapers must have sensed that here was something both very old and very new. Yet all complacently assumed it to be irrelevant, or a periodic recurrence of a colourful old nationalist tradition, or, at most, a healthy bolstering of nationalist strength against government backsliding when the Home Rule Act came to be implemented. None perceived what was being hidden in plain sight, and would be made manifest nine months later.

E. THE CAMPAIGN AGAINST WAR TAXATION, FEBRUARY–APRIL 1916

The coalition government's war budget of September 1915 raised taxation on all classes in Ireland to unprecedented levels. The increased

net financial contribution to the war, though offset to some extent by
the benefit to Irish farmers from high prices for agricultural produce in
Britain, eliminated the deficit in Ireland's favour on which the finances
of the Home Rule Act were based. A retrenchment committee was set
up to examine where cuts might be made in government spending, and
in early January 1916 reductions were announced across a wide range of
grants in agriculture, industry and education. Intensive lobbying of the
Chancellor by Redmond and Dillon ensured that by the end of January
most of the grants were restored. One of the few provincial papers to
give attention to this issue was the *Waterford News*, which viewed it
in apocalyptic terms. On 7 January, it advertised the 'monster' protest
meeting being organised by the Gaelic League against the withdrawal of
grants for the teaching of Gaelic: 'Irish public opinion will show itself
as vehemently opposed to the renewed attempt to strangle Irish nationality through killing the Irish language'. On 28 January, following the
restoration of the grants, its editorial was headlined 'Educational Grant
Restored!' – but no thanks were due to 'the bountiful [chief secretary]
Mr Birrell' as it would not have been diplomatic to withdraw the meagre
educational grants 'while the recruiting authorities are demanding a
blood levy of 52,000 men per annum and the tax collectors are enacting
a demand for £17,000,000'. It was believed, alleged the paper, that the
object of the cut was 'to destroy the growing influence of Gaelic League
ideas on public opinion … the attack on Ireland's oppressors must be
kept up, and we must show our British bosses that they must respect the
rights and integrity of this small nation of ours'.

The taxation measures remained in place, however, and the
Independent's influence encouraged a coalition of prominent nationalists
including Sinn Féin and Irish Volunteer figures, along with two dissident
Irish Party MPs, to launch a nationwide campaign against 'overtaxation'
on 29 February. A public meeting at the Mansion House resolved that
Ireland could not afford to bear the burden of taxes imposed in the
Budget. On 6 March, a meeting of Dublin Corporation voted to call
upon the Irish Party to resist any further increase in taxation. This was

followed by similar resolutions passed at a countrywide series of meetings of public bodies. By late March, Redmond and Dillon, convinced that they had done their best to resist taxation unfair to Ireland, were certain that the primary aim of the instigators of the campaign was to embarrass the Party. Redmond published a letter in the *Freeman's Journal* declaring that the agitation was led by hostile men who were either 'avowedly pro-German' or committed to the 'monstrous doctrine' of Irish neutrality; in either case they were opposed to recruiting. War taxation was a necessity in order to bring the war – 'not only a just war, but Ireland's war' – to a victorious end. His statement brought a change of tone in the public debate, with most public bodies agreeing to entrust the Party with the handling of the issue.

Did the overtaxation campaign influence the regional press? Judging by the coverage of the issue in these papers, it had little effect. Nineteen of the forty-two papers in the sample expressed an editorial opinion on the campaign. Twelve of those made no comment on the unfolding agitation in early March and waited until Redmond's statement before registering their support of the Party and willingness to trust in its guidance. The other seven identified themselves with the criticisms of war taxation being voiced at the campaign meetings or in the *Independent's* columns. The *Midland Tribune* (18 March) published a resolution adopted by the King's County Committee of Agriculture, calling it 'timely' as 'no more important question is now before the country' and arguing that now was the time for Ireland to secure just financial treatment. Later (25 March) it referred again to war taxation and wrote of the 'deep discontent' in the country on this as on the whole Irish question. Of this group of seven papers, only one – *The Kerryman* – directly attacked the Party's handling of the issue, publishing critical editorials on the question on 4, 11 and 25 March and on 1 April. It reported sympathetically on the launch meeting, declaring 'Redmond's Home Rule Act' to be 'hopeless' and complaining that under the 'embalmed Home Rule Act' the taxation of Ireland had more than doubled. Finally, it attacked Redmond's criticism of the agitation as 'bunkum'. It is perhaps significant that most of these seven papers were either already opposed to the Party or would shortly switch allegiance to Sinn Féin. If misgivings were felt in the 'loyal' papers regarding finance, they were presumably repressed.

The above findings are summarised in Chart 2.

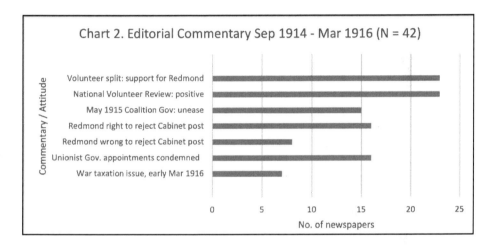

Chapter 4

THE REBELLION AND ITS AFTERMATH, APRIL– DECEMBER 1916

A. RESPONSES TO THE REBELLION

Provincial press responses to the Dublin insurrection of Easter 1916 can be divided under five headings: criticism of the action itself, attempts to extenuate the action, pleas for clemency for the defeated and captured rebels, reactions to the executions of the rebel leaders and attitudes to the Irish Party, John Redmond and Home Rule in the aftermath of the insurrection. These are discussed separately below.

A1. CRITICISM

In common with the Dublin Castle authorities, the British army, the police and the great majority of Ireland's population at large, the provincial newspapers were caught completely off guard by the news of the rebellion in Dublin. Many of their initial reports were hampered by difficulties in communicating with the capital and were consequently sparse in detail and unable to differentiate fact from rumour. Editorial comment, where it was expressed, began in the first week of May, the week after the rebellion's end, when the first executions of rebel leaders had taken place. Of the forty-two newspapers, thirty-four commented on the rebellion itself. Of these, ten condemned it outright while a larger group of nineteen voiced milder criticism, emphasising the madness, foolishness or recklessness of the enterprise. Two preferred to withhold judgment, while the responses of a further three were idiosyncratic.

The strongest criticism came from the *Anglo-Celt* (13 May) which described the rebellion as a 'criminal enterprise', and from the *Westmeath Examiner* (13 May) which called it 'the deepest act of treachery to the Nation's interests'. For the *Roscommon Herald* (29 April), the rebels were 'dupes, victims of evil designing men hired with German gold'. The *King's County Independent* (6 May) combined condemnation with laying the blame on 'Larkinism' (the Irish variant of syndicalism named after the trade union organiser James Larkin whose activities had led to the employers' lockout and street disorders of 1913):

> *The crime against the Government of the country – against Ireland – has been a terrible one. Intensified is it a thousand-fold by the fact that it was committed when our whole energies – the entire manhood and resources – were needed in the life and death struggle against Germany ... As one stands and looks at the terrible scene of destruction, a felling of stupefaction settles, followed by one of bitterest resentment, against the mad fanaticism which has occasioned it ... the agonising picture of so many deaths – amongst the soldiers, the police, the poor dreamers who, deluded by German intrigue, have been guilty of the maddest attempt at Revolution ever essayed in any country of the world ... This was no Irish Rebellion ... it was an outbreak of Larkinism which has terrified and made almost impossible the commercial and industrial life of Dublin and the country for the last four years, backed up, of course, by the wild dreamers – the irreconcilables with which the city is plentiful!*

The fact that 'the country as a whole is loyal to the great constitutional movement places Mr Redmond in a powerful position to ask for consideration and mercy for those concerned'. It was 'the duty of Ireland to plead for Mercy for the misguided young fellows'.

The *Galway Observer* (29 April) recording its 'utmost abhorrence and condemnation', titled its editorial 'Germany's Insurrection'. For the *Derry Journal* (3 May), the insurrection was a 'wild and wicked plot to make the country a catspaw of Germany … no wonder is it, then, that the people as a whole detest such a base attack on their interests, their rights, their hopes, and their principles, though at the same time they may harbour a feeling of pity for the misguided and feather-headed young men who have risked, and, as has been the case with a number of them, have sacrificed their lives. Poor, luckless victims of Prussian selfishness and cynicism!' The *Southern Star* (6 May) strongly deplored and condemned 'this late insane and hopeless Rising which has brought such destruction to life and property' but pleaded for mercy for 'the vanquished and misguided insurgents … [led by] enthusiasts, idealists, visionaries, nurtured on bardic and romantic literature … [whose] pluck, bravery, honesty of motive and high purposed endeavour' none could deny. It would be 'bad policy on the part of the Government to carry the campaign of retaliation too far'. However, in a display of ambivalence that went beyond a clemency plea, it accompanied this with a long and fond eulogy of Pearse by 'A Friend': '… What I hate is to hear cowardly fellows, who would run away from a mouse, casting aspersions on a man like Pearse. He was wrong, he was misguided, but I am sure he meant well'.

The larger group of nineteen papers avoided outright denunciation and fixed instead on the foolishness or recklessness of the action: it was the work of 'a small section of intellectual fanatics' (*Carlow Nationalist*, 6 May); 'Inexplicable Imbecility' (*Tipperary Star*, 6 May); 'very regrettable' (*Wexford People*, 3 May); 'lunacy of the Sinn Féiners' (*Tuam Herald*, 13 May); 'The Mad Mullahs of Dublin' (*Donegal Vindicator*, 5 May); 'the hopelessness, the mad folly, the blind fatuousness of this reckless adventure' (*Irish News*, 1 May); 'misguided and misdirected energy … turbulent spirits … ill-conceived and foolish plans …' (*Drogheda Argus*, 13 May). The *Munster News* (6 May) lamented the fact that 'Lured to their doom … hundreds of ignorant young men, many of them mere boys, have rushed blindfold into a position which none but harebrained fanatics could possibly occupy'. The *Roscommon Journal* (6 May) mourned the physical destruction as if a natural disaster had struck, comparing it to the aftermath of the Paris Commune and the San Francisco earthquake: 'Poor old Dublin is wrecked beyond recovery for many a year to come by the wicked Sinn Féin outbreak … Some of its noblest thoroughfares and most beautiful public buildings are now only heaps of rubbish and ruins.' The *Killarney Echo* (6 May) seemed to indicate something like approval of the rebellion when it published the rebel proclamation next to its editorial; its harshest words for the outbreak were that 'what has happened has cast a pall of despondency over the land'.

Surprisingly for a paper that had made its opposition to Redmond's leadership clear for two years, the *Mayo News* did not try to make capital out of the event, but wrote (13 May) that, although the Irish Volunteer units of that county had been suppressed, none were more surprised than they at the news of the revolutionary events in Dublin. Two other papers would express no disapproval: it was 'not for us to sit in judgment' (*Clare Champion*, 6 May); this was 'no time to waste words in useless moralizing' (*Kilkenny People*, 6 May).

Aside from attitudes to the revolt stood the question of how the papers tried to make sense of such an unforeseen and shocking event. Some appeared to assume that the rebellion was a protest at the delay in the implementation of the Home Rule Act. The *Derry People* (13 May) wrote that on that ground it was 'without justification': the delay in implementation was a 'technical grievance' but those who had won the Act 'understand the circumstances and make no complaint'. The rebellion had prompted an outburst of self-reproach in some British newspapers sympathetic to the Irish cause. The *Kerry Sentinel* (13 May) went along with the 'protest' interpretation when it drew together comments in one of these, the *Daily Sketch*, with sentiments expressed by a London-based Irish journalist and those of John Dillon in the House of Commons the previous day – that he was proud of the courage of the men who had fought in the rebellion – to conclude: 'It will be seen that there is one point upon which all three distinctly agree – that Ireland is, and has been, badly governed'. Naïvely mistaking the motives of the rebel leaders, the *Tipperary Star* wrote, 'It is the pity of pities that the leaders of the people did not take the young men of Ireland in hands with kind advice before it was too late'.

Others seemed to understand the rebellion as a seriously intended, though poorly planned and therefore doomed, endeavour. The *Munster News* (6 May) wrote of it as a 'futile attempt to establish an Irish Republic', and believed that the attempted landing of arms in Kerry and the simultaneous arrival and arrest of Sir Roger Casement corroborated the general belief that Germany was at the back of 'this mad adventure' and 'the slaughter and suffering entailed by a small section in Ireland embarking on the most insane essay in revolution'. In addition, the forces of syndicalism (better known to Irish newspapers at that time as 'Larkinism') had been involved through its 'unfortunate dupes' represented by Connolly's Citizen Army. Summarising, the paper reckoned, 'Those were the forces – Prussian militarism and cosmopolitan advanced Socialism – which were combined in an unholy alliance to bring about, regardless of consequences, an appeal to physical force which, in the eyes of all but lunatics, was foredoomed to failure'.

William O'Brien's *Cork Free Press* as usual ploughed its own furrow. On 29 April, under the title 'The Inevitable', it claimed that it had repeatedly warned the Irish Volunteers against 'this playing at soldiers' and that the object behind their inauguration was from the start 'misguided'. Nevertheless, it would not place all the blame on them. For both Carson's gunmen and Redmond's gunmen there had been official admiration and compliments, but the government was to blame for waging 'a war of persecution' against the Irish Volunteers. The *Kerryman*'s approach was similarly unique: it carried extensive news coverage of the rebellion on 6 May but no editorial comment until three weeks later, when, discussing the royal commission established to inquire into the causes of the rebellion, it resorted to antisemitism in alleging that a chief cause of the rebellion was the appointment of

Sir Matthew Nathan (the under secretary appointed at Dublin Castle by Asquith in October 1914 to smooth the administrative path towards Home Rule) – 'a Jew, despite the well-known dislike of Jews common among Irishmen'.

A2. EXTENUATION OF THE REBELLION

In the search for extenuating circumstances for the rebellion, the press was unanimous in focusing on at least one. Twenty-eight of the newspapers mentioned the example given by the government's toleration of the Ulster unionist threats in 1913 and 1914 to resist Home Rule by force if necessary, and of the mobilisation of the UVF. The *Drogheda Argus* (13 May) had no hesitation in fixing 'responsibility for the slaughter' on Sir Edward Carson, the 'general of the Ulster Volunteer rebels'. The *Westmeath Examiner* (29 April) wrote that Carson had set the example for the Easter rebels by defying the law and 'making force the supreme arbiter'. The *Cork Examiner* went further (9 May), writing that 'the Government's laxity in dealing with the Ulster Covenanters was the primary cause of the recent disturbances'. The *Wexford People* (6 May) wrote that the Carsonites had 'preached sedition and a weak-kneed Government winked at them'; it called Carson the 'true author of the Irish resort to force'.

The *Roscommon Herald* (29 April) placed the 'great weight of fearful responsibility' on the prime minister and Chief Secretary Birrell for allowing the 'wicked system of armed Orange Volunteers' to grow but also for encouraging James Larkin, in the name of the labour movement, to form a so-called 'citizens' army' to arm and drill. Together with the *King's County Independent* already cited, the *Roscommon Herald* and *Tuam Herald* were among a group of papers that saw syndicalism-Larkinism, as one of the driving forces behind the revolt. For the *Tuam Herald* (13 May), the roots of the revolt lay in the 'unpardonable' laxity of the Irish Executive shown not only in Birrell's surrender to the Ulster defiance but also in the 'fatal policy of placation and surrender to Larkin and his gang' begun by 'that wretched wobbler' [Lord Lieutenant] Lord Aberdeen'.

The *Mayo News* wrote (28 April) that the 'root and foundation of all the trouble was permitting armed forces to be formed in the north of Ireland for the open and avowed purpose of resisting Ireland's constitutional demands'. The *Leinster Leader* (13 May) wrote without emotion that the rebel leaders had paid the penalty: 'Over their graves we are silent'. But the inquiry must go back to when the Home Rule controversy had been 'violently plucked from constitutional methods'.

Exceeding all in vitriol was the *Kilkenny People*. This paper had been loyal to the Irish Party up to the rebellion – 'It may be taken for granted that the Irish Party will leave nothing undone to protect Irish interests,' it had written regarding the forthcoming Budget on 25 March, just a month beforehand – but would very soon desert that allegiance. 'Carson and his criminal confederates,' it wrote on 29 April, had been allowed by the Liberal government to arm 'the most violent, the most fanatical and the most illiterate mob in all Europe', igniting a fuse which had resulted in 'this appalling calamity'.

The *Munster News* (6 May) and *Tipperary People* (6 May) were the only exceptions to the general condemnation of Carson, both mentioning that he had joined with Redmond in a plea for clemency for the rank and file and hoping it would produce the desired result.

A3. PLEAS FOR CLEMENCY

Eighteen of twenty-eight newspapers in the sample that commented made editorial pleas for clemency, or, in the cases of the *Cork Examiner* (1 May) and *Limerick Echo* (2 May), amnesty for the rank and file. The *Limerick Leader* wrote on 10 May that twelve executions were enough and it was time for clemency. The *Carlow Nationalist* (13 May) said that, with twelve of the leaders executed, the government 'would do well to cease'. The *Ballina Herald* (11 May) expanded on the theme:

> [M]*any valuable lives have been lost on both sides and non-combatants to the number of several hundred have met their deaths … our sympathy goes out no less to the families of the rebels than to the relatives of the gallant soldiers*

who gave up their lives to quell this outbreak … many young men left their homes on the days preceding Easter Monday without their people being made aware of what they intended doing … It is more than probable that a large number. of these young people had no idea of what was intended … As regards the leaders, those of them who have not met their deaths in battle are having justice meted out to them with an inexorable hand, and already a dozen or so have been executed. We do not cavil at the justice of this, but we think that it is now time to cry halt …

The *Tipperary People* (6 May) reprinted Redmond's appeal to the government 'not to treat with undue hardship and severity the masses concerned in the recent outbreak' and Carson's statement that 'no true Irishman would call for vengeance upon the mass of the insurgents'. It accompanied this with a piece titled 'Tribute to Insurgents', citing a *Daily Telegraph* report that quoted a prominent Dublin unionist who said that the rebels had engaged in no looting and had tried to prevent it, and who praised 'the clean manner in which the Sinn Féiners fought … the more remarkable in view of the bitterness which the revolt has evoked'.

These comments reflect a general, albeit uncomfortable, acceptance of the inevitability, if not the justice, of the execution of the rebellion's ringleaders, coupled with a wish request for lenient treatment of the young rank and file Volunteers who had been manipulated by the secret IRB cabal. This was in line with the response of Redmond himself, who on 1 May had given Asquith his view that, while Casement and the other ringleaders would have to be dealt with 'in the most severe manner possible', the rank and file should be shown the 'greatest possible leniency'. A week later, by which time twelve of the leaders had been shot following court-martial, he asked in the House 'whether the Prime Minister was aware that the continuance of military executions in Ireland has caused rapidly increasing bitterness of exasperation amongst large sections of the population who have not the slightest sympathy with the insurrection; and whether, following the example set by General Botha in South

Africa, he will cause an immediate stop to be put to the executions?'
(The reference was to the suppression of the Boer extremist revolt led by
Christiaan De Wet in October 1914 by the Union of South Africa (Home
Rule) government, after which only one rebel officer was executed).

A4. REACTION TO THE EXECUTIONS OF REBELLION LEADERS

Criticism of the executions was voiced by fourteen of these twenty-eight
papers. Most of it took the form of mild misgivings rather than anger
(the *Clare Champion* wrote that there was 'no need for draconian measures'; the *Derry Journal* warned that 'vengeance is not politic'), while one,
the *Connacht Tribune* (27 May), accused the government of ignoring
the lessons of the South African revolt and, on 3 June, expressed outrage
at the 'severities' put into effect by the military authorities following
the rebellion. The *Clonmel Nationalist* similarly published (20 May) a
letter of protest at the searches and arrests taking place in the locality.
Only two papers expressed outright anger at the executions themselves.
The *Donegal Vindicator* wrote (19 May): 'the sight of Irishmen shot in
cold blood by England's soldiers has made the whole nation see red'; it
added that although the Sinn Féin rebellion had 'left Ireland unmoved
… now we are Sinn Féiners to the last man'. This was a purely rhetorical
outburst for a newspaper which at no stage supported the Sinn Féin
party. The anger of the *King's County Independent* was a different matter
since it signalled the start of a shift away from pro-Party loyalty. The
paper seemed torn between hatred of the 'crime' of the rebellion it had
already denounced and sympathy for those who had perpetrated it. Its
editorial of 13 May seemed deeply influenced by what it called the 'thrill-
ing speech' of John Dillon in the House of Commons the previous day,
in which he denounced the executions and praised the bravery of the
rebels. 'An extraordinary revulsion of feeling in Ireland has taken place,'
it wrote. 'The whole country condemned the rising in Dublin … the
spread of disaffection which is sweeping like an avalanche all over the
country …' Next to this was displayed an article titled 'Irish Volunteers/
Men of Education/Incapable of Acts of Brutality'. The following week it

continued to vent its anger at the executions, saying that 'an altogether exaggerated view was taken of the occurrence' and giving much coverage to a condemnatory resolution passed at a meeting of Roscommon County Council, a body it described as 'thoroughly attached to the constitutional movement … [which] met after fifteen of the leaders, the poets, the dreamers – Irishmen all – God have mercy on their souls – had been summarily executed'.

In evaluating press reactions to the executions, it should be borne in mind that martial law had been proclaimed all over Ireland on 29 April and, although a formal system of censorship did not come into force until the end of May, many editors may have toned down their early responses for fear of prosecution.[1] The radicalisation of the *Kilkenny People*, the first paper to run foul of the new military regime of General Maxwell, illustrates the pressures potentially influencing editors.

Having warned on 6 May that martial law was now in force and that it would be 'absolute madness' for anyone to offer themselves as human sacrifices, the *Kilkenny People* a week later professed itself 'absolutely bewildered' at the recent arrests of peaceful supporters of Sinn Féin and the Irish Volunteers who had caused no disturbance of any kind. On 20 May, it went further: it seemed, it protested, that Kilkenny had been selected for 'an extra special dose of martial law', in contrast with counties such as Cork, Limerick and Kerry, which had been left relatively untouched despite real unrest having occurred there. This elicited a warning from General Maxwell on 28 May, in which he ordered E.T. Keane, the editor, to submit proofs of future editorials for vetting prior to publication. Keane reacted, in the editions of 3 and 10 June, by leaving the editorial columns blank apart from a reprint of Maxwell's letter together with an editor's note saying that the paper's reply had been censored by the 'Military Dictator' and that it preferred to publish no editorial at all. None of the other newspapers in this sample ran foul of the military censorship as early as this (some others did later, in 1917 and 1918), though the pro-Redmond *Donegal Vindicator* protested at a warning from Maxwell that it would be suppressed if it used language calculated to provoke rebellion. It begged Asquith to take it under his protection: 'we are abjectly law-abiding,' it pleaded on 2 June.

If there was a 'revulsion of feeling' sweeping the country as a result of the executions, as alleged by the *King's County Independent*, there is little evidence of it in these newspapers. This is confirmed by a military intelligence report from the south of Ireland in October 1916 noting that the press in general remained 'friendly', the hostile exceptions being the *Kilkenny People* and the *Cork Free Press*.[2] A genuine revulsion of feeling would soon take place, affecting a significant section of the provincial press; however, this would be a response, not to the executions (though of course lingering resentment cannot be excluded as a factor) but to the imminent prospect of the partition of Ireland embodied in the Lloyd George package of summer 1916 aimed at bringing the Home Rule Act into immediate operation (see below).

A5. ATTITUDES TO THE IRISH PARTY AND HOME RULE POST-REBELLION

In the midst of the emotions generated by the executions and the disturbed conditions produced by the arrests all over the country of suspected partisans of the rebels, it was notable that twenty-seven news-papers, directly or by implication, expressed their confidence in the Irish Party and John Redmond in May. 'The swift smash-up of the insane attempt at insurrection is a triumph for constitutionalism,' wrote the *Munster News* on 6 May. 'Mr Redmond and his methods have been fully vindicated ... and for this reason the Irish Leader's plea for clemency will be heartily re-echoed throughout the country'. 'Constitutionalism has not failed,' said the *Carlow Nationalist* (6 May), a paper that would go over to the Sinn Féin camp in the following year. The *Clare Champion*, another paper destined to change its allegiance, wrote sympathetically (29 April) of the 'sorely-tried Irish Leader, whose superhuman endeavours succeeded in placing the Irish case in a position of unassailable power' and on 6 May congratulated the county on its 'magnificent and unan-imous loyalty to Mr. Redmond'. The *Sligo Champion* called Redmond

(27 May) 'the one genuine rallying-centre for the forces of stability and progress'. The *Limerick Leader* declared (12 May) that the country was 'wholeheartedly behind Mr. Redmond and the Irish Party'. The *Cork Examiner* wrote (6 May) that they had 'lived to see our countrysides and roadways, through the exertion and through that alone of the Irish Party, swept clean of hovels, our farmers steadily growing prosperous and fixed in the soil, and poverty rapidly disappearing from the land'. The *Derry People* wrote (6 May) that the rebellion had been drowned in blood, a fact that showed the futility of 'scrapping wise leaders who had won reform'; it had the 'fullest confidence … [in the] securing of that freedom which Mr. Redmond and his Parliamentary colleagues have won for the motherland'. Of the fifteen other papers, none expressed a contrary sentiment (the usually hostile *Kerryman* and *Mayo News* were refraining from comment at this stage).

Related to the question of confidence in the Party and its leadership was the attitude of these newspapers to the Home Rule Act, on the Statute Book since September 1914. In many of the standard accounts of the aftermath of the rebellion, it is stated or implied that nationalist opinion quickly repudiated Home Rule, if it had not done so already, in favour of the independence project of the rebels. In fact, 32 of 36 newspapers in the summer of 1916 reported and commented as if the Home Rule Act on the Statute Book remained the only political option remotely in consideration for Ireland. The only conceivable alternative to the Irish Party, Sinn Féin (despite the misapplication of its name to the insurrectionary movement), had not yet begun to reorganise itself and remained the tiny fringe group it had been for more than a decade. 'Home Rule was never more alive than it is at present, and the necessity for it was never more apparent' said the *Westmeath Independent* (sister paper of the *King's County Independent*, the author of the 'revulsion of feeling' trope) on 29 April. The *Connacht Tribune* looked forward to the Act being 'in operation without undue delay' (13 May) and referred to the 'dream of Ireland as a sovereign state' as 'hopeless' (20 May). The *Clare Champion* insisted that the Act was 'still on the Statute Book and we mean to keep it there'

(29 July). The *Kilkenny People* was supportive but had warned (25 March) that excessive new war taxation in the forthcoming Budget would severely hamper the operation of Home Rule. The *Wexford People*, also a Party supporter, voiced misgivings about some of the financial clauses but also took the opportunity to revisit its unease about the prospects of the Act's implementation in the light of the promised amending bill. The government's 'tinkering', it wrote, had 'disgusted thousands of young men', and many thought it would have been better had Redmond not insisted on the Act being placed on the Statute Book under circumstances in which the government was not prepared to operate it without the amending bill. Of the remaining four papers, the two Roscommon organs were highly critical of the Act's financial clauses as unworkable, while *The Kerryman* and *Mayo News* had long ago voiced their contempt for it.

This commentary on the rebellion in summarised in Chart 3.

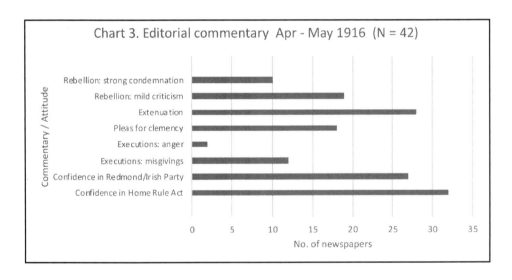

B. LLOYD GEORGE'S HOME RULE INITIATIVE OF JUNE–JULY 1916

B1. THE PARTITION PROPOSALS, JUNE 1916

Following the end of the executions of the rebel leaders and the visit of Prime Minister Asquith to Dublin in mid-May, a new initiative of redress began to emerge at Westminster. All sides accepted that the status quo of suspended Home Rule was no longer viable. Even Tory MPs and newspapers were alert to the effects of the executions on Irish–American opinion. Prominent Tories as well as Liberals had indicated willingness to support a new initiative aimed at settling the question. Redmond and his colleague T.P. O'Connor MP were eager to take advantage of the new mood with a view to immediate implementation of the Home Rule Act. The result of this ferment was Lloyd George's consent to chair a new round of negotiations between the parties that would take up from the point at which the Buckingham Palace Conference had broken down.

On 12 June, the details of the agreement between Redmond, Carson and Lloyd George were published in the press. The county plebiscite provision of 1914 was abandoned, as was the automatic inclusion of the excluded counties after a specified period. The Home Rule Act, modified by an Amending Act, was to come into immediate operation as a war emergency measure with the bloc exclusion of six Ulster counties, to be reviewed at the end of the war. The Irish parliament would consist of the MPs currently representing the twenty-six included counties, while the full 103-MP Irish representation would remain at Westminster. The whole arrangement was labelled 'provisional' – to stay in force until twelve months after the end of the war, but if the Imperial Parliament had not by then made permanent provision for Ireland, its life would be extended by Order in Council 'for as long as might be necessary'. At the end of the war, there would be an imperial conference of dominion representatives, aimed at overhauling the government of the empire, that would consider a permanent settlement for Ireland in that context.

When news of the outline of the Lloyd George initiative emerged in late May, the reactions of the newspapers were largely positive. Of the twenty-nine papers that commented, twenty expressed hopes for a positive outcome for the nationalist cause, six were pessimistic and three were non-committal. Of the five papers from nationalist Ulster, the region with most at stake in the potential outcome, two were positive and two negative, the latter expressing stern warnings. The publication of the detailed provisions immediately changed the pattern of this response, exciting an unprecedented level of engagement with comment from forty-one of forty-two papers in the sample. Most attention was concentrated on the Ulster exclusion clauses, all of it negative. However, the degree of vehemence of the criticism divided the papers into two groups. Of the forty-one newspapers, twenty-three (56 per cent) expressed detestation of partition in varying degrees but all stopped short of outright rejection, expressing a pragmatic willingness to accept it as a step towards the desired national goal, or at least on condition that it not be regarded as a final settlement. The eighteen (44 per cent) papers in the second group reacted in the language of abhorrence, using terms like 'dismemberment' and 'mutilation', and rejected outright any settlement proposals of which partition formed a part, refusing to believe that a 'provisional' or temporary partition measure would not become permanent. In some case, this was coupled with an indictment of the Irish Party leadership for its willingness to have entertained the proposals at all (this was the position of the powerful Dublin-based *Irish Independent*).

Carson, facing objections from unionists outside the six counties, managed with difficulty to convince the Ulster Unionist Council to accept the scheme. The task of Redmond and his northern lieutenant, Joe Devlin, of selling the proposals to Ulster nationalists was made tougher by the implacable opposition of the northern Catholic bishops as well as by the renewed anti-partition crusade of the *Irish Independent* (see Chapter 1). Still suffering from the destruction of its Dublin premises in the rebellion and other organisational problems, the pro-Party *Freeman's Journal* was hamstrung in its response. However, Devlin was able to win a majority for acceptance at a meeting of 1,500 Belfast nationalists on 17 June. A bigger obstacle was a conference of delegates drawn from the six counties scheduled for Belfast on 23 June. Having met the Catholic bishops in advance, Redmond addressed the conference and staked his political career on the result, threatening to resign his leadership if the proposals were not endorsed. The delegates voted in favour by 475 to 265, though those representing the nationalist-majority counties of Tyrone and Fermanagh showed large majorities against. The Irish Party later met to praise the 'magnificent spirit of patriotic self-sacrifice' shown by the delegates.

The newspapers in the first group accepted the Lloyd George scheme with varying degrees of reluctance. One of the earliest to comment, before the publication of the details, the *Ballina Herald* wrote (1 June) that 'Settlement by consent is the only practicable solution of the difficulty. There must be a certain amount of give and take, and from the events of the past fortnight it seems manifest that both Sir Edward Carson and Mr Redmond are prepared to go a long way to meet each other. We do not like a divided Ireland … and it would be lamentable if a large district in the North were severed from the rest of the country. The industrial wealth of the North is essential to the well-being of the country'. The *Southern Star* (24 June) wrote:

> *Frankly, we do not like the partition of this country. We abhor the setting up of a statutory barrier in addition to the unfortunate barriers set up by differences in race & religion …* [However,] *shall we not be stronger and more powerful by setting up some kind of a Home Rule Government in Dublin & getting possession of the Boards and Departments that have too long misruled this country? … it would be unwise and imprudent to reject the proposed solution provided (1) the Nationalists of the excluded counties in free and open convention consent to it; (2) and that it is clearly understood the present plan is only of a temporary character, and that the fiscal side of the question is right.*

The *Killarney Echo* (10 June) asserted, 'Every true lover of Ireland strongly resents any proposal to cut Ireland to pieces in order to patch up a passing settlement ...' Yet a week later, in a thoughtful piece titled 'What Would Parnell Do Today?,' it pointed out the arguments in favour of taking three-fourths of Ireland now: 'we will be in a better position to work it out not only for ourselves, but for those we love and respect in the six excluded counties of Ireland ... Then, if they [unionists] hold hostages of our people in the six excluded counties, don't we hold hostages of theirs in the other twenty-six? ... [H]aving read the numerous protests of public bodies and others against partition, we feel bound to put some view of the other side ...' On 24 June, it reminded readers that 'every enemy of Ireland is also shouting now against division in the hope of destroying any chance open to us under present conditions ... Again we ask is it wise and patriotic to refuse to accept the proposal to confer freedom on five-sixths of Ireland, or should we reject it without hesitation owing to the temporary exclusion of part of Ireland? Let us decide the issue after carefully thinking it out ...'

For the *Sligo Champion*, nationalists 'must be practical'; coercing the Ulster unionists was a bad idea and 'three-quarters of Ireland in Irish hands' was 'not bad for a start' (17 June). The *Clare Champion* reported the county council as having denounced partition as 'the grossest insult to Irish nationality'; if there was to be exclusion, it must be temporary only (17, 24 June). The *Limerick Leader* called on its readers not to reject the proposals (14 June) and applauded the 'unselfish patriotism' of the Ulster nationalists in voting to accept them (26 June). The *Westmeath Examiner* praised the Ulster nationalists for having 'refused to take up the attitude of the dog in the manger' (1 July). The *Longford Leader* wrote that if the nationalists of Ulster accepted the proposals, 'we fail to see why the Catholics and nationalists of the south and west should complain. After all, it is the Catholics and nationalists of Ulster who stand to suffer by accepting this arrangement, and if they are willing to do so, we most certainly have no right to object' (24 June). The *Connacht Tribune* warned at the outset that the Ulster question was the 'stumbling block' (27 May) and that Carson and his Orangemen stood in the way of the operation of the Act and that the government must 'deal with' them. In June, it called for 'sane reasoning and cool heads' and said that the deal was 'worth accepting' and that Redmond's policy was correct.

In its typically measured, even intellectual, editorial style, the *Tuam Herald* (17 June) wrote of the 'cruelly hard sacrifice' demanded of the Ulster nationalists, adding that it was a decision of the greatest and gravest national importance and that nothing should be said or written to embitter the controversy. After the Belfast conference had voted, it said that the Ulster nationalists who had accepted the provisional policy of partition, however distasteful they found it, would earn the 'eternal gratitude' of the Irish people. The rest of Ireland must face the question from their standpoint. To coerce the Ulster opposition meant civil war, and compromise was therefore necessary. The *Cork Examiner* similarly praised the 'high ideals and lofty patriotic spirit' that had impelled the vote at the Belfast conference; the duty of the rest of Ireland was to prove by emulation of this splendid spirit and by excellent administration that they regarded the country as in a state of transition (24 June).

Of the Ulster papers, only the Belfast *Irish News* (as might be expected from an organ close to Devlin) supported the scheme and sought to influence the delegates on the morning of 23 June as it wrote: 'Ireland will not be "partitioned". The partial severance must be temporary in the inevitable course of events. But is Ireland united today – except as an "entity" under Martial Law? ... Has Ireland ever been really united? Certainly, not since the date of the Norman Conquest'.

Of the eighteen papers uncompromisingly against partition, four of the Ulster organs were predictably vehement. The *Derry Journal* had written, 'No Nationalist in Ulster or Ireland would dream of agreeing to the exclusion of one square mile, or even one rood, of the country as a permanent proposition' (14 June) and 'the flow of popular feeling against the detested proposals grows stronger from day to day ... Let the people decide!' (16 June). After the Belfast vote, it recorded its 'Grievous Disappointment' (26 June), lamenting that feeling in the suggested area of exclusion 'has attained to the strength of acute mental distress and dismay'. Speculating on the reasons for the vote, it thought that Redmond's resignation threat and his pledge not to accept any scheme of permanent exclusion had been instrumental, but also that anti-partition statements from southern unionists, some Protestant bishops and Tory die hards might have swayed delegates who otherwise hated partition.

The *Anglo-Celt* wrote (3 June) that there should be no Ulster exclusion; it favoured instead the idea that the Home Rule parliament should sit alternately in Dublin and Belfast. Two weeks later, it was highly critical of the proposals as revealed: their 'temporary' aspect, much emphasised by Redmond and Devlin, only increased their danger. It was the duty of nationalists to judge the scheme calmly, but the paper thought it all 'bound to end in disaster'. It was at pains (24 June) to stress that it did not blame the Party leadership if it was out of touch with Irish feeling, since the Party was required to be 'encamped in the House [of Commons]' by the will of the people. After the 23 June conference vote of nationalists, the paper wanted to know (1 July), 'Why have the Belfast nationalists accepted the exclusion arrangement? … What happened at the Ulster Conference?'

The objections of the *Donegal Vindicator* to the Home Rule scheme were similar to those of the *Anglo-Celt*. If Lloyd George thought, it wrote on 9 June, that Ireland would accept 'the Buckingham Palace proposals plus the disputed counties Fermanagh and Tyrone', he would be no more successful than his predecessors: 'We will not have it; we will have Home Rule, pure and simple, without qualification or dismemberment … Ireland demands it, and England must give it'. In advance of the Belfast conference, it was anxious that only the most able must be selected as delegates to represent Ulster. However, although its anti-partition editorial line aligned it with the *Independent*, it was equally anxious to distance itself from both sides in the war between the two Dublin nationalist dailies. On 16 June, it disagreed with the *Independent*: before deciding that Messrs. Redmond, Dillon and Devlin had proved false to their country, 'there must be evidence'. A week later, it rejected the *Freeman's* claim that those who refused to accept the proposed settlement were 'factionists and enemies': this was false regarding nine-tenths of them, it wrote. On

30 June it wrote that, although it hated the proposals, it would not campaign against the Belfast conference decision to accept them: that would be 'factionism'. Exclusion was an 'atrocity', but it would not believe that Redmond, Dillon and Devlin had 'conspired to bring political ruin on the nationalists of the north-west [sic]', however mistaken they might be. Later it wrote (14 July) that, although the settlement was 'farcical', and Derry would fight exclusion, the paper would not join the anti-Party campaign.

The *Derry People* voiced early hopes (20 May) for the Home Rule initiative, saying that 'only a little intelligence and elementary justice' were needed to bring a settlement. However, three weeks later, it carried two 'special articles' on the Lloyd George proposals, one calling them 'unthinkable … it is asking too much of nationalists to accept dismemberment' (10 June). On 17 June, it pointed to contradictory interpretations of the proposals, titling a news item 'The Exclusion Fog: Permanent or Temporary? Conflicting Statements.' Stating confidently (but without foundation) that an executive for the six-county excluded area was part of the proposed settlement, it asked, 'Why did Mr. Redmond, Mr. Dillon and Mr. Devlin conceal this part of the proposed scheme?'. It was 'an ignoble surrender to Carsonite bigotry'. It would prefer to see Ireland struggle on 'for many weary years', even with martial law, than be dismembered (24 July). Having thus crossed the Rubicon in attacking the Party leadership, it broadened the criticism (and rewrote its own history) by asserting (1 July) that the fundamental mistake had been 'made two years ago when the principle of Exclusion was admitted'.

Outside of Ulster, the *Meath Chronicle* criticised the 'dismemberment plan' and counselled the Irish Party to take the advice of the Ulster bishops and drop it (17, 24 June). The *Nenagh Guardian* (24 June) after the announcement of the Belfast vote, wrote that 'the country rings with vigorous protests against any form of partition, and abhorrence of such measures by the various public boards and national bodies of the country have been recorded'. The *Roscommon Journal* (24 June) quoted the opinion of Cardinal Logue that 'it would be infinitely better for us to remain as we are for fifty years to come under English rule rather than to accept these proposals'. It was pleased to record that Roscommon County Council had 'joined with so many other of the county councils of Ireland and other public bodies in protesting against the partition of Ireland under Home Rule. We fail to see how any Irishman could possibly bring himself to view with equanimity the prospect of a settlement of the Irish question on the basis of a mutilated Ireland … It is all very well to say that it only means the 'temporary exclusion' of six counties, but will it, in fact, be temporary?'. The *Drogheda Argus* wrote 'A nation divided against itself cannot stand, and hence Mr Lloyd George's proposal to isolate six Ulster counties is highly repugnant' (17 June). Citing a statement from the Ulster Unionist Council that the settlement must be permanent, otherwise 'negotiations are at an end', it commented 'If this is to be the Unionist attitude it is sheer waste of time to indulge in *pour parlers*. We have too much confidence in Mr Redmond to believe for a moment that he would entertain such a preposterous and insolent proposal' (24 June).

The *Munster News* (10 June) cited the statement of the Ulster bishops: 'The utmost confidence in the Irish Party is placed on record, and their Lordships express the firm belief that Mr Redmond will be no party to any settlement that will fail to commend itself to the vast majority of the Irish people. This view Irish Nationalists generally will heartily endorse.' Following the Belfast vote, it opined (24 June):

The Nationalist Conference held yesterday … cannot be said to have been in any sense conclusive on the question of the exclusion of six Ulster counties under the Lloyd George scheme … [The vote means that] considerably more than one-third of the representatives of public opinion amongst those most vitally affected are opposed … How can Nationalist Ireland outside Ulster be expected to favour a plan that has met with such strong opposition? … It will cost supporters of the Irish Party many a pang to find themselves unable to agree to these proposals; but, much as they may regret the step, their duty to their country will oblige them to hold that the scheme which Mr Redmond in an evil hour was induced to accept must meet with uncompromising opposition.

The editorial went on, however, 'in the interests of fair play', to register its 'deep indignation at the methods used by the *Irish Independent* to mislead the country in this crisis'.

Some papers changed their minds in the course of the national debate on the proposals. The *Carlow Nationalist* (17 June) was 'totally and unreservedly against the exclusion of one square inch of Irish ground from the benefits of self-government', though it had confidence that the Irish leaders should know best what was in the interests of the Irish nation. A week later, it held that 'temporary exclusion is far better than the suspension of constitutional government' and the 'essential point is to get the Irish Parliament set up' (24 June). It threw its support behind the 'strictly provisional arrangement', writing that 'three-quarters of a loaf is better than no bread' (1, 15 July). Similarly, the *Midland Tribune* had begun with 'emphatic protest' (10 June) but later advised that 'Nationalists should keep their heads' (17 June). After the Belfast vote, it reckoned that the outcome showed that 'the Irish Party now occupies a stronger position than throughout the negotiations', and there would be 'no stampede of nationalist opinion away from the course indicated by the Irish leaders'. The *Kerry Sentinel* changed its stance in the opposite direction. Beginning in moderation – 'There is, so far, not the least reason for apprehension of any kind … Whatever concession might be given to secure the establishment of Home Rule at once could not … derogate from the full national claim, which will remain until it is satisfied' (10 June) – it moved within a few days to denouncing a scheme that was 'satisfactory to Carson and his followers, and, what is much more regrettable, satisfactory to Mr Redmond and his Party', and warned the latter that 'No Irishman worthy of the name will stand idly by and see his country dismembered …' [It would be] 'far far better … to leave our country as it is at present' (14 June).

For some newspapers in the rejectionist camp, the entire partition controversy was the catalyst for a decisive break from their previous loyalty to the Party. The *Kilkenny People* sounded an early warning well before the terms of the Home Rule scheme were known. On 27 May, it hoped that Lloyd George could succeed where others had failed, but added: 'Any settlement which leaves out Ulster could not possibly have the support of Irish nationalists'. On 10 June, having seen the terms, it commented, 'it is not Home Rule at all, and ... can settle nothing, though it will probably unsettle a great deal. The Home Rule Act is to be torn up ... and the six counties, including two with a clear nationalist majority, are to remain subject to and at the mercy of the hereditary enemies of our race and creed'. Despite the government's statement that the scheme was only provisional, it wrote on 17 June, 'the central fact is that we are called upon to sanction the dismemberment of Ireland, which, so far as any guarantee to the contrary is concerned, may continue not for a year or two years, but for all time'. In advance of the Belfast conference, it sympathised with the 'very difficult' situation in which Ulster nationalists were placed, while it reprinted the trenchantly anti-partition views of two Ulster Catholic bishops (24 June). On 22 July, with the final outcome still in the balance, it claimed that the Carson and Redmond versions of the deal contradicted each other. In the same editorial, it criticised Redmond's leadership for the first time, wielding a dagger where the *Derry People* had used a bludgeon: 'No Irish Leader in our history has rendered such devoted service to the British Government and no other Irish Leader is ever likely to do so again. And what return is he receiving for his loyal service? ... [only] the chicanery of the Government'.

The *Waterford News,* like the *Kilkenny People*, had been broadly supportive of the Irish Party (though it had taken a combative approach to the overtaxation issue in March). Now, galvanised by the partition issue, it executed a dramatic about-turn. On 7 July, under the heading 'The Great Betrayal', it objected to:

the way in which the pronouncements of the Bishops of Ulster have been treated by Catholic Members of Parliament, Catholic public bodies, and, perhaps worst of all, by certain Nationalist newspapers. It may be assumed – at any rate by Irish Catholics – that the Bishops of Ulster are in a better position to judge what is good for their flock than any whippersnappers down South ... Our Parliamentary representatives and their followers are recklessly stating that six counties in Ulster have consented to Exclusion. Apart from the question as to how the majority vote was obtained in Belfast – of which the less said the better – the fact was that two of the counties, as well as the city of Derry ... rejected [the proposals] *by a large majority and in spite of blandishments and threats.*

By 14 July, it had discovered that the Home Rule Act itself would 'have to be scrapped or it will have to undergo a process of wholesale reformation' and that the confidence placed in Irish party representatives had been 'misplaced'.

Five other newspapers had no motives of loyalty to the Irish Party to restrain their opposition to the Lloyd George proposals from the outset. The *Leinster Leader* was a pro-Home Rule paper unsympathetic to republicanism. Its criticism of the Party was similar in theme and tone to, though more muted than, that of the *Independent*: it inveighed against its 'discredited convention system ... machined resolutions of our public administration boards ... the waning power of the Irish Party' (17 June). For this paper, there could be 'no permanent dismemberment under any circumstances'; if there had to be temporary exclusion, it should be done to all of the nine-county province of Ulster (3 June). However, its editorial of 24 June presented both sides of the case regarding the Home Rule scheme, while allowing that there was a 'big body of public opinion' against the Party's efforts to reconcile the country to temporary exclusion of the six counties. On 1 July, it accused Redmond of getting his majority at the Belfast conference vote by a 'subterfuge' (his threat of resignation). It also wanted to know why unionist Ulster should not be coerced, though it did not suggest a practical way to achieve this. On 15 July, it assailed the Party again: since consent of unionists was to be a precondition for the inclusion of the six counties, partition would be permanent and Ireland would be left with 'this travesty of a Home Rule legislature' plus martial law.

The *Roscommon Herald* was also in the constitutionalist camp although it made no secret of his antagonism to the Party's leadership. The paper was apt to mix militant pro-war sentiment ('All the Asquith gang [are] only fit for the scrap-heap ... totally unfitted for the conduct of the War', 9 December 1916) with anti-Party scurrility (it repeated on 5 August the dissident MP Laurence Ginnell's allegation that the Party's members had cheered the executions in the House of Commons). 'The problem for statesmen in this critical hour,' it warned on 27 May, 'is the judicious handling of the two races or the two creeds ... Mr. Redmond knows that Home Rule with Ulster out would be flung back with scorn by the Irish people'. On 24 June it quoted an *Irish Times* report that Carson had got an undertaking from Lloyd George in writing that the exclusion of Ulster was to be definite and permanent. Not since the days of the Parnell split, it wrote, had the country been 'so profoundly moved as at present. The outcry against Mr. Redmond has grown in intensity ... The setting up of two nations within the ring of our shores concerns everybody north and south'. 'Ireland Mutilated' was its editorial headline on 1 July: the country was to be 'chopped into two parts'.

The *Kerryman* had already denounced the Home Rule Act before the rebellion as 'hopeless'. On 17 June, in response to the exclusion proposals, it inveighed against the 'weakness of the "Leaders"' and the fact that the Party bosses were now leaving it to the people to decide on their 'supine concessions'. A week later, it published a long letter on its front page under the title 'Barterers of a Nation's Birthright', with an editorial alleging a conspiracy between Lloyd George and Redmond. The most extreme newspaper of the four, the *Mayo News*, had long dissented from mainstream constitutional nationalism. Under the heading 'The Great Betrayal' (24 June), it greeted the proposals with a storm of hyperbole. 'Lloyd George's proposals for the dismemberment of the Irish nation' had found willing tools in the Irish Party and Redmond to accomplish his difficult task; they had 'sold their country as Judas sold his God … Oh, for a Parnell or a Davitt to lead the Irish people! What a use they would have made of the splendid opportunities which the present circumstances afford'. The Irish Party had become obsessed with 'the Imperialistic idea' and Redmond was 'but a puppet in the hands of the Government'.

The *Cork Free Press*, the paper of William O'Brien and his ally T.M. Healy, did full justice to its founder's characteristic hyperbolic style in its critique of the Lloyd George proposals and Redmond's role. If the Irish Party joined O'Brien even now in 'offering generous concessions to unionists, short of partition,' it asserted on 3 June, 'the question would be permanently settled in a day'. A later editorial alleged that the whole scheme was concocted 'to gratify the wild vanity of Mr Redmond to go down as the man who gave Ireland her freedom'. Another was titled 'The Attempt to Destroy the Nation' (10, 17 June). The Belfast convention had been 'carefully packed', it alleged on 1 July, and the vote had made the British press exultant, as they saw 'the destruction of the ancient Irish nation'.

B2. THE BREAKDOWN OF THE HOME RULE INITIATIVE, JULY 1916

On 20 June, reports emerged of acute internal dissension in the Cabinet on the Home Rule package. Deputations of southern Irish unionists had been lobbying the government. Three ministers – Lords Lansdowne and Selborne and Walter Long, all with extensive land interests in Ireland –threatened to resign, citing their concern at unrest and Sinn Féin demonstrations in Ireland under what they assumed would be a weak Home Rule government. Carson tried to quiet their objections, and Lloyd George urged Asquith to threaten that, if they insisted on governing Ireland by coercion, he would go to the king and nominate Long to be prime minister. However, Asquith staved off the threatened resignations by promising a committee to draw up necessary safeguards for British military and naval facilities in the event of another outbreak. Redmond agreed to these safeguards, most of which were already in the Home Rule Act, on 1 July.

The settlement proposals had still to be put to parliament in amending bill form. On 10 July, Asquith reiterated that the bill was 'a provisional measure', but also paraphrased his pre-war statement that Irish unity 'can only be brought about with, and can never be brought about without, the free will and assent of the excluded area'. Carson asked him whether the six counties, after the provisional period, could be included [under Home Rule] by a bill. Asquith replied that 'they could not be included without a bill'. The assurance that there would be no automatic inclusion was already implicit in the agreed proposals, and Redmond made no objection.

The following day, Lansdowne stated that the amending bill would 'make structural alterations' to the Home Rule Act and would therefore be 'permanent and enduring in its character'. In the Cabinet on 19 July, Lansdowne and Long secured agreement that the exclusion of the six counties be made permanent from the outset. When this 'irreversible' decision was presented to Redmond on 22 July, the deal was dead. By scuppering the creative ambiguity of the proposals, it made Redmond's continued assent impossible. Clearly, 'provisional now with permanent arrangements later' was something he could – with difficulty – sell to Irish nationalist opinion. 'Permanent as of now' he could not. A furious Redmond promised Asquith 'vehement opposition' to the measure, and the bill was abandoned.

Less than ever before had separated the two sides. But the agreement had been torpedoed, not by hardline nationalists or extreme Ulster unionists, but by a group that had featured little in the Home Rule debates of 1912 to 1914, the anti-partition southern unionists. The allies of this group in the Cabinet were traditional Tories, more concerned with the security of imperial interests in the whole of Ireland, worried by the rebellion and the swing of nationalist sentiment now under way and inclined to view the Home Rule scheme as an unwise concession to extremism.

The breakdown of the Lloyd George agreement on 22 July, like its earlier announcement in June, excited a very high level of comment, with thirty-seven of the forty-two newspapers expressing reaction. The commonest response, expressed by twenty-four (65 per cent) of these, was that the breakdown was a betrayal and a demonstration of bad faith by the British government. A majority of these, seventeen, were papers that had been willing to countenance the scheme as a provisional measure; the other seven, somewhat illogically, were papers that had been uncompromising in their opposition. 'Once again England has broken her treaty with this country … has thrown [the Irish members] overboard … Never has any English Government sank so low, or committed a more cynical breach of faith than has the present Coalition Government' (*Southern Star*, 29 July); 'Another Broken Treaty' (*Killarney Echo*, 29 June); 'Betrayed! Home Rule Proposals Smashed Up! … The Irishmen in the British Army were deceived, and now in death betrayed' (*Clare Champion*, 29 July); 'Perfidious Albion!' (*Wexford People*, 29 July). For the *Drogheda Argus* (29 July), the result might be summed up in three words: 'disappointment, disgust and dishonour'. For a smaller group of thirteen (35 per cent) papers, ten of which had opposed the partition scheme under all circumstances, the reaction was one of relief. The *Anglo-Celt* (29 July) was 'delighted at the result' and 'thankful' it was all over; 'Good riddance will be the universal comment of the people' wrote the *Derry Journal* (26 July). The *Midland Tribune* wrote (29 July) that the proposals had 'died an unregretted death as far as Ireland was concerned … [they were] thoroughly unpopular from first to last'. 'Thank goodness the Partition Bill is dead,' agreed the *Tipperary Star* (29 July).

Embedded in attitudes towards the breakdown was the question of where the blame should be laid. Of the thirty-nine papers that commented on this, twenty-two (56 per cent) attributed all the blame to the British government and none to Redmond or the Party; of these latter, seventeen had assented to the partition proposals while five had opposed them. However, another fifteen (38 per cent), of which thirteen had strongly rejected the proposals, laid at least some of the blame at Redmond's door, in comments ranging from veiled or moderate criticism to outright denunciation.

In the 'no blame' camp were the *Southern Star* (29 July): 'Little good can now be gained by recriminations amongst brother Irishmen'; and the *Limerick Leader* (26 July): the breakdown was a 'base betrayal' that showed the bad faith of the government but Redmond and his Party had been 'wise and far-seeing'. The *Cork Examiner* represented the views of many papers when it wrote (25, 26 July) that neither Redmond nor Carson could be held responsible for the breakdown, but Asquith and Lloyd George had acted with 'deplorable weakness' and the full report would reinforce the feeling that Englishmen were not to be trusted. The *Munster News* (31 July) asked, 'Has a deeper depth of degradation ever been reached, even in British public life? Mr Redmond strained to breaking point the allegiance of his followers in Ireland in order not to do anything which would embarrass the Government during the war, and this is the result ... He trusted the Coalition Cabinet, and it has proved to be devoid of honour or principle ... Is it any wonder that deep distrust of everything English should once again fill the hearts of the Irish people?' The *Tuam Herald* (22 July) defended Redmond against the 'unfairness and dishonesty' of the charge that he had 'weakly submitted to the cruel necessity' and could have averted six-county exclusion. Even then, it refused to give up hope: the two Irishmen Redmond and Carson, neither of whom was to blame for the breakdown, now had a 'grand opportunity' to do better than the Welshman Lloyd George (29 July). The *Donegal Vindicator*, while it registered the general sense of outrage (28 July), refused, like its sister Ulster paper, the *Anglo-Celt*, to join the *Irish Independent*-led hue-and-cry for the head of Redmond, and accused that paper of 'a ruthless disregard of decency' for attacking the Party and its leader as traitors (4 August). These two papers were not alone in counter-attacking the *Independent*: all but one of the pro-Party papers did so, either explicitly or in coded language. The *Carlow Nationalist* was another organ that condemned the government's backsliding but believed 'that Mr. Redmond in accepting exclusion for the six counties did so in the best interests of Ireland' (29 July).

Of the fifteen critical papers, the mildest was the *Meath Chronicle* (29 July), which advised that Redmond 'will be wiser to attract still closer to him the public opinion of nationalist Ireland'. The *Tipperary Star*, a paper unused to political commentary until the eruption of the partition controversy, wrote that Redmond had been 'too easy, too hopeful, too trustful, too gentlemanly, if you like, and he is now suffering for it' (29 July). The *Connacht Tribune*, while standing by Redmond, wrote that the Party had been 'led into a trap and tricked and duped' (5 August); the constitutional movement had 'got out of touch with a considerable section of the people' (9 September). In the view of the *Wexford People* (29 July), 'a huge mistake was made through Mr Redmond being too hopeful and through his not facing the situation boldly, and telling the people of Ireland, at the outbreak of the war, that Home Rule was impossible so long as Ulster objected'. For the *Derry Journal* (26 July), not merely the younger generation but veteran nationalists, 'were amazed and filled with chagrin that the Irish Party had not promptly rejected the invitation to "negotiate" upon such degrading terms'.

The *Drogheda Argus* wrapped its critique of Redmond's actions inside a blistering attack on Asquith and a recital of recent history back to the 1910 Budget and the 1911 National Insurance Act (Liberal enactments received with enthusiasm by the British masses but which had added to the grievances of conservative Irish nationalists). 'In his anxiety to placate the northern Unionists, the Prime Minister, who was kept in office longer than any other British Prime Minister, by the Nationalists … listened to the diatribes of Lansdowne and the threats of Carson before the platitudes of Redmond and the denunciations of Dillon' (29 July). A week later, it echoed much of the *Irish Independent* case against the leadership, though it stopped short of demanding Redmond's resignation:

One thing clear from the House of Commons debate is that the Irish Party should not put its trust in any British party but remain absolutely independent and free to walk into the Division lobby at any time against either of the two great British parties. As Dillon said, instead of getting thanks from the

Government, they get nothing but kicks. But what else could he expect as an experienced politician?

Why had Lloyd George tricked the Irish Party, and given Carson a secret assurance, the paper asked, and why had the prime minister winked at this trickery? The obvious reason was that 'the Irish Party trotted into the lobbies on every division to keep Asquith in office, and remained passive and hopeful' (5 August). In a cryptic expression of a wish for a change of leader, the *Killarney Echo* wrote (29 July) 'We would appeal to all real Nationalists to keep steady, and calmly consider as far as it is possible to do so … to go ahead unitedly, under the command of men whose thoughts and hopes and affections are for Ireland first and last and all the time …' The *Roscommon Journal* (29 July) chimed with this theme in a reference to 'the present time, when our country and country's cause is losing so heavily, owing to the weakness of the Party and its leaders'.

The *Kerry Sentinel* (26 July) framed the question on all nationalist minds in an editorial titled, 'What Next?': 'What Mr Redmond said at the conclusion of his statement let us all echo and re-echo: "from this time forth we feel it our duty to exercise an independent judgment in criticising the ever-increasing vacillation and procrastination of the Government, which seem to form their only policy, not only with reference to Ireland, but with reference to the whole conduct of the war."' For the *Clare Champion,* there was only one policy for the Irish Party in future: independent and unqualified opposition. But all was not yet lost: Home Rule was 'still on the Statute Book and we mean to keep it there' (29 July).

For three papers, the *Derry People,* the *Kilkenny People* and the *Waterford News* (the last circulating in Redmond's own constituency), the entire episode of the Lloyd George negotiations – the discussion of his Home Rule scheme, its ultimate rejection by the Irish Party and its abandonment by the government – was the chief catalyst for their turn against the Party at this early post-rebellion stage and their gravitation to a radical critique of constitutional nationalism. The *Derry People* (29

July) wrote that betrayal was invariably the fate of those Irish leaders who trusted in the promises of English politicians. For the *Kilkenny People*, the collapse of the process was the signal for a caustic attack on the entire history of the Irish Party–Liberal alliance, as far back as the fall of Parnell. The Irish leaders had fallen into the government's trap: Lloyd George had told one story to Sir Edward Carson and another to the Irish Party. It was now clear that the Bishop of Derry and the other Ulster bishops were 'absolutely right, and Mr. Redmond and his colleagues absolutely wrong'. It hastened to add that the latter had acted in good faith: they had thought they were dealing with honourable men, but 'how they came to think it mystifies us' (29 July). The *Waterford News* (28 July) drove the knife in further. It was only to be expected, it wrote, that 'the Irish Party – exposed and humiliated as never an Irish political organisation was before – should endeavour to shift the blame ... It is now perfectly clear that the alleged provisional character of the Exclusion was a false statement ... And Mr. Redmond, it will be observed, has not resigned. It is difficult to understand how Irish Nationalists can place further confidence in those who have so grossly deceived them'.

Finally, the five papers already hostile took their cue from the *Independent* in throwing off all restraint as they used the collapse of the deal to pronounce anathema upon the Party. The *Leinster Leader* described the breakdown as leaving the Party in a plight 'to which their vacillation and supineness foredoomed them' and which the 'weak and menial attitude' of its leader deserved. It accused Redmond of forgetting Ireland at the start of the war and thinking of it only as a centre of recruiting in his 'zeal for the interests of the Empire'. Yet, despite the harsh rhetoric, the paper did not conceive of an alternative to constitutional politics: the Home Rule Act on the Statute Book was 'the only foundation for peace and reconciliation'; the Party must return to militant methods. Redmond and his followers had 'abandoned the path of Irish nationality in 1914', but it could still allow for a future 'reunion of the people and their Parliamentary representatives' (29 July). The *Roscommon Herald* greeted the breakdown with the heading, 'A Burst

Bubble', claiming to know that 'Mr. Redmond was constrained by the force of Irish public opinion to drop any further association with this sad business. It was very foolish of Mr. Redmond the first day to touch such a question. It has undoubtedly injured his popularity in a grievous manner, and it is questionable if he will ever recover from the blow' (29 July). For *The Kerryman* (29 July), 'The game of humbugging the Irish people has ended. The obvious course is for Mr. Redmond and his lieutenants to resign. It is no excuse to say they were misled ... they threw away countless chances to secure Irish legislative independence'. The *Mayo News* ('The Bubble Burst', 29 July) described the fiasco as the result of the 'combined efforts of a back-boneless prime minister, aided by a pliant and weak-kneed Irish Leader and Party ... Redmond as a leader of the Irish people has become impossible ... [he] has run his ship for years on Asquith's word without even getting one inch nearer the promised land'; the restoration of Castle rule shortly afterwards was 'the reward which Mr. Redmond has got for his grovelling to the Liberal Ministry' (5 August).

Chiming with the *Independent*, the *Cork Free Press* (29 July) head-lined its post-breakdown editorial 'The Collapse of the Partition Plot'. Redmond had been thoroughly defeated in Ireland and had 'wriggled out of the scheme by rejecting it on a quibble'. He had already accepted the permanence of partition on 10 July in the House of Commons, it alleged, but 'that was before the roar of protest from the people'

This commentary on the Lloyd George initiative is summarised in Chart 4.

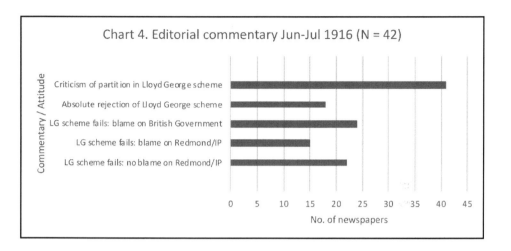

Chart 4. Editorial commentary Jun-Jul 1916 (N = 42)

B3. REDMOND'S RETURN TO PUBLIC LIFE, OCTOBER 1916

Following the collapse of the summer's Home Rule initiative, Redmond retired, bruised and demoralised – and worried for the safety of his brother and son, both in the thick of the fighting at the Western Front – to his Aughavanagh home. After ten weeks of seclusion, he emerged to deliver an address in his Waterford constituency on 6 October to mark the twenty-fifth anniversary of the death of Parnell. A force of police was present at City Hall to guard against disturbances as he arrived, and a violent melée broke out after two girls hoisted tricolours and called for cheers for the republic, prompting *The Kerryman* to report the remark of a priest comparing the men who 'assaulted the young ladies' to 'aborigines of Patagonia'. Redmond's address lamented the setback to national progress and hopes occasioned by 'the insane ideals of men who invited Ireland once again to take up arms against the British Empire'. He deplored the 'scandalous bad faith' shown by the government in the recent negotiations, repenting his own participation, and announced that he would go into no more negotiations on the matter. The new policy would be 'open and vigorous opposition', and he called on the government to: '"Appease the inflamed feelings of the Irish people; withdraw martial law; make it plain that the Defence of the Realm Act was to be administered in Ireland, not as at present, but in the same spirit as in Great Britain; treat the Irish prisoners of the unfortunate rising as political prisoners." In the meantime, 'Home Rule is safe if Ireland is sane,' he concluded.

The oration received a mixed reception. The *Irish Independent* set the tone for the opposition by sneering at Redmond's '"new" policy of belated firmness', but the speech had a much-needed rallying effect on Party supporters. Of the thirty papers that commented, nineteen (63 per cent) voiced support, four (13 per cent) were critical in varying degrees and six (20 per cent) were antagonistic.

The Waterford-based *Munster Express* (14 October) gave generous coverage (14 October) to Redmond's 'royal and most enthusiastic reception in Waterford'. The other local organ, the *Waterford News*, by contrast, barely noticed Redmond's arrival and reception in the city; it then published two pieces of criticism of the speech without reporting the speech itself (6, 13 October). In a later issue, it referred to Redmond's 'chairmanship of the Partitionist Party' (20 October).

The *Anglo-Celt* (14 October) wrote that the leader had now 'admitted he made a mistake' and that 'the majority will forgive Mr. Redmond and thank heaven the nation escaped the peril … [of the] abhorrent proposals'. The *Carlow Nationalist,* a paper that would switch allegiance in the following year, remained on board for the moment, hailing 'the magnificent lead given by Mr. Redmond … [who] certainly spoke for nationalist Ireland' (14 October). The *Dundalk Democrat* (14 October) thought that Redmond had been 'too long silent' and was not surprised at the 'fury' of the *Independent* and T.M. Healy. The *Connaught Telegraph* (14 October) thought that he had never delivered 'a more masterly or courageous' address. The *Cork Examiner* (7 October) commended its 'lucidity and breadth of view' and its 'wise words'. *The Wexford People* (11 October) was glad that the speech had 'cleared the air very considerably'. Nationalist Ireland was now divided in three sections, it claimed, and

Redmond's words would reassure the middle group whose confidence had been shaken.

The *Roscommon Herald* was dismissive: the address had been delivered 'in the Hebrew language – it could be read backwards or forwards and you could take what meaning you please' (14 October). The *Kerryman* (14 October) was scathing on 'Redmond's "Sanity" Stunt'. The *Mayo News* (14 October) claimed that Redmond had spoken as a man who had realised his failure – a case of 'a brilliant career dimmed by abuse of popular confidence'. The *Kilkenny People* (21 October), which, exactly two years previously, had hailed 'the wonderful demonstration of Wexfordmen' at Redmond's Wexford recruiting rally and looked forward to a repetition at Kilkenny the following Sunday, noted that much of his speech had been taken up with the blunders of the military authorities that had held back recruiting, and commented sourly, 'he should feel glad his advice wasn't taken, given that recruits are now bewildered at finding themselves fighting for the rule of Sir John Maxwell'. (Martial law was revoked and Maxwell recalled in November.) Meanwhile, the *Cork Free Press* (14 October) saw in the address only 'the mendacity of the traitor fresh from this deliberate continuous and undeniable course of perfidy to his country'.

One other paper was a new recruit to the opposition. The *Midland Tribune*, which had been in the 'no blame on the Party' camp in late July, now (14 October) executed a radical change of stance: 'The Party and its leaders have been weak and flabby when they should have been firm. [Redmond's] new threat of opposition … may be taken with the proverbial grain of salt. Mr. Redmond is too fond of toadying to English opinion to expect anything very material otherwise from him now'. It went further to allege that 'the Irish Party and Mr Redmond long ago smashed the Volunteer movement, and in that way are largely responsible for the rebellion'.

Not only the opposition papers, but most Redmondite ones, as they endorsed the leader's 'no more negotiations' stance, seemed to lose sight of the issue at the core of the controversy – the refusal of Ulster unionism to accept Home Rule in their own region. Only two papers in the sample appeared to grasp the realities. The *Tuam Herald* wrote, 'The demand of the Irish Party to put the Home Rule Act into operation cannot be met ... it is impossible, however desirable, unless the Orange Party acquiesces. That stern fact of their resistance cannot be got over or got under. People talk lightly of coercing the Orangemen of Ulster, but no government will deliberately put an Act in force which will provoke civil war and cripple its capacity for carrying on its present defensive war for Imperial safety'. Anticipating the idea of the Irish Convention, which would be embraced by Redmond and moderate nationalists the following year, it concluded that 'the only way forward is Irish parties reaching a common settlement by themselves' (14 October). The *Galway Observer* put it more succinctly: 'the anti-partitionists are now the factionists ... one of two extremes that do not want a united Ireland' (14 October).

At the end of the year, as Lloyd George replaced Asquith as prime minister and the rebels of Easter were sent home from their British internment camps, the comments of one paper reflected the general inability, in the fevered post-rebellion atmosphere, to map out a clear path ahead. The *Clonmel Nationalist,* a journal that largely focused its editorials on farming and business matters and only sporadically engaged in political commentary, summed up the year's developments on 23 December by lamenting that the 'Orange ascendancy gang' had succeeded in blocking the operation of the Home Rule Act – a summary not quite accurate if by 'Orange ascendancy' it meant the Ulster unionists. It was 'truly deplorable to see it hung up at the behest of a miserable section of political and sectarian partisans' and Lloyd George's 'half-hearted attitude and prayerful wishes' were of no help.

Chapter 5

THE DECLINE OF THE IRISH PARTY AND THE TRIUMPH OF SINN FÉIN, 1917–18

A. THE NORTH ROSCOMMON BY-ELECTION, FEBRUARY 1917

The political events of the first eight months of 1917 form a continuum, a set of interconnected events which represented the playing out of the rebellion's aftermath combined with the Home Rule debacle of July 1916. The release of the interned rebel prisoners at the end of 1916 facilitated the unprecedented defeat of the Irish Party in the North Roscommon by-election in February. This was followed the next month by the Home Rule debate in which Lloyd George made clear that the Home Rule Act could be implemented immediately for nationalist Ireland but that unionist Ulster would not be coerced to submit to an all-Ireland parliament: in short, that Home Rule would not be an all-Ireland settlement. The debate in turn supplied the issue that determined the outcome of the second by-election, another defeat for the Irish Party in South Longford in May. Soon afterwards, the prime minister invited Redmond to choose between immediate operation of the Home Rule Act with Ulster exclusion or the setting up of a convention of all Irish parties and prominent non-politicians charged with negotiating an agreement on an all-Ireland settlement. Redmond rejected the first option out of hand but accepted the offer of the convention.

The demand for the creation of an atmosphere conducive to the convention led to the release in June of the convicted rebel prisoners from British jails. One of these, Éamon de Valera, delivered a crushing blow to the Irish Party when he won a huge landslide victory in the July by-election in East Clare caused by the death of Major Willie Redmond MP in the fighting at Messines, Flanders. The coda was provided by a fourth Sinn Féin by-election win, in Kilkenny City, in August. These political events were accompanied by two landmarks in the reorganisation of the previously tiny but now burgeoning Sinn Féin party as the Irish Party went into decline.

The year 1917 was just six weeks old when the by-election in North Roscommon delivered the Irish Party its first electoral defeat at the hands of fellow-nationalists since its reunification in 1900 and, for the first time since Parnell had turned the Irish Parliamentary Party into an effective political weapon, gave victory to an advocate of unconstitutional methods. The anti-Party candidate was Count George Plunkett, not a registered Sinn Féin candidate but the father of one of the executed rebel leaders, Joseph Mary Plunkett. The combination of the efforts of recently liberated prisoners of Frongoch and disgruntled Irish Party supporters gave Plunkett 3,022 votes to the Party candidate's 1,708. Many sympathisers and members of the Party (though not Redmond) dismissed the result, attributing it to a sympathy vote for the count. (Only when elected did the winner announce his intention to adopt the Sinn Féin abstentionist policy of not taking his seat at Westminster, to the objections of his more moderate followers.)

Press commentary on the result was roughly evenly divided between the pro-Party sentiment of thirteen of twenty-six papers (50 per cent) that tried to explain the result away or place the blame on outside forces, the mostly sympathetic criticism of six (23 per cent) and the jubilation or *schadenfreude* of seven (27 per cent).

The local *Roscommon Herald* (10 February) (Jasper Tully was one of the by-election candidates) pulled no punches with a cartoon captioned, 'The strong boot of North Roscommon with 3,709 votes … sent the Redmond Machine to everlasting smash with one well-delivered kick on polling day'. The accompanying editorial opined that the vote 'demonstrates in the first place the true feeling of the country towards Mr Redmond's Irish Party, which 'must be promptly consigned to the scrap heap'. The neighbouring *Westmeath Independent* (10 February), a paper in the midst of a full-scale about-turn since its 'Bravo England!' headline of August 1914 and its gushing praise of Redmond a mere year earlier, asked 'Why has Roscommon, by taking this dramatic action, sent a thrill of pride vibrating through Ireland?' The *Derry People* called it 'a sledgehammer blow to the Irish Party'. The *Kilkenny People* (10 February) hailed the result 'with profound joy and satisfaction from one end of Ireland to the other at the magnificent blow that has been struck against tremendous odds for the freedom of our own small nation', though it added that 'it would be absurd to read into that answer a wholesale condemnation of the constitutional movement'.

Of the loyal Redmondite newspapers, most treated the result as an anomaly, either ignoring it or describing it variously as 'a natural reaction to martial law' (*Connacht Tribune*, 10 February), 'Ireland's verdict on the executions' (*Sligo Champion,* 10 February) or the result of 'very exceptional circumstances' (*Irish News*, 10 February). A disconsolate *Westmeath Examiner* (17 February) could only take refuge in the thought that the 'extreme Unionist press' was jubilant at what they saw as the beginning of the 'smash-up of the Irish Party', something that could only mean the end of Home Rule. For the *Wexford People* (10 February), the result was retaliation for the shooting of the candidate's son and his own internment after the rebellion. Offering its customary moderate criticism, it wrote that there was 'a very considerable number of constitutional nationalists who appear to have lost confidence in the wisdom and ability though not in the honesty or patriotism of the Irish Party in the handling of Home Rule'. The *Donegal Vindicator* (9 February) thought that the Party's decision to contest the seat had been 'ill-advised': it should have let the seat go to Count Plunket.

In the wake of the unprecedented defeat, Redmond prepared a personal manifesto to the Irish people that considered the implications for the future. If the vote indicated not just an expression of emotion but a deliberate change of principle by the people, it raised an issue 'clear and unequivocal, supreme and vital' that must be 'brought to the test' as soon as possible in every constituency, he wrote. His colleagues, convinced the release of the manifesto would be disastrous, persuaded him not to issue it to the press.

B. THE HOUSE OF COMMONS DEBATE, MARCH 1917

Of greater significance was the debate in the House of Commons on an Irish Party motion in T.P. O'Connor's name calling on the government to confer 'free institutions' on Ireland without delay, to be followed by the second by-election of the year, in South Longford. Proposing the motion on 7 March, O'Connor drew on the recent speech of US President Wilson, which had set out the principles that must guide the post-war settlement – the rights of small nations to self-determination and government by consent. He was seconded by Major Willie Redmond, making his third visit to the House from the Front, who made a moving plea to the government, described by the *Manchester Guardian* as 'a masterpiece of simple eloquence', in the name of the Irishmen in the trenches, to rise to the demands of the situation: 'in the name of God we here who are about to die, perhaps, ask you to do that which largely induced us to leave our homes … to do that which we all desire, make our country happy and contented …'

Sir John Londsale, MP for Mid-Armagh, replying for the Ulster Unionist Party, understood recent statements of Redmond and Dillon to mean that nationalists still contemplated the coercion of Ulster, or believed that Ulster might yet assent to Home Rule. He asked:

Do the events of the last twelve months justify them in expecting that we should be more ready to come under Home Rule today than we were before the War? Are we to be blamed if, having regard to all that has occurred, we prefer to trust the British people and the Imperial Parliament?

Lloyd George declared that any settlement acceptable to the Irish people as a whole would be welcomed with delight by the whole people of the United Kingdom. In line with the principles of self-determination, the people of Britain were determined to confer self-government on the parts of Ireland that unmistakably demanded it, but there could be no question of compelling the population of the north-east to submit to the rule of an Irish parliament. The debate ended when Redmond, saying that he had listened to the prime minister with 'the deepest pain', led his MPs out of the chamber. After the debate, the Irish Party issued a manifesto accusing the prime minister of adopting a position of 'the denial of self-government to Ireland for ever', having accepted the principle that a 'small minority' should have a veto against self-government for a united Ireland.

Even more than the breakdown of the Home Rule negotiations the previous July, this debate laid bare the real nature of the obstacle blocking the path to the implementation of the Home Rule Act of 1914. No longer was it the prolongation of the war itself, as might have appeared to be the case in 1915 and early 1916. The issue of the exclusion of unionist Ulster from Home Rule, unresolved and placed in abeyance in September 1914 when the Act went on the Statute Book, was now once more in the open. Since the partition of the island loomed as the inescapable accompaniment of any Home Rule implementation, the partition issue became the dominant one in Irish politics in late 1916 and early 1917 and the weapon wielded with ever-increasing success against the Party by its enemies. The passions centred on this issue were articulated far more widely and more intensely, with deeper implications for public opinion as expressed in the press, than those arising from the executions of the 1916 rebels or the subsequent repressions.

Since nationalists of all hues considered the concession of one square inch of the island to be unthinkable, treasonous and a blasphemous insult to the nation, they understood the unionist refusal to accept Home Rule for Ulster as a veto on Irish self-government *in toto*. The refusal of the British government to enforce the Act on the Ulster community that rejected it was taken to be identical to a refusal to implement it at all in any part of Ireland. The pragmatism that had briefly blossomed in the provincial press had gone out of fashion. Newspapers that had been willing in June 1916 to tolerate some form of exclusion of Ulster counties now had no option but to line up behind the Party's new stance. Had its pragmatism brought Home Rule into being the previous year, things would, no doubt, have been different. As it was, Redmond and his colleagues were saddled both with the failure to make Home Rule a reality and with the taint of concession on partition, and their new intransigence won them little or no credit.

Since many newspapers, even those critical of the constitutional movement, were still reporting on proceedings in the Westminster Parliament, the debate received wide coverage. Of twenty-seven papers commenting, sixteen (59 per cent) were supportive of the Irish Party's action or expressed anger at Lloyd George and the government policy, five thought the debate had discredited the Liberal alliance and three the Party, while three more thought the prime minister had nullified the Home Rule Act. The *Connacht Tribune* (10 March) registered its 'anger and despair' at the refusal of Lloyd George to coerce Ulster. The *Westmeath Examiner* (10 March) interpreted the prime minister's reply to the debate to suggest that 'the question of Irish freedom be entirely at the decision of Sir Edward Carson and the Orange Ascendancy gang … [that the rights of Ireland] should be treated with contempt and handed over to the tender mercies of the arch-rebel against Ireland and against loyalty – Sir Edward Carson' (10 March). The *Irish News* (8 March) also despaired, summarising the debate result under the title, 'The Ways Have Parted'; the prime minister had committed himself to a policy that meant 'the Irish question must be regarded as insoluble'. The *Longford Leader* approved the decision of the local executive of the UIL to continue its support for the Irish Party in parliament, calling it the opinion of the 'sane and sound Nationalists in this part of Ireland' (10 March). The most deeply constitutionalist (and still pro-war and pro-recruiting) of this group of papers was the *Tuam Herald*. It had seen the Roscommon outcome as 'the parting of the ways between constitutionalism and 'the fatuous course and sad tale of defeat, death and disaster'. Every subject people in Europe that had tried insurrection in the 1840s, 1860s and 1870s, it wrote – Poland, Bohemia, etc. – had turned to constitutionalism. The outcome of the Home Rule debate, though disappointing, only emphasised the need for 'wise leadership' (10 March). It reserved its spleen for the Ulster unionists, 'that narrow-minded, intolerant and uncompromising body ... the true Bourbons of Irish politics' (17 February).

Nothing better illustrates how the partition issue was being seen through new eyes in 1917 than the reaction of the *Donegal Vindicator* to the Home Rule debate. Bitterly, it lamented that majority rule was to be set aside and the will of the minority was to prevail. It had seemed that Asquith at least was sincere and determined to grant Home Rule, but they had been wrong about him: 'His opinion we now know to have been that the coercion of Ulster was unthinkable'. The paper apparently forgot that these words of Asquith had been a matter of public record since he had uttered them on 14 September 1914, when it had professed itself as having no fear of an amending bill!

For the *Leinster Leader* (10 March) the Roscommon result and its welcome by 'public bodies all over the country' indicated the changed popular feeling that had set in. This, it asserted, 'tends to the lifting of the Irish question from the sphere of domestic political problems and its elevation to one of international importance capable of settlement by the belligerent powers jointly'. Noting the failure of the Irish Party to make an impression on the government, and its repeated humiliation, it alleged that 'the Home Rule Act is, in effect, pronounced null and void, inasmuch as the Premier has declared ... that "the Government are not prepared to force the North-East portion of Ireland to submit to government by a population with whom they are out of sympathy. Any attempt to coerce Ulster would be a curse to Ireland". Yet Ireland has been dragooned and coerced in the attempt to make North-East conceptions of government acceptable to the overwhelming majority of the people.' The *Kilkenny People* (10 March) was sceptical of the Party's walkout: 'the Irish Party have adopted the Sinn Féin policy for one night only,' it sneered. It claimed it had been betrayed, but 'what else did they expect? What else did they deserve?' Showing no self-reproach for its own history of Redmondite enthusiasms, it wrote that Lloyd George had kicked them but 'the Irish Party has been blacking the boots [at Westminster] for over twenty years' and T.P. O'Connor was 'the boot-black-in-chief'. The *Mayo News* (3 March) mocked the 'staged event in the House of Commons'; the *Roscommon Herald* (10 March) dismissed the 'play-acting in Parliament'.

C. THE SOUTH LONGFORD BY-ELECTION, MAY 1917

The next electoral contest was held in the South Longford constituency. The nominee of the Sinn Féin committee was Joseph McGuinness, a 1916 rebel in prison in England. The Irish Party's campaign was hamstrung by prolonged bouts of illness afflicting Redmond and the fact that there were three rival candidates for nomination, one of them backed by the local bishop. It was two weeks before a plea to the three to allow Redmond to select the strongest candidate bore fruit. In the meantime, an army of young pro-Sinn Féin activists had poured into the constituency, well equipped with motor cars and American money. It became known that large numbers of the younger Catholic clergy were working actively for the Sinn Féin candidate. In the campaign, Party leaders cited the legacy of social reforms won in the past by the Party and fought the charge that the Party had agreed to partition as well as the (untrue) accusation that they had cheered the 1916 executions. Voting intentions up to the final day seemed evenly split. Then, on 8 May, the day before polling, a petition letter signed by eighteen Catholic and three Protestant bishops, opposing any form of partition for Ireland, temporary or permanent, was published in the press. One of the signatories, Archbishop William Walsh of Dublin, published his own letter on polling day, which carried the sensational message that, 'Anyone who thinks that partition, whether in its naked deformity, or under the transparent mask of "county option", does not hold a leading place in the practical politics of today is simply living in a fool's paradise ... the mischief has already been done, and the country is practically sold.'

The intervention of the archbishop was probably decisive. The result was a victory for McGuinness by thirty-seven votes (1,498 to 1,461). The Sinn Féin leader Arthur Griffith pronounced it 'the greatest victory ever won for Ireland at the polls', and a defeat for the 'partition plot' referred to by Archbishop Walsh. The defeat of the Irish Party candidate can be taken, at least in part, as the response of grass-roots nationalists to the outcome of the Commons debate.

Polarisation of press opinion after Longford was more pronounced than after the Roscommon result, with eleven of thirty-two commenting papers (34 per cent) celebrating the outcome or otherwise expressing opposition to the Party, and most of the remainder too shocked, or too concerned to place blame, to rally support for the Party. The majority on both sides, either explicitly or implicitly, identified partition as the key issue on which the voters had pronounced a verdict.

The local *Longford Leader* (12 May) mourned the outcome as another blow at the constitutional movement and the Irish Party. Its news report highlighted intimidation practiced against the Party's supporters and the 'bizarre colours and motor madness of our Sinn Féin friends'. Editorially, it expressed 'profound concern' at the fact that '1,500 men of mostly mature years have voted to disenfranchise themselves' [that is, by voting for an abstentionist candidate]. It was hard to judge the ultimate effect but it was too hasty to suggest that the Irish Party should resign in a body and let Sinn Féin take over, as they were 'a headless lot of young men without a policy'; it was better to wait for the general election, it advised. (It should be remembered that the expanded franchise that would allow non-householding young males and many women to vote had not yet come into effect, and these by-election results reflected disenchantment among the traditional electorate that had until now given the Party its large majorities.) The *Donegal Vindicator* (11 May) wrote that Archbishop Walsh's letter was a 'mean sort of stab in the back of the Irish Party'.

The *Connacht Tribune* wrote that the result was due to 'distrust of English statesmanship' (12 May). For the *Sligo Champion*, 'Carson and Ulster block the way' (5 May). The *Anglo-Celt* wrote that South Longford should give the Irish Party 'the incentive to make plain to Lloyd George that no Home Rule will be accepted that is not all-Ireland Home Rule' (12 May). The *Munster News* (19 May), alluding to the common belief that Lloyd George was anxious to settle the Irish question in order to appease American opinion now that US entry into the war was imminent, quoted the *Freeman's Journal* hyperbole that 'the north-east corner is now in arms, not against Nationalists, but against the public opinion of two hemispheres'. The *Wexford People* (16 May) saw the result as a 'protest against the Government, Carsonism and the Irish Party' and correctly reckoned the bishops' anti-partition letter to have been crucial to the Sinn Féin victory. This paper, although it would maintain its allegiance to the Party's policies right up to December 1918, once again had critical words for its leader, who had led nationalists into a fool's paradise by 'declaring so often Home Rule was safe, that the position was impregnable, and in paying the price for Home Rule before the goods were delivered'. The *Tuam Herald* claimed that 'the intolerant Orange party alone are causing all this trouble' and wrote in fatalistic tone that there must now be a further postponement of the Home Rule settlement: the 'unique pronouncement' of the Catholic and Protestant bishops during the election meant that partition in any form was impossible (12 May). The *Ballina Herald* (17 May) reflected:

The onlooker sees most of the game, and we may as non-politicians claim to be onlookers in the present struggle between Sinn Féin and orthodox Nationalists, and to our mind the defeat of the Party candidates in the recent elections was due not to any senseless turn over of the populace to revolutionary methods, or to an equally senseless allegiance to the cause of an Irish republic, but to the fact that, rightly or wrongly, the Irish Party are believed to have more than coquetted with the idea of partition.

All of these papers followed Irish Party policy in backing Redmond's rejection of Lloyd George's offer of Home Rule with partition. They also tended to support calls for the amnesty of the remaining rebellion prisoners. However, the shift of opinion and allegiance in a significant section of the provincial press that had begun after July 1916 was well under way after the South Longford result. The *Meath Chronicle* (19 May) interpreted it as 'the last nail into the coffin of partition'. The *Carlow Nationalist* interpreted Lloyd George's reply to the Commons debate to mean 'there could not be Home Rule for the Irish nation, because there was a minority against self-government' (10 March). Having been willing to accept 'three-quarters of a loaf' the previous year, it now warned against any partition: 'every square inch of Irish soil belongs to the Irish Nation' and the minimum demand of Ireland was for 'full legislative, administrative and fiscal independence' (5 May). The paper's conversion to Sinn Féin was signalled when it wrote that South Longford was 'the handwriting on the wall' and Irish public opinion now wanted the Irish nation's claim to be heard at the Paris Peace Conference (12 May). The *Clare Champion*, which had grudgingly accepted the need for temporary Ulster exclusion in 1916, was on the cusp of its change of allegiance after the Commons debate, writing that 'If the Irish Party ever go back to that House of trickery and dishonesty, it must work for Ireland alone'. It claimed that Lloyd George had 'torn to shreds the Home Rule Act' by stating he was not prepared to use force to include any part of Ireland that refused to accept Home Rule (10 March).

The *Derry People* and *Kilkenny People* had already deserted the constitutionalist camp in 1916 (see above). The former drew from the Home Rule debate the lesson that 'the policy of trusting the Liberals has ended in ghastly and ignominious failure, and the Irish Party stands today disgraced and discredited before the civilized world' (10 March). 'Well done, Longford!' was its greeting for the by-election result as it simultaneously warned against a 'new Partition Plot' on the parts of Lloyd George and Edward Carson (12 May). The *Kilkenny People*, in its characteristic emotive style, hailed 'the magnificent blow' struck for freedom in North Roscommon, which had brought 'profound joy and satisfaction from one end of Ireland to the other' (10 February). South Longford had 'triumphed over the Orangemen and partitionists'. If Ireland acted up to the lead given there, 'a stern account will be exacted from the politicians who put their country up for sale ... The partitionists are the men who betrayed their trust. They were elected to fight for Home Rule for Ireland, not to barter away part of our birthright' (12 May).

The consistently neutral *Clonmel Nationalist* (3) took the lesson of South Longford to be 'a fierce outcry by Nationalists and Unionists against any form of partition'; the constituency had manifested 'the abhorrence of the country for partition [and] its desire for more vigorous parliamentary action, including amnesty for political prisoners' (12 May).

D. THE IRISH CONVENTION AND THE EAST CLARE BY-ELECTION, JULY 1917

On 15 May, just before he made a long-awaited statement on the government's plan for dealing with the Irish impasse, Lloyd George sent two alternative proposals to Redmond (soon to be published as a White Paper). The first involved a plan for the immediate operation of the Home Rule Act, with exclusion *en bloc* of six Ulster counties, to be reconsidered by parliament after five years if not already terminated by a council of Ireland comprising all the MPs for the excluded area and an equal number from the Home Rule parliament. The Act would contain completely revised financial terms to take account of wartime taxation. Lloyd George recommended this option as one that 'will give immediate self-government in Ireland to those who wish for it, and will at the same time create and keep continuously in being the means whereby a final reconciliation between the two sections of the Irish people can at any time be brought about'. The alternative proposal involved the assembling of a convention of all Irish parties 'for the purpose of drafting a Constitution for their country which should secure a just balance of all the opposing interests'. Redmond rejected the first proposal out of hand but told Lloyd George that the second had 'much to recommend it'; the vision of Irishmen meeting together to draft a constitution was 'a high and blessed ideal'. Soon afterwards, the Irish Party accepted the second option and preparations began in London and Dublin for the assembling of the convention.

The tasks of agreeing on a basis of representation and finding a chairman were time consuming, and it was a month before Lloyd George, on 11 June, announced to the House an agreed scheme of membership. The total number of the convention was to be 101, with the chairmen of all county and borough councils to be invited. Also included were two representatives of the urban populations of each province, the chairmen of the Dublin, Cork and Belfast Chambers of Commerce and five representatives of Labour from those cities. The clergy would be represented by four Catholic bishops, two Church of Ireland bishops and the moderator of the Presbyterian Assembly. On the advice of Carson, the Ulster Unionist Council (UUC) decided to send delegates. However, although invited to attend, Sinn Féin declined to participate. After further delays, the convention finally opened in Trinity College Dublin on 25 July under the chairmanship of Sir Horace Plunkett.

Overshadowing the opening of the convention was the question of its democratic legitimacy in the light of the by-election results and the resurgence of Sinn Féin. In the weeks since South Longford, Sinn Féin clubs had mushroomed throughout nationalist Ireland. The East Clare by-election in July pitched Éamon de Valera, the only 1916 rebel commandant not executed, less than a month out of Lewes prison, against the Irish Party. De Valera's election rhetoric added a fresh element to the political discourse: as well as the intransigent opposition to partition heard in the previous contests, there was now a militant emphasis on the demand for 'sovereign independence' for Ireland and 'the vindication of the ideals of Easter Week'. Any voices pointing out that the new goals were liable to entrench partition further were unlikely to be heard. The Irish Party candidate called the demand for an Irish republic an 'impossible dream' in current circumstances and the rebellion 'criminal folly', and claimed that the Party's presence at Westminster was the only safeguard against conscription. The verdict on 11 July, a landslide Sinn Féin victory over the Party by 5,010 votes to 2,035, left no doubt as to the direction in which public opinion was moving.

Of thirty-three papers that commented on the convention between May and July, a small majority of eighteen (56 per cent) greeted it with responses ranging from enthusiastic to hesitantly hopeful. Of the remainder, seven were sceptical and another seven dismissive. The pro-Party papers were almost all in the first group, those disenchanted with it in the latter two groups. Opinion on the East Clare result was almost equally divided, with sixteen of thirty-four papers (47 per cent) gloomily registering the magnitude of the Party's defeat, while fourteen (41 per cent) celebrated it and predicted the end of the Party.

Just how much hope was being invested in the convention by thinking constitutionalists was manifest in the editorial of the *Ballina Herald* (19 July) titled 'Convention Prospects':

The eleventh hour efforts which have been made to create what is called 'atmosphere' for the All Ireland Convention seem to have had a result quite the reverse of what was intended ... it is perfectly plain from the stupendous majority obtained by the Sinn Féin candidate in East Clare that the atmosphere is far from likely to act as a health-giving tonic to the Convention ...

Admittedly East Clare has been a big and staggering blow, but, we submit, it is no fatal blow to constitutionalism. That fatal blow can only be dealt by constitutionalists themselves, and the failure of the Convention to devise a satisfactory settlement may achieve what the Sinn Féiners cannot. Moderate men have now to pin their faith solely on the Convention.

The *Sligo Champion,* having welcomed the convention, wrote without enthusiasm of de Valera's victory as 'the beginning of a new epoch in the political history of this country' (14 July). The *Longford Leader* had little doubt that the convention would be 'a most historic and epoch making assembly'(21 July). The *Wexford People* laid the blame for East Clare on Carson and the government for 'refusing the demands of the Irish people' (14 July). The *Galway Observer* (14 July) was certain that 'the Government is making Sinn Féiners'. The *Dundalk Democrat* ((14 July) deplored 'the forgetfulness and ingratitude' of the rural population, adding that Clare had always been a region of 'lawless unrest'. It was useless and foolish, wrote the *Westmeath Examiner,* to minimise the importance of the East Clare result, which was 'a serious blow to the prestige of the Irish Parliamentary Party and to the constitutional movement. Those who have helped to deliver it have assumed a grave and terrible responsibility'. If it was an indicator of general opinion, Ireland was 'about to plunge recklessly into the abyss of revolution' (14 July). For the *Tuam Herald*, optimism about the convention's prospects waxed and waned, but East Clare was 'a debacle for the imperiled cause of law and order' (14 July). Only one Party-supporting paper would not accept the result. The *Irish News* (12 July) wrote, 'We hold that the sane public opinion of the whole country has been misrepresented, not truly interpreted, in North Roscommon, South Longford and East Clare. If this view is wrong, then the end of the Parnell–Davitt movement cannot be long deferred'. But the *Cork Examiner* (12 July) thought that though the by-election defeats 'must fill every man with disquietude … Ulster's unyielding position … naturally has goaded our young men into fury'.

The *Clare Champion* (19 May), now fully in the Sinn Féin camp, called both of Lloyd George's options equally bad; the convention proposal was 'an insult to this country'. Greeting the de Valera victory, it claimed that the spirit of patriotism 'has always in times of great crisis unerringly guided the voters of East Clare' and 'Ireland's claim to Absolute Independence must and shall be considered at the [Paris] Peace Conference' (14 July). The *Kerry Sentinel* (26 May), a Party supporter until the Roscommon vote, reckoned that, unless a general election were held first, the convention would be 'nothing more than a farce'. The *Kilkenny People* wrote that the convention as outlined could not be seriously considered: any acceptable convention must be based on manhood suffrage. The Irish Party 'have no claim or authority to speak or to negotiate on the part of the people of Ireland' (19 May). The convention was another Lloyd George plot, but Sinn Féin would not play along. It was 'nominated and gerrymandered' and 'grotesquely at variance with and in denial of the fundamental principle of constitutional government' (26 May, 16 June). Of the by-election result, it wrote: 'East Clare has now held its Court-martial and delivered its verdict, and that verdict is one of 'Guilty' against the Irish Party on a charge of high treason to Ireland ... He [de Valera] and his Party, and not the Parliamentary Party, are the genuine spokesmen of Irish national sentiment' (14 July). (After this editorial, the *Kilkenny People* was suppressed by the government until its re-appearance on 13 October. Its moderate counterpart, the *Longford Leader*, reported that it had been seized by the military, adding that its editor, E.T. Keane, 'though a fine fellow has developed from being a strong supporter of the Irish Party into being a most violent Sinn Féiner' (21 July).)

The *Tipperary Star* (14 July), only mildly critical of Redmond in 1916 (see above) now, after East Clare, excused its tardiness in nailing its colours to the Sinn Féin mast: 'while the soul of the nation was being trafficked away ... no man who realized the tragedy dared raise a finger of warning without serious consequences to himself, such was the destructive power of the corrupt political machine ...

[he] had to sing dumb or face social outlawry and perhaps material ruin'. The republican *Mayo News* headlined its report on East Clare (14 July) 'Ireland Has Triumphed' and commented: 'The English-nominated kill-time Convention may now sit but will not block the onward march of Ireland'. The *Waterford News* (13 July) proclaimed that 'the [Sinn Féin] movement has captured the people of Ireland. The voice of the generation which has grown to full manhood while the Party has been selfishly wasting precious time in Westminster is heard all over the land'. The *Midland Tribune* saw it as 'the death-knell of Parliamentarianism' while for *The Kerryman*, it was 'a mandate to the Irish Party to clear out'. Striving for balance, the *Leinster Leader*, which wrote (26 May) 'whether the Convention succeeds or not, this attempt of the Government to escape their responsibilities cannot succeed', a month later hailed the release of the jailed prisoners as 'magnanimous' and praised 'this latest remarkable policy of conciliation' (23 June). (Alone among the expanding cohort of anti-Party papers, the *Leinster Leader* would continue to support the convention.)

After another Sinn Féin victory at Kilkenny City in mid-August confirmed the verdict of East Clare, the *Galway Observer* (18 August) wrote that, if there were any more results like this, 'we will have to take it that the minds of the people in this country are changing, or have changed … as if we were going through a peaceful revolution'. Presciently, it added: 'We are not so certain that it is going to end peacefully'. The *Midland Tribune* (25 August) claimed that 'the Party is now a living lie'. The *King's County Independent* (18 August) took time to look back on the previous decade to enumerate the many mistakes of the Irish Party it now discerned for the first time, and, incidentally, to rewrite its own history. Deploring 'the jingoism let loose on the country' in 1914, it omitted to mention its own front-page 'Bravo England!' headline of 8 August that year as Britain and tens of thousands of Irishmen went to war.

E. THE ASHE AFFAIR, REDMOND'S CENSURE MOTION AND THE SINN FÉIN CONVENTION

The chief events of the last third of the year 1917 were the progress of the Irish Convention, taking place behind closed doors in Trinity College Dublin with occasional visits to Belfast and Cork, about which hopes and speculation flourished but little hard information emerged; the hunger strike and death in Mountjoy prison, due to forcible feeding, of the 1916 rebel leader Thomas Ashe, one of those released in the summer amnesty; and Redmond's House of Commons censure motion in October on the government's Irish policy, which coincided with the triumphant second convention of Sinn Féin in Dublin.

All the newspapers were inevitably sparse in their coverage of the Irish Convention but those supportive of the Party were united in hoping for a positive outcome. One of the few papers to take an attentive interest was the *Tuam Herald*, which carried almost weekly editorials in late May and early June and many more thereafter, their flavour often conveyed by such titles as 'A Fateful and Grand Opportunity' (26 May), 'Duty of Helping the Convention' (28 July) and 'The Convention Winning' (8 September). On the last date, it wrote that there was 'every evidence it is growing daily in public confidence, and close contact is breaking down the prejudiced views of unionists and nationalists'. On 27 October, it claimed that 'all Ireland is in sympathy with the work of the Convention'. A month later, when its proceedings had hit a crisis, the paper worried about 'unpleasant rumours that it will not come to an agreement', but it had high praise for the southern Unionist members, whose constructive contributions under their leader, Lord Midleton, were to their 'eternal credit' (24 November).

The pro-Party papers tended to play down the story of the Ashe death or see it as another British blunder. The *Wexford People* (27 October), the *Westmeath Examiner* (20 October) and the *Munster News* (24 October) all echoed the conspiratorial tone of the *Freeman's Journal* in seeing it as the work of a provocateur or 'Hidden Hand' in the Castle administration seeking to foment anarchy and undermine the constitutional movement and the convention. For the *Sligo Champion*, Ashe was 'another martyr to the cause of Irish patriotism' (29 September). For the *Cork Examiner*, the tragedy showed 'the absolute sincerity and determination of the men who are making sacrifices for their principles' (29 September). The *Longford Leader* (29 September) openly lamented Ashe's death, extolling his personal qualities 'whatever differences may divide us' – his 'manly courage, honour, sterling patriotism … a hero of whom any country would be proud'. The *Cork Examiner* (29 September) averred that 'the tragic fate of Thomas Ashe will be deplored by those who may not agree with Sinn Féin methods'. The *Irish News* (1 October) counselled calm: 'If we surrender ourselves to one transient passion after another we shall inevitably find ourselves side-tracked when the great readjustment takes place'.

Of the eighteen papers (thirteen of them recent recruits) in the anti-Party camp, most were dismissive of the 'Convention Humbug' (*Derry People*, 16 June) but reverential if restrained in their comments on the Ashe death, probably from fear of sharing the fate of the *Kilkenny People*. The latter paper returned to publication in October with a belated reference to Ashe as a victim of 'the terrible doings within the walls of the Dublin Torture Chamber'. The *Mayo News* left its editorial space blank when it published news of the death (29 September). A month later, it seemed stoic about the tragedy, writing that no reform was ever secured without sacrifices, 'often bloody sacrifices' (27 October). Only the *Clare Champion* responded with a call to action, appealing to the men and women of Clare to come to Ennis the following Sunday to join 'not a mere demonstration of welcome to a great leader [de Valera] [but] solemn and earnest expression of horror and condemnation of the treatment of Irish Political Prisoners which has sent a brave and noble patriot like Thomas Ashe to a martyr's grave' (29 September). The *Kilkenny People* blasted the 'utterly discredited and egregious collection of humbugs and charlatans styling themselves "the Irish Parliamentary Party" who were trying to see 'if they cannot reap some posthumous benefits from the tragedy which they did nothing to avert and for which they were indirectly responsible' (20 October).

The verdict of the inquest into Ashe's death was published in early November. It found unanimously that the death had been caused in the first place by mistreatment in the prison, then by subjection to forcible feeding, and it censured the deputy governor. The *Roscommon Herald* and *Midland Tribune* published the fact that Redmond's son-in-law, Max Sullivan Green, was chairman of the Irish Prison Board. The former in true Jasper Tully style used the fact to claim that 'the two Johns' [Redmond and Dillon] were in control of the board, with Green as the 'Head Turnkey', and that, by implication, they shared responsibility for Ashe's death (3 November).

On 23 October in the House of Commons, Redmond moved a motion of censure of government policy, putting the case that the situation of 'extreme gravity' in the country resulted from provocation by government officials that drove otherwise moderate people into the arms of Sinn Féin. Twelve of the twenty-three papers (52 per cent) that carried comment were generally supportive of his speech (it would turn out to be his last major parliamentary performance). Most of them focused their ire on the familiar shadowy array of villains, from malign officials at Dublin Castle to Unionists in the Cabinet, echoing the insinuation of the 'Hidden Hand' at work to undermine the Irish Convention. The other eleven (48 per cent) of these papers either ignored or dismissed the speech, the *Carlow Nationalist* (27 October) calling it 'milk and water ... the negation of Irish Nationality' while the *Clare Champion* (27 October) described it as 'weak and timorous', and the *King's County Independent* (27 October) called it 'a craven appeal to England'.

Redmond's censure speech almost coincided with, and was overshadowed by, the triumphant second Sinn Féin convention of the year, held in Dublin on 25 October. An earlier conference in April, before the South Longford election, had attracted an attendance of 1,200, but of 257 public bodies invited to attend, less than a third had sent representatives and a mere seventy-one Sinn Féin clubs were represented. This time, flushed with its four by-election victories and the propaganda boost of the Ashe affair, the new party staged an impressive display, with at least 1,700 delegates representing 1,009 clubs. The convention elected de Valera as its president, with Arthur Griffith and Count Plunkett standing aside. In his acceptance speech, de Valera declared that his election for East Clare and accession to the Sinn Féin leadership were monuments 'to the brave dead, and this is the *post factum* proof that they were right, that what they fought for – the complete and absolute freedom and separation from England – was the pious wish of every Irish heart.'

Press reaction to the Sinn Féin convention was the inverse of that for Redmond's Commons performance, with twelve of twenty-five commenting papers (48 per cent) hailing the new party's ascendancy, ten negative and three neutral. The *Kilkenny People* (3 November) found 'inspiration, hope and encouragement' in the gathering. The *Westmeath Independent* (27 October) contrasted the Irish Convention 'called together by the English Government' with the Sinn Féin Convention – 'a real convention' – with its manifestation of 'intense sincerity and earnestness'. For the *Meath Chronicle* (27 October), the convention had been 'thoroughly representative of organised nationalist opinion in Ireland'. For the *Mayo News* (3 November), de Valera was now 'the leader of the Irish race'. The *Midland Tribune* (27 October) reckoned that 'with De Valera as president, the country will agree that the best man is at the wheel'.

The Sinn Féin proceedings allowed the party's policies to come under detailed scrutiny for the first time. The *Irish News* (27 October) warned that the Irish people must not be deluded: if they thought that the ascendancy and triumph of the MacNeill–Griffith 'Hungarianism' [a reference to Griffith's early espousal of the Austro–Hungarian dual monarchy model for Ireland at the time of his founding of Sinn Féin in 1904] removed the possibility of disaster, they would 'dream in a fool's paradise'. Calling the 1916 rebellion 'a terrible and indefensible deed', it wrote that only the people could now save Ireland from 'an irreparable disaster' – the pitting of peasants with ten-foot pikes against machine guns and howitzers. The

Tuam Herald (29 September) was an early critic of some Sinn Féin policy planks, writing before the convention that the Poles, Czechs and Yugoslavs did not expect to be represented at the Paris Peace Conference, so that the expectations of the advanced sections in Ireland were 'to say the least, illusory'. The *Cork Examiner* (26 October) tried to be fair to the new party, giving impartial consideration to its policies. It contained many men of ability, it wrote, and it could not question its sincerity of purpose. But there was no evidence that the Peace Conference (assuming the Allies won the war) would issue a fiat to Great Britain to establish an Irish republic on her trade routes. Neither France nor the US had championed the Sinn Féin programme, and there was 'not the remotest possibility' of that demand being conceded. Sinn Féin policy was 'bankrupt in statesmanship and bereft of common sense'. For the *Donegal Vindicator* (26 October), whatever its views on Sinn Féin policies, there was no doubting 'the straight, fearless honesty of the present leaders' who deserved all praise. But the paper would continue to support the Irish Party as the new party had 'no backbone, no firm policy'. The republic was an ideal, but an impossibility, and the abstention policy was mistaken.

As 1917 came to an end, the pattern of opinion on Irish politics in the provincial press showed a remarkable shift from that exhibited only eighteen months earlier. Following the early lead of the *Kilkenny People,* the *Waterford News* and the *Derry People* in June–July 1916, eight others of thirty-two papers that had been broadly supportive of Irish Party policies had swung against the Party to champion the new forces that burgeoned after the failure of the Lloyd George Home Rule initiative. Another, the *Southern Star*, would shortly join the pro-Sinn Féin camp, having been bought out in December 1917 by a consortium that included Michael Collins and three others.[1] A further two former Party-supporting organs had adopted a neutral position. The result was that a press sample that comprised thirty-two pro-Irish Party, four anti-Party and six neutral newspapers in mid-1916 had come to comprise eighteen pro-Party, twenty anti-Party and four neutral newspapers at the beginning of 1918. These changes of allegiance are shown in Table 2, with a shift of one other pro-

Table 2. Changing policies of sample of provincial Irish newspapers 1916–18 (N=42)

1. Pro-IP throughout	2. Pro-IP at start, swung to SF	3. Pro-IP at start, became neutral	5. Neutral at start, swung to SF
Drogheda Argus Dundalk Democrat Longford Leader Westmeath Examiner Wexford People Cork Examiner Limerick Leader Munster Express Munster News Ballina Herald Connaught Telegraph Connacht Tribune Galway Observer Tuam Herald Anglo-Celt Donegal Vindicator Irish News & Belfast Morning News (17)	Carlow Nationalist Kilkenny People Meath Chronicle Midland Tribune King's County Independent Westmeath Independent Clare Champion Kerry Sentinel Nenagh Guardian Southern Star Waterford News Derry People & Donegal News (12)	Clonmel Nationalist Derry Journal Sligo Champion (3)	Leinster Leader Killarney Echo Roscommon Journal Tipperary Star (4)
		4. Neutral throughout	**6. Critical of IP throughout, embraced SF**
		Limerick Echo Tipperary People (2)	Cork Free Press The Kerryman Mayo News Roscommon Herald (4)

Note: IP=Irish Party; SF= Sinn Féin.

Party paper, the *Sligo Champion,* to a neutral stance at the end of 1918. It should be added that some of these shifts of loyalty may owe as much to local factional differences or family feuds, perhaps predating the war, as to differing stances on the politics of the moment. This certainly seems to explain the divergence between the *Roscommon Herald* and the *Westmeath Examiner,* both of them initially pro-Home Rule papers but for long locked in a mutual antagonism that reflected the animosity between their respective ownerships, the Tully and Hayden families. It is possible that similar local factors may explain the rift between the *Munster Express* and the *Waterford News,* two pro-Home Rule papers of that city which by 1917 had come to hold very different views of their local MP, John Redmond.

F. THE IRISH CONVENTION AND THE DEATH OF REDMOND, SEPTEMBER 1917 —MARCH 1918

In its first two months of leisurely deliberation under the chairmanship of Sir Horace Plunkett, the Irish Convention considered several schemes of all-Ireland self-government suggested by members. Helped by the conciliatory oratory of Redmond and others, these debates had the effect of improving personal relationships and removing some of the bitterness of religious and cultural issues from the arena of nationalist–unionist controversy. In late September the convention adjourned, having appointed a committee of nine, consisting of five nationalists, three Ulster unionists and one southern unionist to get to grips with the details of a new Home Rule scheme. The differences were soon narrowed down to questions of finance. A system of complete fiscal autonomy, with full Irish control of customs and excise, was favoured strongly by most of the nationalist members (in line with nationalist opinion, which saw the terms of the 1914 Act rendered obsolete by the huge wartime increase in taxation). Such a scheme, proposed by the nationalists on 5 November, raised the spectre of protectionist tariffs under Home Rule and was rejected out of hand by the Ulster unionists on the grounds that it would separate their interests from 'the great industrial people' of Great Britain from whom they refused to be divorced. A compromise scheme proposed by the southern unionist delegate Lord Midleton that would have left excise under Dublin control, but customs in the hands of Westminster, failed to attract united support from either the nationalist or the Ulster unionist delegates. After many weeks of debate, Redmond tried to break the deadlock in January 1918 by seeking the support of his fellow-nationalists for the Midleton scheme, but found himself isolated, having lost the backing of prominent Irish Party colleagues. Increasingly incapacitated by illness, he ended in February by throwing his support behind the nationalist demand for full fiscal autonomy. The Convention had reached the end of the road and the end of any further hope for an all-Ireland constitutional settlement.

Until the breakdown of the nationalist consensus in mid-January, the convention's proceedings were closed to the press. However, nine of the eighteen pro-Party newspapers and one neutral tried to read the signs and expressed alternating hope and concern. The *Limerick Leader* (4 January) had begun the year heralding 'brighter hopes' for its deliberations, a prospect preferable to the policy of 'placing all our hopes on the Peace Conference and of relying on the "gallant allies in Europe"'. The *Cork Examiner* (15 January) wrote that 'Irish nationalists cannot reasonably expect the Convention to agree upon a scheme which will embody their maximum demands. Our minimum demand is … a Parliament for all Ireland, with full jurisdiction over purely Irish affairs, and administration by an Executive or Government responsible to that Parliament alone … [Within that there is] plenty of scope for reasonable concessions'. Four papers noted that the Ulster question was once again blocking the way to agreement. The *Drogheda Argus* (9 February) drew pessimistic deductions from the resignation from the Cabinet of Carson, announced on 21 January, and his return to Ulster to rally his forces: 'In this crisis Sir Edward has not hesitated to resort to the old rallying cry of "no surrender", despite the fact that he is willing to send back his delegates to the convention, and notwithstanding the knowledge that if a National settlement does eventuate there must be more or less a surrender on both sides, since the very basis of a settlement must be a compromise of principle …'

For the *Westmeath Examiner* (26 January), the issue was one of 'national common sense versus moonshine'. The *Connacht Tribune* (26 January) wrote that 'Ulster must not be allowed to wreck the Convention'. The *Wexford People* (26 January) expressed the 'serious alarm' of well-wishers of the convention and saw it as a 'grave scandal' that Carson had had such a prominent place in the Government. Only the *Cork Examiner* (24 January) adopted a moderate, even respectful, tone in hoping that Carson would 'choose to throw his weight against extremist counsels in Ulster' and promote conciliation. In the midst of such uncertainty, the *Tuam Herald* (9 February) found escape from the Irish impasse by identifying itself with a different national struggle. In an editorial titled 'The Cause of Bohemia', it found that 'The Czechs are an especially gifted and cultured people, and wherever they go they impress every one with their superior qualities'. It would later find an analogy with Ireland when it drew a parallel between the Sudeten Germans of Bohemia, 'that foreign German element in its population', and the 'Orange gang, denying to the entire country its right to independent existence' (6 July).

The increasing disorder in many parts of the country worried some of these papers. The *Sligo Champion* (2 March) blamed the rise in raids for arms, attacks on the police and land seizures on Sinn Féin, a movement the paper now saw as an Irish incarnation of the Bolsheviks. 'It would be an affectation of ignorance or indifference,' wrote the *Tuam Herald* (2 March), 'to refrain from recognizing the very serious condition of things that unhappily exist in parts of the south and west and particularly in certain districts of this county … the Bolshevists in our midst'. The *Donegal Vindicator* (8 March) wrote, 'Sinn Féin runs riot over Ireland … the future is dark, indeed'. Such sentiment was not confined to the pro-Party press. The *Leinster Leader* (2 March) recorded its concern at the growing disorder as manifested by 'cattle driving, land-commandeering and political disturbances'. However, the *Clare Champion* (9

March) bridled at the suggestion of disorder; the situation there was 'grossly exaggerated' and did not warrant the 'military occupation' that had almost cut off the county from the rest of the country. Sinn Féin, it claimed, would have put an end to the cattle driving and arms-raiding if the military had not come in. (This paper was suppressed by the censor between 30 March and 28 September 1918.)

Opinion was predictably divided on the result of the by-election in South Armagh in early February, which gave victory to the Irish Party candidate. Of twenty-nine papers commenting, eleven (38 per cent), including many of those still loyal to the Irish Party, evinced a brief revival of morale. The *Irish News* (30 January) had forecast a Party victory – otherwise there would be 'a suicidal surrender to the madness of Markieviczism'. The *Westmeath Examiner* (9 February) saw the victory as calling 'a halt to the policy of wild and reckless revolution'. The *Dundalk Democrat* (9 February) reckoned it 'a turning point of the mad revolt against unity and sanity'. For the *Donegal Vindicator* (8 February), the win was 'a necessary setback to the Sinn Féin enthusiasts and their madcap idea of a pretty little Republic'. On the other side, another seventeen (59 per cent), including many of the pro-Sinn Féin papers, saw the defeat as a merely temporary setback or the result of an alliance between the Irish Party and Ulster Unionist Party to keep out Sinn Féin. The *Derry People* (26 January) predicted, 'If Redmondism holds South Armagh, it will be no victory ... [it will] only be a prolongation of Redmondism's death agony'. The *Midland Tribune* (9 February) commented, 'Devlin's [Ancient Order of] Hibernians are now in open alliance with Kick-the-Pope Orangemen to oust Sinn Féin candidates'. The *Clare Champion* (9 February) agreed: 'the entente between the Irish Party and Orange Unionists has won them a seat but lost them their honour and even their pretensions as Nationalists'. However, the *Cork Examiner* (4 February) claimed that it was fairly obvious that the 2,680 'Orange' voters had not in fact voted, making the possibility of a Hibernian–Orange coalition 'utterly fantastic'; rather, it drew the lesson that nationalist electors were 'not duped by Sinn Féin nostrums' and had repudiated that party's 'gallant allies in Europe'.

The *Southern Star,* the last of the formerly Redmondite papers to go over to the opposition, showed the extent of its change of editorial policy under its new owners. The previous year, as the convention began its work, it had warned (11 August), 'If the Convention fails to effect the object for which it was summoned … then we may look forward to chaos.' Later, its hopes had risen (29 September): 'It is sufficient to know from prominent members of the Convention in public addresses that all goes well within closed doors … It is highly gratifying to know that a feeling of optimism as to its ultimate outcome prevails all round, and that much better results are expected from it than were at first anticipated.' Later still (27 October) it appealed to Sinn Féiners to give the convention a chance: 'We do not ask them to retract or forego one iota of their beliefs, we simply ask them to possess their souls in patience while the Convention is sitting – to encourage that body to come to a conclusion that will be generally accepted …' As recently as 3 November, it had convinced itself that 'the language of the Sinn Féiners is becoming more sober, moderate and restrained … In fact, Sinn Féin is settling down to be quite a very sensible proposition'. By February 1918, these policies and any concern for the convention had been jettisoned. Commenting on South Armagh, it counselled 'There is no need for us to be downcast. The cause of Sinn Féin has suffered no serious or permanent set-back. The rejoicings and the boastings of the Redmondites will speedily lose their point'. The following week's editorial (16 February) was titled, 'The Folly of Constitutionalism'. The paper was suppressed by the military authorities in early March.

The death of Redmond on 6 March united the non-Sinn Féin papers in mourning. The *Clonmel Nationalist* (9 March) announced that 'the people mourn the passing of a great tribune, remarkable for his constructive statesmanship'. The *Connacht Tribune*, its columns edged in black, called him 'a great man' who had 'towered head and shoulders' above his contemporaries (9 March). The *Cork Examiner* (7 March) wrote of him as 'a faithful servant of his country ... always tolerant and broadminded to a fault'. The *Sligo Champion* recalled the death of Parnell in headlining its eulogy 'The Dead Chief': 'Under his able leadership the National Party have been able, by constitutional agitation, to practically create a new Ireland' (9 March). In the view of the *Wexford People*, Redmond's burden had been 'worsened by the treachery of those in high places whom he trusted, and of a certain section of his countrymen at home who stooped to the foulest epithets' (9 March). For the *Donegal Vindicator*, he was 'an ideal leader of men. He knew no fear, and a cause was never lost until it was won ... [he had] statesmanship *in excelsis*, and his Party were loyal as to no other' (8 March). For the *Ballina Herald* (14 March), 'Calamitous is not too strong a term to describe the tragedy to Ireland of the passing away at this juncture in its history of Mr John E. Redmond, leader of the Irish Party. Mr Redmond took up the mantle of Parnell, and for nearly thirty years carried it with untarnished dignity, and he has laid it down at a moment when his experienced and far-sighted statesmanship was never more required to save the country from what is likely to accrue from unfulfilled hopes.' In the estimation of the *Tuam Herald*, 'history will place him side by side with Grattan, O'Connell, Butt and Parnell ... a wise, experienced, far-seeing statesman' (9 March). The *Dundalk Democrat* (9 March) agreed with the comparison with O'Connell and Parnell, adding that, 'In some respects he was the greatest of the three ... [and] deserted by large bodies of his ignorant and ungrateful fellow-countrymen'.

The most seasoned anti-Party papers, *The Kerryman,* the *Mayo News* and the *Leinster Leader* reported the death but made no comment. The *Roscommon Herald* mixed a modicum of sorrow with sarcasm: 'Everybody is sorry for him as a man, but as a political leader, the question is entirely different ... Fr. Bernard Vaughan declared that Mr. Redmond's death is a great loss to the Empire and to the cause of Imperialism. Fr. Vaughan is right.' However, many of those papers that had recently shifted allegiance, while critical of Redmond's political legacy, carried obituary editorials infused with a certain personal sympathy. The *Westmeath*

Independent (9 March), under the title 'A National Loss', wrote that it had 'no heart for a polemical discussion', instead eulogising 'a brave, amiable, generous, chivalrous soul … no man served Ireland with a purer or more unselfish purpose'. The *Carlow Nationalist* referred to 'circumstances over which he had no control'; the lesson of his fate was the folly of the 'Trust England' policy. The *Derry People* saw the circumstances of Redmond's death as resembling to some extent those under which O'Connell and Parnell had died. 'The time for a true estimate of Mr. Redmond's character and of his life's work,' it wrote, 'is not yet … [He was] a clean political fighter. He never descended to abuse, and never said a harsh or an unkind thing of a political opponent.' The *Nenagh Guardian* (9 March) managed a very gracious obituary in which it noted that Redmond had 'filled a great place in Irish life' and remarked on the strange similarity between the ending of his career and that of Daniel O'Connell. The *Kilkenny People*, the first loyal paper to switch allegiance to Sinn Féin, focused on the positives as it saw them:

> [O]*ne of the most notable personalities in the public life of Ireland for nearly forty years … for ten years, as a member of the united Party under the most powerful and determined constitutional leader that Ireland ever produced he rendered brilliant service to his country. Then the 'split' came and Redmond remained faithful to the Chief … When the Party had reunited under his leadership, 'the fight was carried on by John Redmond* [on Parnell's lines] *for a couple of years, and then the inevitable thing happened, the thing that happens to every Irishman who remains long enough in the British Parliament breathing its 'mephitic atmosphere'.*

A note of forgiveness concluded the obituary: 'Let us remember that when Parnell had few friends, John Redmond was one of them … if he made mistakes and committed errors of judgment he was but human'.

The *Kerry Sentinel* (9 March), a paper that had uttered no word of criticism of Redmond before late 1916, pretended that it had not seen 'eye to eye' with him 'during the last eight or nine years of his political life'. The *Tipperary Star*, initially uncommitted but now firmly in the Sinn Féin camp, wrote that 'Mr. Redmond doubtless meant well, but … in trusting so unquestioningly to British promises he, to a large extent, lost the confidence of his own people'. However, 'his difficulties were well-nigh unsurmountable … a charming gentleman in every respect … his bitterest political enemies pitied him rather than blamed him'.

G. THE CONSCRIPTION CRISIS, APRIL-AUGUST 1918

On 21 March, the German High Command launched Operation Michael, a massive spring offensive on the Western Front with sixty-five divisions, freed from the Russian front by the peace treaty of Brest–Litovsk, pitched against twenty-six divisions of the British Third and Fifth Armies, making a large breach in the Allied lines. British losses were exceeded in severity only by those of the first day of the Somme battle. Among the worst-hit units was the Sixteenth (Irish) Division, whose under-strength battalions suffered an average of ten per cent fatalities and lost large numbers of prisoners. By 3 April, when it was finally relieved, it had taken 7,149 casualties, including over 1,000 dead, the highest of any division engaged since 21 March, and no longer existed as a fighting force. The scale of the Army's losses gave a new urgency to the conscription issue.

On 16 April, the threat of Irish conscription became real at last when the House of Commons passed a conscription bill for the whole of the United Kingdom. The decision generated the biggest political event of the year before the general election of December. The furore convulsed nationalist Ireland for almost five months, and had the potential, had the threat been followed through, to ignite a violent insurrection with the kind of popular mandate that the 1916 rebellion had lacked. All of nationalist Ireland was united in opposition. Of thirty-three papers that commented, thirty-two advocated resistance. Most of the pro-Party papers reacted with reflexive denunciations of 'Prussianism' (*Connacht Tribune*, 13 April), 'a very grave blunder' (*Wexford People*, 11 May) or 'a policy of madness … [originating in] inherent hatred of the country which our ruling classes have shown for many centuries' (*Longford Leader*, 13 April). Adapting the nineteenth century anti-Russian music hall song, the *Galway Observer* (13 April) cried 'We don't want to be Sinn Féiners, but by jingo if we do, we will, like Carson, threaten to break every law in the realm before we are coerced into conscription'.

Only the *Tuam Herald* made any attempt to understand the government's motives in the context of the war. It called the move 'one of the most momentous and most important decisions respecting the future peace and progress of this country'. Never had things been so desperate in the war, and 'the Democracy of Europe will go down in dust if the enemy succeeds'. But, although absolutely necessary, conscription was being done in the face of the wishes of the representatives of the Irish people. The proper course would be first to establish an Irish government, which could then be 'trusted to do its duty' (13 April). Tully's *Roscommon Herald* had its own antisemitic conspiracy theory to hand to explain the government's decision: 'It cannot be forgotten since the Marconi scandal, that Lloyd George is in the net of a low type of Jewmen in England. It was Jewmen of that blend that left Russia prostrate and dismembered. There were just 700 Jewmen in the intrigue that brought Russia to her knees … the notorious jewman Kerensky … his fellow Jewmen Lenin and Trotsky' (Trotsky, in fact, being the only Jew among the three). The paper had its own slant on the epoch-making British defeat of the Ottoman Turk army and General Allenby's entry into Jerusalem in late 1917: 'generals and men and guns were sent from the Western front to Palestine to conquer Jerusalem for the Jews … Perhaps it is the same Jew finger that is prompting the trouble in Ireland' (13 April).

On 16 April, Redmond's successor, John Dillon, led the Irish Party out of the House of Commons and back to Ireland to join the anti-conscription campaign. Two days later, a well-attended conference at the Mansion House led to the setting up of the nine-man Irish Anti-

Conscription Committee and a declaration against conscription by the Catholic hierarchy. With all non-unionist elements in Ireland pledged to resist the measure by all means necessary, support for the committee was unanimous. The issue dominated the provincial press editorials for many weeks. The *Limerick Leader* (22 April) was at one with the *Tipperary Star* (27 April) in calling conscription 'a declaration of war' on the Irish people. The *Connacht Tribune* wrote that 'the manhood of Ireland awaits attack' (11 May).

Such unanimity did not, however, prevent constitutionalist and revolutionary sections from using the crisis to advance their own particular interests, and this sparring was reflected in the newspapers. The death of Redmond had triggered two further by-elections, one in his Waterford City constituency, contested by his son Captain William Archer Redmond, the other for the East Tyrone seat vacated by the latter.

The by-elections gave two victories to the Irish Party over Sinn Féin, and a few papers reverted to the hopes they had derived from the South Armagh result: 'The tide has turned, as we knew it would' (*Connaught Telegraph*, 6 April); 'The country is returning to sanity from the Sinn Féin whirlwind' (*Limerick Leader*, 5 April). However, anti-Party papers blamed the same Irish Party by-election victories for misleading the government into underestimating the degree of resistance to conscription. The *Roscommon Herald* and the *Mayo News* both claimed that it was these three results, in particular the election of Capt. Redmond to his father's seat, that had brought the Conscription Bill to pass (4, 11 May).

When Arthur Griffith was nominated as Sinn Féin candidate for the East Cavan by-election, the *Limerick Leader* (13 May) accused him of 'inviting disaster' at a time when national solidarity was needed, and the *Anglo-Celt* (11 May) called on him and his Redmondite opponent to step down in favour of an agreed 'national unity' candidate; the *Carlow Nationalist* (18 May) threw back the charge by impugning the Irish Party's contesting of the seat as the cause of disunion. When Griffith won the seat handsomely, restoring the run of Sinn Féin electoral successes of the previous year, the *Donegal Vindicator* (28 June) wrote that he should not have been nominated, but the *Carlow Nationalist* (29 June) hailed the victory with 'Well done Cavan – Brilliant Stroke for Independence' and the *Roscommon Herald* wrote that had the Irish Party candidate been elected, conscription would now be in operation. The united anti-conscription front notwithstanding, the *Herald* was in no mood to observe the spirit of truce: 'Nothing was a bigger strain on the public last Sunday [when more than a million people had signed an anti-conscription covenant] than the appearance of the 400 Pounders [the derogatory Healyite term for Irish Party MPs, paid £400 a year] on the anti-conscription platforms'.

The uproar surrounding conscription submerged the news of the collapse of the Irish Convention, which had held its final votes in late March. Lloyd George's response was to frame a new twin-track policy, Home Rule combined with conscription, a move that had the immediate effect of finally discrediting Home Rule as traditionally understood in nationalist eyes. A nine-man cabinet committee chaired by the southern Unionist Walter Long met on 15 April, charged with drafting a new Home Rule Bill on the lines recommended by the convention.

The very moderate *Ballina Herald* (18 April) commented:

For nine months the members of the Convention, Unionists and Nationalists, sat together, and the result of their labours was anxiously awaited, but with inevitable fatality, it has arrived at a time when the people are solely interested in one vital thing – conscription … If we are to have Home Rule, it should be Home Rule in fact as in name, and half measures will never reconcile the people, or encourage them to loyally co-operate in the affairs of the Empire. It may be that the Government will carry through a measure of self-government, based on the majority report, but we fear very much, in the present temper of the people, it is foredoomed to failure.

The unpalatable fact for moderates was that Home Rule as traditionally understood had come to be seen by a significant section of nationalists as itself a half measure and, when further modified by partition or coupled with conscription as it was now, unworthy of consideration.

Those few papers that commented at all dismissed the Lloyd George package out of hand; some saw it as the latest government excuse for avoiding implementing Home Rule. For the anti-Party papers it was more straightforward: the *Carlow Nationalist* (4 May) wrote that 'the new Home Rule simulacrum' would be repudiated in any event, but especially when accompanied by conscription'. A similar divergence was shown between pro- and anti-Party papers in their comments on the 'German Plot' arrests in mid-May, based on manipulated intelligence of an alleged Sinn Féin conspiracy to launch another insurrection with German military aid, when 150 activists, including Griffith, were detained and deported to England. The *Cork Examiner* (21 May) was moderate, urging that 'the Irish administration owes it to itself and the public to clear the air at once … Misgovernment, insincerity and injustice are the fount from which plots and plotters spring'. For the *Longford Leader*, the arrests were another government blunder; for the *Sligo Champion*, merely 'further excuse to shelve Home Rule' (both 25 May). For the *Carlow Nationalist*, however, they were an attempt to discredit the Sinn Féin movement at home and abroad, while the real leaders of the Irish nation were in British prisons (25 May, 27 July). For the republican *Mayo News* (25 May), they signified that 'the only argument that has any weight with the British Government is the fist to the nose'. The *Kerryman* (25 May) wrote that the arrests had 'made Ireland still more Sinn Féin than it was' and it was 'now a certainty that Sinn Féin will sweep the country'.

Now that conscription was the new obstacle in the way of nationalist acceptance of Home Rule, there was much less mention of partition, the bugbear of the previous year. It was as if the issue had served its purpose in bringing down the Irish Party, and the Sinn Féin camp's awareness that it too would soon be answerable on it made it not quite politic for them to mention. In the pro-Party camp, since there had been no advance in understanding of the Ulster position or in willingness to consider territorial compromise, it was inevitable that scapegoats should be sought. The *Connacht Tribune* wrote that Home Rule had been withheld from the Irish people (6 July) and the fate of the Act on the Statute Book was 'another shameful page' (3 August). It reserved a special venom for Lloyd George, writing that 'no man has so earned the contempt and reprobation of all decent Irishmen' (6 July). The *Tuam Herald* (3 August) preferred to disparage the 'Scots–Irish … ancestors of the chosen people of the Covenant, the ungodly descendants of an ungodly lot under a clever lawyer who is not even an Ulsterman … the men who are helping more than anything to hamstring and hold up the full force, manhood and power of Ireland today, are keeping this country in turmoil and denying the Irish people their rights'. The *Wexford People* (29 June) and the *Anglo-Celt* (6 July) noted Lord Curzon's statement that Home Rule had been dropped due to the resistance to conscription, a move the former paper called 'another piece of black treachery towards Ireland'.

H. THE GENERAL ELECTION CAMPAIGN, SEPTEMBER—DECEMBER 1918

The German Spring Offensive petered out in July without decisive success, and the arrival of US troops at the Front changed the balance of forces and allowed a successful Allied counter-offensive to begin in August. An end to the war was finally in sight. The turn of the tide removed the pressure for conscription and, although some newspapers occasionally warned that the threat had not gone away, less was heard of the issue. Opposition to conscription did not always blunt an overall pro-recruiting stance. The *Donegal Vindicator* (13 September) called for a new voluntary recruiting drive as the 'only sane policy' to avoid conscription. The *Munster Express* (24 August), under the heading 'The Call of the Irish Regiments', helpfully provided information on the various branches of the service an Irishman could join. There followed what would prove the last surge in Irish enlistment during the war, the *Sligo Champion* (12 October) reporting approvingly that, in a few weeks, almost 10,000 men had enlisted.

As the tenuous unity of the anti-conscription coalition crumbled, the polarity of the constitutionalist and revolutionary wings of nationalism was restored by the imminent prospect of a general election, one which Sinn Féin approached in confident expectation of a resounding victory. The Sinn Féin win in East Cavan was hailed sardonically by the *Longford Leader* (22 June) with 'Praise to Allah! Another great Sinn Féin victory on the road to Irish freedom'. Home Rule was now a mere scrap of paper, and why? 'Because of the imbecility and insanity of the Irish people themselves'. The Irish Party's return to Westminster just before the summer recess was welcomed by the *Wexford People* and the *Tuam Herald* (both 3 August). The Party had returned sadder and wiser, wrote the latter, having realised that abstention only 'played the enemy's game'. A direct appeal against conscription and for national self-determination, signed by all parties in Ireland and sent to President Wilson from the Mansion House Conference in time for 4 July, received support from newspapers on both sides of the divide.

In the four final months of the year, the provincial press divided in roughly equal proportions according to their views on the binary choices facing the nationalist electorate. Broadly, the pro-Sinn Féin papers supported the making of a renewed appeal for Ireland's admission to the Paris Peace Conference as opposed to the Irish Party's advocacy of a renewed campaign at Westminster for self-government, and the former's framing of the demand at that conference as one for full or sovereign independence (though not a 'republic') as opposed to the latter's call for dominion (colonial) Home Rule (to replace the 1914 Home Rule Act).

For the papers in the Sinn Féin camp, acceptance of abstentionism was so self-evident as not to require comment. However, they had plenty to say on the substantive question of the national demand. The *Mayo News* (27 July) urged the new Sinn Féin clubs to 'make ready for the fray' by accounting for every voter. Yet this most republican of newspapers did not call for a republic. Self-determination meant that the Irish people alone were entitled to decide on the form of government for the country – a republic, dominion Home Rule or 'a step-child in the Empire'. The mildest comment came from the *Clare Champion* (5 October, 9 November) when it welcomed the Irish Party's declaration in its election manifesto for 'national self-government for Ireland ... including full and complete executive, legislative and fiscal powers', a formula it described as 'a big jump from partition'. However, it asked why the Irish Party still wanted the word 'Dominion' 'written across the map of ancient Erin'. Its own policy was 'self-determination versus Home Rule of any kind, and the Peace Conference versus the British Parliament'. (The term 'self-determination', as the right of small nations emerging from imperial rule, had appeared in 1917 as the buzzword of US President Woodrow Wilson's policy proposal for the post-war settlement. The Clare newspaper seemed to interpret it to mean absolute independence rather than the right of a people to decide on their form of government.) The national demand was variously formulated by other papers as 'sovereign independence' (*Carlow Nationalist*) and 'free and unfettered development along the lines of national self-determination' (*Kilkenny People*). The *Tipperary Star* (30 November), urging support for the Paris Peace Conference strategy, wrote that a vote for Sinn Féin would be 'a revolution of thought but not a revolution by force of arms', which would be 'impossible and foolish'.

An important part of the Sinn Féin election campaign was to keep up an unrelenting attack on John Dillon as leader of the Irish Party. 'Mr. Dillon is the danger,' wrote the *Waterford News* (2 August). 'If Mr Dillon continues to usurp a position as the alleged leader of the Irish people, the struggle to defeat Conscription cannot succeed ... His impudent assumption to speak for the people of this country makes him the most insidious enemy possessed by Ireland during the present crisis'. The *Kilkenny People* (29 June) dubbed him 'Old Man Garrulous' and accused him of lying about his closeness to Parnell in the 1880s. The *Derry People* attacked him for his dismissal of the option of a republic and his espousal of colonial Home Rule (6 July). The *Midland Tribune* (29 June) wrote of Dillon's demand for full control of all internal Irish affairs including customs and excise as 'somewhat belated' and claimed that his East Cavan rout had caused him 'to throw the 1914 Home Rule Act overboard'. The *Roscommon Herald* (19 October), as so often, found a low tone when it carried a cartoon showing Dillon climbing a pole marked '£400 a year' with the text, 'The leader of the Irish people at home and abroad finds he cannot climb the greased pole of a General Election because the grease of his speeches in favour of Conscription, Partition and jobs in Dublin Castle is sticking too close to it'. It went on to castigate him for his 'conduct' on the 1906 Education Bill and the 1908 bill to set up the national university when he had supposedly tried 'to impose godless education' on Catholics. When the Irish Party's manifesto used the language of self-determination, the *Mayo News* (2 November) wrote that the people would not be fooled by Dillon's efforts to steal planks from the Sinn Féin platform.

The Irish Party was now in competition with Sinn Féin, not only adopting as intransigent a stance on partition but distancing itself as far as possible from 1914-style Home Rule and arguing for independence within the empire on the model of Canada or Australia. The *Drogheda Argus* (5 October) tried to flesh out the dominion Home Rule idea:

> *We are far from thinking that Home Rule would act as a panacea for all the evils which centuries of misgovernment have brought about, nor do we expect that with the passing of an Act of Parliament the country would be immediately converted into an El Dorado ...* [referring to a recent article by Geddis, editor of the *New Zealand Times*]. *The system he outlined would give Ireland Dominion Home Rule in a scheme of Imperial Federation. This was Parnell's idea of Home Rule. That is what the Nationalists of Louth demanded at the huge demonstration that was addressed by Mr Joseph Devlin ... at Ardee on Sunday last. It is what every sane and sensible and disinterested man*

demands, not only in Ireland, but throughout the British Dominions. And in addition to the claim for Colonial Home Rule, we also demand equality of treatment for all classes and creeds. We object to the handing of Ireland over to the representation at Westminster of the Ulster Unionists, and we object to the Ulster Unionists being allowed to retain their arms and ammunition, or, as in pre-war days, to Carson & Co. being allowed to plot with the Germans, or to invoke foreign aid in their attempt to subvert law and order …

The pro-Party papers were uniformly critical of the policies of separatism and abstentionism in the Sinn Féin platform. The *Tuam Herald* (14 September) wrote that 'vicious talk of a republic', together with lawless excesses, were 'embittering the trouble in Ireland' and were 'the sublimest folly men could adopt'. It decried the intolerance of the young, inexperienced men who denied freedom of speech to alternative nationalist views. The *Limerick Leader* (7, 16 August) attacked the lies being told about the constitutional movement, especially about its representative T.P. O'Connor MP who had been touring the United States since the previous year. In an editorial titled 'Ireland at the Cross Roads', it summarised its policy in the phrase: 'The constitutional road leads to complete Dominion Home Rule; the republic road leads to nowhere'. For the *Wexford People* (9 November, 14 December), which also called for dominion Home Rule, separation and a republic were 'absolutely unattainable'. The *Connaught Telegraph* (2 November) warned that the expected result of the general election 'will make Ireland's condition a thousand times worse than it is now, as we are showing determination to boycott Westminster and leave a free field to our enemies'.

However, not all the constitutionalist papers rejected the Sinn Féin Paris Peace Conference policy outright. Of fourteen pro-Party papers that carried a comment, seven (50 per cent) supported, under certain conditions, an appeal to the conference. The *Connacht Tribune* (2 November) was in favour, but insisted that the demand put to it must be 'rational'; there was no room for 'Sinn Féin's republic extravagance'. The

Irish News (9 November) thought that the probability of Sinn Féin delegates being admitted alone to the Peace Conference was 'so remote that it need not be reckoned with'; that policy therefore spelled disaster for Ireland. However, if the leaders on both sides in the election were to present 'a united and solid front ... to the Peace Conference and the world', it would be a different matter: 'the representatives of the other free victorious nations will extend the hand of welcome'. The *Sligo Champion* (2 November) similarly lamented 'the divisions among Irishmen' and called for a national conference of all parties to formulate a united claim to be put to the Peace Conference, but noted that Sinn Féiners were perceived as pro-German and unsympathetic to the Allied cause whereas the Irish Party had never wavered. Given the hubris in the Sinn Féin camp, with the *Midland Tribune* (7 November) headlining an editorial 'The Party Must Go', such calls for unity were unlikely to be heeded.

The other pro-Party papers were either sceptical or dismissive. A frequent theme among them was their sense of vindication at the fact that the Allies had proved victorious and that the Sinn Féiners had 'backed the wrong horse'. Despite the *Midland Tribune*'s (9 November) denunciation of 'the atrocious calumny that Sinn Féin is pro-German', this feeling seemed to bring them a momentary boost in morale in the face of the advancing Sinn Féin tide. The *Anglo-Celt* (9 November) wrote that Sinn Féin predictions of a German victory had been 'hopelessly at fault' and it was better to 'stick by the British democracy', which would be 'supreme' after the war. Most of these papers focused their criticism on the Sinn Féin abstention policy, the *Wexford People* (11 December) writing that it only 'hands over the administration of Ireland to Sir Edward Carson and his Orange friends'. The *Donegal Vindicator* (22, 29 November) wrote that Ulster nationalists would not vote for an 'orgie [sic] of Carsonism at Westminster'; the issue of the election was representation: was it to be Westminster or vacant seats? The Irish Party policy was active, that of Sinn Féin passive. The *Tuam Herald* (23 November) lamented the fact that 'Ireland has left herself without a friend' by the will of 'an apparent majority of our misguided people'.

In the midst of these exchanges, the *Clonmel Nationalist* (13 November, 18 December) veered between purple prose ('Junkerism still prevails in England', 'Ireland lies bound and bleeding in the grip of ascendancy') and its efforts to maintain a tone of impartiality between the parties. Ireland's hopes, it wrote, were now largely fixed on the Paris Peace Conference 'to which her people are appealing and at which the principal arbiter will be President Wilson, the grandchild of Irish parents and the true friend of democracy'. The paper did not discuss the relative merits of the competing policies but was glad that, although people were sharply divided, the election was being fought in an orderly manner.

Six weeks before the election, the Irish Party at Westminster essayed a final sally for the constitutional strategy. On 5 November, in a reprise of his motion of March 1917, a resolution in the name of T.P. O'Connor proposed that 'before the British Government takes part in any proceeding for the resettlement of Europe on the conclusion of peace, the Irish question should be settled in accordance with the principles laid down by President Wilson … and that by the application of these principles the system of coercion and military rule, under which Ireland is at present governed, should be brought to an end'. The debate took place on the day that Lloyd George announced the terms of the armistice with Austria–Hungary. Amid many tributes and felicitations, the prime minister offered his congratulations 'to the Czecho–Slovak and Jugo–Slav peoples, who have thrown off the yoke of their oppressors, and joined themselves openly with the Allies. These little nations, which have stood out so long and with such heroism against Germanic domination, may rest assured that the Allies intend to come to their aid as fast as they possibly can'. O'Connor took up the 'little nations' theme, asking the House to 'help another small nation – another small oppressed nation – to be congratulated on its early liberation from another form of oppression'. Attempting to dismiss the obstacle posed by the Ulster problem, he compared the 18-20 per cent of Ireland's population that comprised the 'Orangemen of Ireland' with the 35 per cent German minority in Bohemia. 'I have spoken of Ulster standing between Ireland

and her liberation,' he said. 'Of course she is. But Ulster does a little more than that. Ulster stands between this Empire and its honour and its security'.

The chief secretary, Edward Shortt, in reply referred to the inescapable difficulty: 'The Irish Convention has sat ... the Irish Convention has failed to agree. The Irish Convention has failed to obtain that which my right hon. Friend put in the forefront of the difficulty – the acquiescence of Ulster in any form of settlement ... It is as true today as it was two years ago, I presume, that it is unthinkable to coerce Ulster by force. If that is so, what is their proposal with regard to Ulster? Are they going to coerce Ulster by force or are they not?' Dillon retorted: 'Let Ulster obey the law like every other part of Ireland'. When Shortt persisted with his challenge, the young Irish Party MP Richard Hazleton declared, 'From the Government downwards, in the United States of America, throughout the length and breadth of that great country, there is hardly a single man to be found who does not wonder why the right hon. Member for Trinity College [Carson] was not put up against a wall and shot'. As before, no meeting of minds was possible, and the resolution was defeated by 196 votes to 115. The sterility of the debate was final testimony that the Irish Party had run out of options; its forty-four-year constitutional project had foundered on the rock of Ulster.

Of twenty-four papers that commented on the debate, the pro-Sinn Féin press could hardly be bothered to pay attention to it, though the *Carlow Nationalist* (9 November) viewed it as evidence in favour of abstentionism and the *King's County Independent* (9 November) announced it as the death of 'Parliamentarianism'. It was left to ten of the pro-Party papers to register dismay at Lloyd George's failure to deliver something to the Party that might rescue it from its fate. The *Tipperary People* (9 November) wrote that the resolution had been 'treated with contumely'. The *Irish News* (6 November) commented, 'The British Government's message was essentially that they will never be parties to a League of Nations based on Wilson principles'. The speeches of Shortt and Bonar Law were 'beneath contempt' – they had fallen back on 'the old hackneyed cry, or threat, of "Ulster", which deludes no one now'. How much this characterisation of the Ulster problem by nationalists was a helpless cry of anger leading nowhere was demonstrated by the *Sligo Champion* (9 November) when it attacked Shortt's speech in similar language but a few weeks later (30 November) challenged Sinn Féin to say how it proposed 'to compel Ulster unionists to submit to the laws of an Irish Republic' – the very question Shortt had challenged the Irish Party to answer!

As the election approached, forty-one of the sample of forty-two newspapers gave advice to the voters (the *Cork Free Press* had ceased publication after 1916). Of this number, eighteen were pro-Party, eighteen pro-Sinn Féin and five took a neutral stance (the hitherto consistently pro-Party *Sligo Champion* joined the neutral camp at the last minute in order to advocate for a united deputation to the Paris Peace Conference). The *Connaught Telegraph* (7 December) was confident 'the people will not abandon the only weapon left them for securing their rights'. But the *Westmeath Independent* (30 November) sensed 'there is a thrill of hope pulsating through the length and breadth of Ireland today'. The *Kilkenny People* (7 December) could not wait for the vote: 'Like a rotten tree swept away by an angry flood the so-called Irish Party, which had long forfeited any right or title to that designation, is disappearing from view and in less than a fortnight nothing will remain of it but an ugly memory'. On nomination day, it was announced that the Irish Party would not contest twenty-five constituencies held by its MPs, the majority of them in the southwest. A deal brokered by Cardinal Logue allotted each of the nationalist parties four Ulster seats in which contests would be avoided to prevent Unionists benefiting from a split nationalist vote.

There remained only the verdict. Although voting took place in most constituencies on 14 December, many results were not obtainable until the days after Christmas. In an election characterised by personation and intimidation, and in which two-thirds of the electorate were first-time voters, Sinn Féin won forty-eight per cent of the vote to the Irish Party's twenty-three per cent and the Unionists' twenty-eight per cent.

Reckoned as an all-island vote, Sinn Féin support fell just short of a majority. However, there can be little doubt that a vote in the twenty-five uncontested constituencies would have brought its total to over 50 per cent. And within the nationalist electorate, it was a resounding two-to-one victory over the Irish Party. The first-past-the-post system translated it into seventy-three seats for Sinn Féin and a mere six for the Irish Party, of which four were in the six-county area soon to be partitioned. The Irish Party's democratic mandate had decisively passed to Sinn Féin – a mandate to advance the case for independence for nationalist Ireland at the Peace Conference, but not a mandate to use violence nor to speak for unionist Ulster.

When the full extent of the rout was obvious, anti-Party papers were exultant. The *Derry People* (21 December) wrote that 'Last Saturday the majority of the Irish people pronounced with the greatest possible emphasis for complete freedom … Ireland is out of the slough of despond. The old order is dead'.

On the other side, some of the pro-Party papers ignored the news, some were circumspect and some defiant. The *Wexford People* (25 December) felt that it was Carson and his friends who had really carried the day, and refused to believe in the practicability of the Sinn Féin programme. The *Longford Leader* claimed that Sinn Féin had no plan if the Paris Peace Conference strategy should fail. The *Westmeath Examiner* (28 December) was sure that when responsibility for the future of the nation was placed on the Sinn Féin movement, 'the hopelessness and futility of the whole thing will be quickly apparent to the people', and they would rally to the old standards of Parnell and Davitt. And the *Tuam Herald* (28 December) found refuge from unbearable realities by hailing the self-government just achieved by what it called the 'four gallant brother nations' of Bohemia, Serbia, Poland and Romania; it had a special greeting for the Czechs and their leaders Kramar and Masaryk – '"Nazdar", as they say themselves in their own beautiful language'.

Press commentary for the 1917–18 period is summarised in Chart 5.

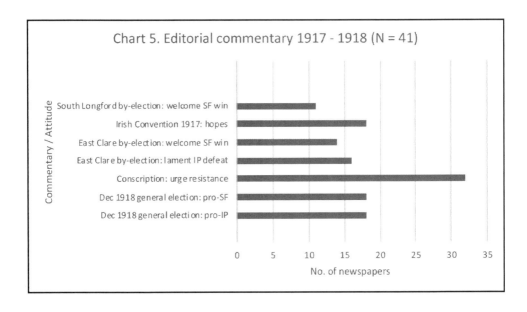

Chapter 6

REVOLUTIONARY VIOLENCE
AND REPRESSION,
JANUARY–DECEMBER 1919

A. DÁIL ÉIREANN

Following their party's established policy, the Sinn Féin members of parliament elected in December 1918 declined to take their seats in Westminster Parliament. Instead they met in Dublin on 21 January 1919 at the Mansion House and constituted themselves as An Dáil Éireann (Gaelic for 'the Parliament of Ireland'), with themselves designated as 'TD' (teachta Dála, or 'member of the Dáil'). Of the 69 TDs elected in December, only twenty-seven attended, since thirty-four were in prison and eight otherwise unavailable. The event was covered by journalists from the Irish and international press and the public gallery was crowded.

The meeting adopted four documents. The first was a provisional 'Dáil constitution' designating itself the parliament of a sovereign 'Irish Republic' that claimed jurisdiction over the whole island of Ireland. The second was a declaration of independence that ratified the proclamation of the republic issued at the beginning of the Easter 1916 rebellion and pledged 'to make this declaration effective by every means at our command'. It asserted 'that the elected representatives of the Irish people alone have power to make laws binding on the people of Ireland, and that the Irish Parliament is the only parliament to which that people will give its allegiance'. Thirdly, it adopted a 'Message to the Free Nations of the World', which appealed for Ireland to be allowed to make its case for independence at the Paris Peace Conference and defined an 'existing state of war between Ireland and England' which could 'never be ended until Ireland is definitely evacuated by the armed forces of England'. Finally, it adopted a 'Democratic Programme' – an outline of social and economic policy.

Provincial press reaction to the event was predictably divided. Of the forty-one remaining newspapers in this sample, twenty-three carried an editorial comment. Nine of these were enthusiastic, five expressed sympathy, seven struck a neutral or factual tone, while two expressed scepticism. The *Kilkenny People* (25 January) called it an 'epoch-making event', asserting that 'the action taken by the duly elected representatives of Irish public opinion is in the highest and only proper sense of the term strictly constitutional'. The *Waterford News* (25 January) exulted in the 'first fruits of victory' and claimed that the apathy of the Irish Party era had disappeared. The *Meath Chronicle* (25 January) wrote that it marked 'the definite enunciation, both in fact and in spirit, of Ireland's status as an independent nation, whose full national life and development is only arrested by sheer force of a strong military force', and the Dáil was 'the only democratic body that can be recognised as having the essentials upon which moral government rests, namely, the unfettered allegiance and consent of the people'. These papers were joined by others, such as the *Midland Tribune* and the *Sligo Champion*, in recognising the historic significance of the event. The latter, however, warned (25 January) that 'until [the Dáil] becomes a reality by international guarantees, its enactments, whatever they be, will have comparatively little influence on the current of Irish affairs. To convert the shadow into a reality by a successful appeal to the Paris Peace Conference or to the Council of the League of Nations must be the first duty of An Dáil'. The *Kerryman* (25 January), while equally supportive, warned nationalists not to expect much from President Wilson.

The *Derry People* (4 January) had begun the year, in an editorial titled 'The Nation's Responsibility', with advice that seemed to come from within the Sinn Féin camp itself. 'The responsibilities resting on the shoulders of Sinn Féin are henceforward increased a thousandfold … The parliamentary divisions have been captured … But for the practical expression of our will to freedom much more is required. Firstly, we must now force the county councils, the corporations, the Poor Law Boards, and the other public bodies to obey the will of the people … we must make preparations for the capturing by honest fearless men of all possible seats on these bodies … There must, therefore, be no cessation of hostilities on the part of any of the Sinn Féin clubs and branches'. Secondly, they must bring the machinery of law and order under the control of the people: 'Let us set up our own courts. Let us obey and respect our own laws, and let us prove by definite demonstration that in all things concerning the public weal we are the most law-abiding people in Europe'.

Among the sceptical organs, the *Dundalk Democrat*, in line with its previous allegiance to the Irish Party, dismissed it as the work of 'extremists'. The *Westmeath Examiner* felt that Home Rule, despite the election result, was not dead and must return to the political agenda when disillusionment set in with the abstentionist policy. However, most of the former Redmondite press was now trying to accommodate itself to the new reality. The *Tuam Herald* (4 January), writing before the Dáil's convening, was prepared to allow Sinn Féin a chance to put its new policy to the test: 'How far they may succeed in doing what the Irish Party conspicuously failed in doing, and whether it was their fault or not, remains to be seen and shown'. Abstention might be open to reconsideration, it thought, 'but a Republican policy is, if it be persisted in, absolutely futile and time-wasting'. To succeed, (i) it must have a decisive majority categorically demanding it and (ii) England must be prepared to concede it as the outcome of constitutional agitation:

Force, external or internal, is out of the question as a means of securing such a radical change … But it is not at all unlikely, if the Sinn Féin Party play their part well and wisely and adopt constitutional methods that, being as they are, a compact homogeneous body of active and intelligent young men, sincerely honest and unpurchaseably patriotic, they may yet become the means … of bringing to this country the fullest measure of self-government which is possible under conditions under which alone it can be workable, that is making and keeping Ireland within the Empire as much part and parcel of it as the self-governing colonies of Canada, Australia and South Africa.

The *Irish News* (22 January) began its response to the event by drawing a historical lesson from the very convening of the Dáil:

It is England's business to reflect that four years ago 95 per cent of the people whose representatives met in the Mansion House on 21 January 1919 were looking forward with hope and eagerness to self-government within the British Empire and enlisting by the thousand to fight and die for the cause that Empire had made its own. The direct results of the policy deliberately adopted by England's rulers in their dealings with this country were displayed in Dublin yesterday – and the demonstration was impressive and historic, however impracticable it may be deemed.'

The paper went on to dissect the Mansion House proceedings. It did not believe that either the Sinn Féin policy or programme 'will ultimately commend themselves to a majority of the Irish people'. But in another sense, 'nothing was accomplished'. Of the 'Three Manifestoes' adopted by the meeting, 'the first is indisputable (that Ireland is a free people)'; but as for the ratification of the republic proclaimed in Dublin on Easter Monday:

'Mr John MacNeill & Mr Arthur Griffith cannot consistently subscribe [to it] since the Irish people knew nothing about it, MacNeill did all in his power to prevent it and Griffith said it would cause "a holocaust of the young men of Ireland' to which he would never consent"'; yet the TDs ratified it and pledged themselves to make that declaration effective by every means in their power. 'What "means" are "in our power"? The [Paris] Peace Conference? The Address to the Free Nations? An eloquent document, a presentation of principles appealing for a hearing at the Peace Conference. Previous representatives of the Irish people have done the same with a far greater measure of national authority but circumstances have defeated them. A pledge to use "every means at our disposal" is really meaningless … The Address is little better than a waste of energy.'

If the documents adopted by the Dáil meeting, particularly the declaration of independence and the 'Message to the Free Nations', were intended to be the opening gambits in a possible negotiation process with the British government, the latter's reference to an 'existing state of war' between the two countries was not an encouraging sign. Although no such state of war existed in reality, but only in the minds of the ideologues for whom the 'republic' declared at Easter 1916 was already a reality, such a statement in an official document amounted to an effective declaration of war.

Despite this reference and the pledge in the declaration of independence to use 'every means at our command' to establish the republic, the new Dáil made no explicit statement that it was prepared to wage war or to sanction the use of armed force. No such mandate had been sought or given during Sinn Féin's general election campaign, which had emphasised the demand for self-determination and 'national independence' rather than a republic, and focused on the appeal to the Paris Peace Conference. However, the Irish Volunteer force, the body from whose Dublin membership the bulk of participants in the 1916 rebellion had been drawn, and which had since supplied much of the electioneering manpower that ensured the Sinn Féin election victories of 1917 and 1918, was a quasi-military body not under the control of the Dáil set up by the victors of those elections. During those years it had begun to expand its weapons arsenal, mainly by stealing or buying guns and ammunition from members of the now defunct Redmondite National Volunteers. Before the Volunteer split, in the early summer of 1914, Redmond had seen the need to bring the Volunteer movement under democratic control at a time when it was growing by 2,000 recruits each day, not only to prevent its becoming a threatening unconstitutional political force in nationalist Ireland, but to prevent the possibility of armed clashes with the Ulster Volunteer Force (See Chapter 2). No similar step was taken in January 1919 by the Sinn Féin party leadership or the Dáil formally to subject the Volunteers to civilian control. Charles Townshend suggests that this was due to the prevalence among some members of both the Dáil and the Volunteer executive of the traditional IRB (Fenian) view that politicians were not to be trusted and might come to retard the struggle for the republic; the resistance to pressing an oath of allegiance on the Volunteers was led by Michael Collins, the Dáil's Minister for Finance who would shortly co-direct the military campaign against the British and who was also president of the IRB Supreme Council. As it turned out, the Dáil approved the oath in August 1919 but would begin to administer it only a year later in the autumn of 1920.[1]

B. THE CAMPAIGN OF ASSASSINATION

The danger of armed bodies acting on their own initiative was not slow to manifest itself. On the very day of the Dáil's convening, a small band of Irish Volunteers in south Tipperary, intent on starting their own war, ambushed and killed Royal Irish Constabulary (RIC) constables James McDonnell and Patrick O'Connell as they escorted a cartload of gelignite to a stone quarry at Soloheadbeg near Tipperary town. Although the action lacked the authority, not only of the Dáil, but of the Volunteers' own leadership, it would come to be viewed in retrospect as the first engagement of the 'war of independence'. At the time, it shocked the country. It received coverage in fourteen of the newspapers in the sample, including four which condemned it, two which reported it as a 'tragedy' and three which described it as a 'sensation'.

In its editorial titled 'The Solohead Outrage' the *Clonmel Nationalist* (25 January) wrote of the event as a 'shocking tragedy … a very painful sensation … A truly deplorable affair, it is regarded with horror and indignation by all right-thinking men. Our county has for many years been happily free from outrages of this kind, and of late had enjoyed a remarkable record for crimelessness … The taking away of human life suddenly and ruthlessly is against all law, human and divine'. A few days later (29 January) its news page, under the headline 'Tipperary Outrage/ Condemned by Archbishop and Clergy/ "Cold blooded murders"', it reported that Archbishop Harty of Cashel, at Mass in Thurles Cathedral, had called the murders an 'offence against the laws of God and … against the fair name of our county and our country. We all, without distinction of political party, look with horror on the deed, and express our deep sense of the outrage which has been committed against Christian morals.'

The *Clonmel Nationalist* had taken a neutral position between the Irish Party and Sinn Féin. Two other local papers that condemned the killings were closer to the latter party. The *Tipperary Star* (25 January), in the same editorial in which it commented on the Dáil meeting, wrote:

> *Not since the callous murder of poor Sheehy-Skeffington* [by a British officer during Easter 1916 in Dublin] … *has anything so deplorable been committed as the shooting … of two policemen of good repute, engaged in the prosaic duty of conveying badly needed blasting material to a county road quarry. Whoever the masked band of headless men may be who committed the awful deed they are no friends of Ireland … That such a crime should be committed on the very day that peaceful patriotic Irishmen were meeting in the Capital to speed the cause of Ireland before the Free Nations in Conference in France … is the most heart-breaking stroke to which our country has ever been subjected.'*

A third Tipperary paper, the *Nenagh Guardian* (25 January) wrote that the news had sent 'a thrill of horror' through the country:

Policemen are Irishmen; they often spring from good homes; they are sometimes men of high moral worth; in an Ireland free or unfree they are a necessity; they have onerous and often unpleasant duties to perform; and though the system they represent is one of the most evil and anti-national in the entire world the Irish people, as a whole, have recognised that it is the alien spirit in control and not the ordinary constable who is at fault. It is more than painful to think of these two constables walking out beside this cart, little expecting the tragic fate that was before them.

Only the *Tuam Herald* (25 January) could hazard a guess at the wider meaning of the incident, from which it drew a prophetic conclusion: 'A spirit of lewd lawlessness is abroad … The hot bloods, however, are about, seeking too often mischief, and they may soon assert themselves and cause trouble. God grant that good sense and prudence will prevail … [otherwise] not only will thousands lose their lives and millions worth of property be destroyed but the chances of a change in the present order will vanish into thin air.'

Almost ten weeks later, on 29 March, in Westport, County Mayo, came the year's second political murder when the local resident magistrate, J.C. Milling, was shot several times through the window of his home in the centre of the town and died the following day. As with the Tipperary incident, the fullest coverage and strongest denunciations were carried in the papers in closest proximity to the outrage. A total of seventeen papers carried comment or news coverage, of which eleven voiced condemnation. The *Longford Leader* (5 April) news report appeared under the sub-heading 'Public Sympathy/Crime Denounced' alongside a second report of a public meeting condemnatory of the outrage held in the town hall, Castlebar, with the parish priest, Canon Fallon, presiding. The priest had said, 'no matter what their politics were … murder was a thing which they all abhorred'. A third report was headed 'Westport Crime/Horror Expressed by the Archbishop of Tuam … This Dastardly Crime/Archbishop of Tuam's Message to Priests and People of Westport'. In the view of the *Ballina Herald* (3 April):

All right-thinking people, and they are the overwhelming majority, condemn the foul and cowardly murder of Mr J.C. Milling, RM, and in Mayo the feelings of the people are wrought to the highest pitch of indignation … the dastardly deed … a gallant and honourable gentleman, whose only crime appears to be that he did his duty … The outrage is generally condemned throughout the country and particularly in Mayo, where Mr. Milling's sterling character was fully appreciated. As a resident magistrate he was fearless in the execution of his duty, just to the last degree, and not at all harsh. Nothing in his character could have provoked or warranted any injury to his person and the motive underlying the dastardly crime, which brings disgrace on Westport, is inexplicable.

This comment appeared alongside a news report headed, 'Cowardly Murder of Mr. J. C. Milling/ General Condemnation'.

For the *Connaught Telegraph* (5 April) it was a 'ruthless assassination … a disgrace to a civilised country … [the murderer presumably was] but a mere catspaw selected to carry out the sinister designs of others, on whom the blood-guilt must equally fall and remain to curse and torture them until the grave closes over them … to destroy a young man whose boyhood was spent in the district; who was popular … a capable official who never exceeded the bounds, and above all, one bubbling over with the essence of good-fellowship, and devoid of the least guile.' A follow-up editorial in the paper a week later lamented one consequence of the assassination: the proclamation of the Westport area would mean the 'absolute ruin' of the town 'as all fairs and markets will be stopped and the supplies of seeds and manures the merchants have in stock will remain unbought'. However, it admitted that 'there is no gainsaying the fact that the people of the area affected showed little regard lately for law or order; outrages and brutal assaults, such as the blowing up with dynamite of Lord Sligo's yacht, the burning of Mr. Milling's yacht, the attack on District Inspector Neylen, the smashing of windows in Westport and the murderous assault recently on Mr. Mulley's foreman, were mere incidents in a campaign of terrorism'. The *Connacht Tribune* (5 April) mixed

Sinn Féin 'state of war' propaganda with genuine denunciation: 'No more terrible crime has occurred in the west of Ireland for many years … So far as the murderer is concerned, his identity is shrouded in mystery … So long as the British authorities maintain by covert and overt acts a state of war between England and Ireland, so long shall we have crimes and … courts and turmoil and progress-destroying strife … But whatever political views we may hold, all of us are at one in condemning this dastardly crime.'

The paper closest to the location of the assassination, the Westport-published *Mayo News*, whose republican editor, P.J. Doris, had been jailed by Milling, denounced the murder and was keen to dissociate the Sinn Féin movement from it, whether from genuine revulsion or to avoid suppression by the military authorities.[2] Under the title 'A Foul Crime' it wrote (5 April), 'Mr Milling as RM held an office not always popular, but his discharge of his duties could scarcely have created for him an enemy so bereft of Christian feeling as to desire to take his life.' The unionist press was trying 'to give the crime a political tinge' and to fasten it on the 'popular organisation', but this was no 'Sinn Féin raid for arms'. Mr Milling 'would be the last man to suggest that the people of Westport were the wild murderous race that the Unionist chronicles would now paint them. We can only hope that the truth may be brought to light, and that justice may overtake the perpetrator of as brutal a murder as has ever stained the fair name of our country. It is difficult to write calmly of such an occurrence … The popular feeling is clearly disclosed in the whole-hearted sympathy extended to the widow of the victim.' A follow-up editorial on 17 May alluded to the effects of the martial law proclaimed in Westport since the murder, which would form 'one of the blackest chapters in the very black history of the so-called Irish Government … They have adopted in this peaceful district the methods attributed to the Germans in the occupation [of Belgium] … [and] set all the military and police forces to the task of victimising an unarmed and peaceful people to camouflage their own ineptitude'.

Some newspapers avoided moral disapproval in their editorial comment on killings of police, or drew a different moral. The *Westmeath Independent* (12 April), commenting on an incident at Limerick Hospital in which a policeman had lost his life and another was injured as they tried to prevent the rescue of a prisoner (who was also shot and later died), wrote that 'the sad tragedy stands out by itself – apart from recent happenings in other parts of the country – as a melancholy illustration of what incompetent political administration, supported by the forces of prejudice and reaction in authority, can produce'. Following the Tipperary and Westport killings, other papers began to push back against the practice of publishing clerical denunciations of such actions. In April, Bishop Denis Kelly of Ross (a man of wide abilities who had been closely associated with the Irish Party as an expert adviser on the finances of Home Rule) gave a homily in the pro-cathedral in Skibbereen, in which he condemned 'deeds done in Ireland that were greatly against the doctrine of Our Lord' and that only invited further coercion. The *Southern Star* (26 April), now effectively a Sinn Féin organ, reminded readers that, three years previously, the bishop had called the Easter rebellion 'murder pure and simple' and the work of German agency. Referring to 'the imperialistic Bishop of Ross', it asked, 'has there been a word of condemnation from His Lordship of the Power responsible for the present state of affairs – the Power that proclaims its desire to see justice prevail, while here in Ireland it makes a mockery of justice?' When the homily was attacked shortly afterwards in the pages of the 'Catholic Bulletin', *The Kerryman* (17 May) reprinted the critical article.

By late August, 14 policemen had been shot, nine of them fatally, in ambushes and assassinations. Local clerical condemnation often, but not always, followed these incidents. At the level of the senior clergy, however, a firm condemnation of violence was not forthcoming. In October, the head of the Catholic hierarchy, Cardinal Logue, Archbishop of Armagh, who had called republican violence 'lawlessness, retaliation and crime such as any man guided by God's law must regret and reprobate', sought to obtain agreement from his fellow bishops on a united statement of denunciation, but had to drop the idea, having failed to win unanimity. According to Charles Townshend, the number of recorded public statements of clergy for or against republican violence in the years 1919–21 is very small, but denunciations outnumbered statements of support by almost three to one (144 Irish priests spoke against IRA military actions as against fifty who spoke in support, together representing about 5 per cent of a total of 3,700 Irish priests).[3] However, since those priests who spoke out tended to be located close to the areas of most intense violence, notably the south-western counties, this figure probably under-represents the real incidence of clerical denunciation.

Lay condemnation was also voiced at meetings of elected public bodies. The *Irish News* (12 August) reported on a meeting of Dublin Corporation that had passed a resolution condemning 'the outrages which are and have been occurring in Dublin and throughout the country' and commented 'The Government's responsibility for evil conditions in Ireland cannot be denied by anyone who has not abandoned all regard for truth; but no one can seriously contend that anything of which even the British Government are capable could justify, excuse or palliate deeds as cowardly as they are odious, as harmful as they are criminal'. The *Cork Examiner* (22 August) published a report of the quarterly meeting of Westmeath County Council, which had unanimously adopted a resolution condemning 'in the strongest terms our language can afford the murders and outrages occurring throughout the country'. The proposer, P.M. Kenna, Justice of the Peace, said that 'A storm of indignation should go forth from the elected representatives of the people. The instigators of these crimes are no acquisition to any political party or organisation … we believe they are inspired by dangerous pests of society'. The *Derry Journal* (17 December) reported on an ambush at Dungloe that had left four policemen injured and added: 'Yesterday the Donegal county council adopted a resolution from the Tipperary county council expressing horror at the outrages that have occurred in that county and throughout Ireland generally. We condemn, the resolution added, in the strongest possible manner such outrages and register our belief that such acts are the acts of irresponsible persons, with whom no responsible member could have the slightest sympathy'. Such condemnations would diminish after 1919 as the shock value of violent incidents wore off amid an ever more chaotic situation, and the policy of Crown force reprisals took hold with the introduction of the Black and Tans and Auxiliaries in the second half of 1920 (see below, p. 212)

On 2 September, a party of the Irish Republican Army (IRA, the name now used by the Irish Volunteers) ambushed an RIC patrol at Lorrha, north Tipperary, killing a sergeant and wounding a constable who died shortly afterwards. The attack was immediately denounced as murder, from the pulpit and elsewhere, by the parish priest, Father Gleeson, who urged the parishioners to help the authorities in having the perpetrators brought to justice: 'The sin of Cain has been committed in the peaceful parish of Lorrha; the widow and children are plunged into lifelong grief by the murder of their father. The brand of Cain lies on the assassins … the murderers, if they escape human justice, will not escape divine justice … Their fate is worse than the fate of the man who has been shot'. The *Midland Tribune* (13 September) on its front page carried reports of the shooting and of its denunciation by Fr Gleeson. Inside, its editorial took issue with the priest on the grounds that his sermon had been praised by the 'ultra-Tory' London *Morning Post*. It challenged him to substantiate his claim that 'fifteen men are appointed in each district to shoot the police', and to give the names of those who had told him.

The *Westmeath Independent* (13 September) would pass no moral judgment on such violent acts, but claimed that the real cause of violence in Ireland was that the country had been 'deprived of civil government' for the previous three years and was 'occupied by a foreign army as Belgium was occupied by Von Bissing [the Prussian governor general of occupied Belgium from 1914 to 1917] and his Germans during the war period. It was through that occupation the civil peace had been so disturbed'.[4] A second editorial, titled 'Tarnishing Our Own', dealt with the subject of clerical condemnation:

By some extraordinary kink in the composition of the national character readily understandable in the case of those running the Unionist Press, whose mission is obvious, there is a too ready acceptance by others – who ought to be friendly or, at least, impartial of the belief and opinion – that these happenings [shootings and reprisals] *are the work of the people. In a recent issue we were obliged to comment on the attitude of the Westmeath county council in this respect* [see above]. *In respect to the death of the police sergeant at Lorrha, who was a stranger to the district, and for whose death there was, from the people's standpoint, not even the suggestion of motive, we cannot help feeling pained and disgusted at the acrimonious invective harangue of the Parish Priest, Fr Gleeson, on Sunday last, to which the English Tory Press and the Irish Unionist Press have given conspicuous prominence.*

The *Donegal Vindicator* (12 September), however, would not ignore the assassinations. Attempting to condemn them without causing offence to Sinn Féin, the paper hinted at dark conspiracies: 'But who has given the excuse? Who prompts the deliberate and unjustifiable murder of policemen on patrol, and who orders the shooting of soldiers going to church? … the police and military act as recruiting sergeants for Sinn Féin, or whatever other organisation is working the outrages. We hardly believe it is Sinn Féin, and would not be surprised in the least if time should reveal a great Sergeant Sheridan conspiracy. We all know that these shootings are the only possible way to prevent some measure of liberty being given to Ireland. Why then should Sinn Féin adopt cold-blooded murder as its policy? We do not believe it has, and never will believe it.' It seems that such speculative distancing of Sinn Féin from the violence was judged too mealy-mouthed by part of its readership, since two weeks later the paper claimed that its last comments had been misunderstood: 'We hold firmly the opinion that Sinn Féin as an organisation has no hand in the dastardly murdering of police or soldiers from behind fences', which was being done to turn American opinion against the Irish claim to Home Rule or independence.

C. THE PARIS PEACE CONFERENCE

The Paris Peace Conference convened at the Palace of Versailles on 18 January 1919, and the processes and treaties generated by it went on until 1923, but most of the participation of senior statesmen took place between January and June 1919. Apart from the Great Powers – the United Kingdom, France, Italy, Japan and the United States – the only subject peoples invited were those formerly ruled by the defeated Central Powers – Germany, Austria–Hungary and the Ottoman Empire. Delegates of nations seeking independence from the victorious powers, such as the Irish and Vietnamese (the latter from French Indo-China), were not summoned. For an issue that had been central to Sinn Féin's general election campaign, the question of the presentation of the Irish case to the conference received surprisingly little coverage, with only five papers expressing hopes or support, and one scepticism, for the venture. The *Kilkenny People* (5 April) wrote that the conference must address Great Britain's denial of Irish freedom: 'Even if British rule in this country had been tolerable, the claim of Ireland to the right of self-determination would be none the less impregnable … If the Peace Conference is really determined to create a new order of things, if pious sentiments are not its stock-in-trade, if it is anxious to deal out even-handed justice – as it admittedly has the power to do – it will put an end to this state of things'. The *Donegal Vindicator* (4 April) was sure that the Irish case could not be ignored:

> *The Peace Conference is not too peaceful and, unless a speedy decision is arrived at, there is danger of much trouble, and always with the possibility that disagreements may crop up … The situation as regards Ireland has developed during the week. An influential delegation from the Irish Conference in America has been given passports, and the three members are well on their way to Paris. They cannot be ignored, if it should happen that the big Four are still in session, and that the peace terms have not been definitely settled. 'Ireland*

is not at the Conference, but Ireland cannot be kept out', is a phrase destined to become historical.

The *Leinster Leader* (5 April) based its optimism on what it took to be the state of foreign public opinion:

The Irish case for self-determination is gaining a growing sympathy amongst the delegates of the nationalities at the Peace Conference. The French press is also practically unanimous in the advocacy of the Irish cause, and this despite the propaganda carried on against it. America, as latest particulars allowed to filter through reveal, has undergone an extraordinary transformation from the pictures presented to us by the British press during the war, of the hostility to Ireland owing to the refusal of the people to follow the lead of the Irish Parliamentary Party, and identify their country with the war against the Central Powers. The neutral countries too have forgotten their resentment and animosity, and Ireland, so far from being isolated and friendless, lacks nothing [in] goodwill among the nations today.

A week later, however, as the *Connaught Telegraph* reported (12 April), the hearing of the Irish case was the last thing on the conference's mind:

Things are not going very smoothly at the Peace Conference; on Monday a 'smash-up' was reported ... After five months' deliberation the delegates have not been able to achieve anything while Bolshevism has swept all before it, and a big outbreak is hourly expected in Germany ... For months the Peace Conference was like a mutual admiration society, but learned platitudes, champagne suppers, banquets and grand opera did not feed the starving, satisfy the revolutionaries and now we have the result ... Evidently the PC has been a fiasco, despite all we were told, and this was expected having regard to the condition of Russia and Germany.

The *Sligo Champion* (17 May) put its modest hopes in a delegation of Irish–Americans that had toured Ireland during April. During their brief stay, it wrote, they had come in close touch with 'tyrannical methods, under an alien government, by which those aspirations [of the Irish people] are being repressed and thwarted'. 'Their progress through the country was one long triumphal march,' it added, perhaps incongruously for a country groaning under alien tyranny. They had seen 'two typical displays of the power of might over right': firstly, 'Prussianism' in its most aggressive form when their way to the Mansion House civic reception was blocked by 'a small army of British soldiers with ... all the apparatus of war'; and later when they were prevented from entering Westport (during the aftermath of the Milling murder). 'On their return to Paris,' wrote the paper, 'the Commissioners will have something to tell the international peacemakers—on their return to the United States they will have something to tell the Americans.' However, on the same day, the unapologetically Redmondite *Longford Leader* was claiming that the Peace Conference was already 'over and its work done'. With bitter *schadenfreude*, it added: 'the one painful fact that emerged from its deliberations is that the name of Poor Ireland, the most enslaved and persecuted, as well as the oldest nation in Europe was not so much as mentioned at the conference from beginning to end. The so-called Irish Ambassador in Paris never got inside the door of the Conference ... This is the end of all the blatherskite with which Ireland was deceived and betrayed up to the last moment. Nonentities whom a malign fate has, for the moment, put in a false position in Ireland have gone about the country telling the fools who believed them that Sinn Féin would force the doors of the Peace Conference and insist on Ireland's case being heard'.

The *Longford Leader* was a little premature in writing off the conference, as not all diplomatic initiatives had yet been exhausted. In June, Sinn Féin sent a two-man delegation to Paris to present a 3,000-word letter titled 'Official Memorandum in support of Ireland's demand for recognition as a sovereign independent state' to the French Premier Georges Clemenceau.[5] Much of the document, in asserting Ireland's nationhood and right to self-government, advanced positive reasons as to why its independence would benefit the international order. However, it failed to mention Ulster, an obstacle that, if anything, had been strengthened by the fact that the Irish demand had moved beyond Home Rule. And more importantly for the immediate reception of the submission, it included an acid jibe at British motives in the recent war that might have gone down well at election hustings in Ireland (though not in August 1914) but exhibited a remarkable tone-deafness to the requirements of international diplomacy in 1919:

The Irish people have never believed in the sincerity of the public declarations of English statesmen in regard to their 'war aims', except in so far as those declarations avowed England's part in the war to have been undertaken for England's particular and Imperial interests. They have never believed that England went to war for the sake of France or Belgium or Serbia, or for the protection or liberation of small nationalities, or to make right prevail against armed might.

To expect Premier Clemenceau, whose country had just emerged from four years of unparalleled suffering shared with the British allies who had unquestionably gone to war to defend it, even to read beyond this point was naive in the extreme, and it can be no surprise that the memorandum received no reply.

By early August, hopes were fading that anything would come of the initiative, and the *Kilkenny People* (9 August) was writing of the 'so-called Peace Conference'. The *Derry People* (30 August) kept flickering hopes alive:

'It is generally recognised in political circles here that the British Government has decided on letting matters go on just as they were, and that nothing whatever can be hoped for until the voice of America is heard unmistakeably in support of the demand for National freedom. Mr Lloyd George is completely in the hands of the Tory reactionaries in England ... and so he is content to wait and see how far America is prepared to go before formulating any scheme

of settlement. It is not generally known that all during the Paris Conference the relations between Mr Lloyd George and President Wilson were not by any means of a friendly character. A leading US journalist … informed me recently that after the first weeks the British Prime Minister and America's President were scarcely on speaking terms.

The *Connacht Tribune* (20 September) shared with readers its intelligence on the reasons for Ireland's failure to gain a hearing at the peace conference – 'now revealed for the first time by President Wilson'. He had been forced to this revelation by the pressure of his political opponents in the States:

The contention of British politicians, which their own attitude on the Irish Question has prevented them espousing openly, is that the relations of Britain with this country being purely a 'domestic concern' could not in any way or at any time affect the peace of the world. Therefore the Question remained to be settled in England's own good time … Let us examine President Wilson's attitude on the Question. It is worth quoting in extenso the direct answers that he has just given to [one of the] questions put to him by the San Francisco Labour Council:

'Q: Why was the case of Ireland not heard at the Peace Conference, and what is your position on the subject of the self-determination of Ireland?

A: The case of Ireland was not heard at the Peace Conference because the Peace Conference had no jurisdiction over any question of that sort which did not affect the territories which belonged to the defeated Empires. My position on the subject of self-determination for Ireland is expressed in Article XI of the Covenant, in which, I may say, I was particularly interested, because it seemed to be necessary for the peace and freedom of the world that a forum should be created to which all people could bring any matter which was likely to affect the peace and freedom of the world.'

It was now evident, said the *Tribune*, that the only means for the Irish case to receive a hearing depended on its being brought to another table under the wing of one of the Great Powers, the most likely candidate being, of course, the US. Regarding whether the president's last answer offered a way for Ireland to progress, the paper outlined the obstacles:

> *We do not wish to buoy up our people with false hopes, already shattered at the Peace Conference, at whose doors the Irish and American delegates thundered in vain. President Wilson speaks of a forum, but the first thing that must strike the critical Nationalist, who passionately desires to see the Irish Question settled once and for all in an international tribunal is how is Ireland to gain a hearing at that forum when she failed to gain a hearing at the Peace Conference? What right of entry shall she have? None, it would appear, except upon the initiative of a nation that is a member of the League ... Will the US undertake to bring the case of Ireland before the League of Nations? That is the real question at issue ...*

Even then, there was another barrier: Great Britain would have the right of veto against the raising of 'any matter affecting their internal concerns', and it was almost certain this veto would be exercised against Ireland. In sum, the paper was not convinced that the League of Nations would right the 'century-old wrongs of Ireland'.

The *Roscommon Herald* (13 September) could explain why it was in the US president's interest to sponsor the Irish case but was even more pessimistic for the League of Nations route: 'Sir Edward Carson's last campaign inciting to potential rebellion in Ulster has already lost President Wilson the Irish vote in the US, and without the Irish as a backbone, the Democratic Party ... will be badly beaten at the next Presidential Election. Wilson cannot make any headway with his absurd "League of Nations" project, which has been practically killed by the US Senate. He attributes his defeat to the hostility of the Irish–Americans.'

The *Sligo Champion* (20 September), the paper that in 1918 had tried to bridge the Irish Party–Sinn Féin divide by calling for a bipartisan submission to the Peace Conference, now contemplated the ruin of Irish hopes. The people of Ireland had hoped that the presence of President

Wilson 'would have a telling influence on the members of that august body, and help considerably towards the realisation of Ireland's dream. The result has been a sad disappointment. Not only did he never make mention of the name of Ireland when speaking of the small nationalities of Europe, but he never even vouchsafed any explanation for the omission.' By the end of the year, disillusion was complete. The *Roscommon Herald* (20 December) quoted from a letter by the Cambridge economist J.M. Keynes under the headline 'Wilson the Dupe of the Peace Conference/Bamboozled by Lloyd George'. It was hard to deny the truth of the *Irish News* prediction that the whole episode had been 'little better than a waste of energy'.

D. REPRESSION

As hopes faded for the Paris Peace Conference initiative, the violence of the IRA escalated. In the last third of the year, thirteen more members of the RIC and the Dublin Metropolitan Police would be shot – almost as many as in the first eight months – six of them fatally. The government responded by giving the lord lieutenant, Lord French, what he had been demanding for many months as the killings increased – extended military powers and the suppression of separatist organisations. On 4 July, following the murder of an RIC district inspector in June, Sinn Féin, the Volunteers, Cumann na mBan (the Volunteers' women's organisation) and the Gaelic League were all declared illegal in Tipperary. This paved the way for the proscription of these bodies, and Dáil Éireann itself, throughout the country in September.[6] Newspapers were not long in reacting to the heightened repression. The *Donegal Vindicator* (12 September) placed the chief blame for unrest on the 'military terrorism' of the government: 'Just what Lord [Lieutenant] French thinks he is doing we fail to understand … [he is] converting moderate Nationalists into rampant Sinn Féiners by the thousand … A reign of terrorism it is in truth.'

The *Irish News* (13 September), in an editorial titled 'No One Terrified' that seemed to mix mockery of the military authorities and of Sinn Féin propaganda in equal proportions, wrote:

There seems to have been an almost unusual absence of 'excitement' throughout the country yesterday, though a large proportion of the military and police Army of Occupation were employed by Lord French in 'raiding' Sinn Féin meeting – places and clubs and the homes of private citizens from one end of Ireland to the other. Lord French has not been a soldier for nothing. If the primal war campaigns in Belgium and France had been planned by the Allies with a tithe of the completeness and attention to detail displayed by the brilliant strategists who organised the 'raids' from Cushendall to Castletownbere yesterday, an end would have been made of the war before All Saints' Day, 1914. But, of course, Lord French had the advantage of his lively, if not lengthened, experience at the French and Belgian front before he came to take charge of the Irish front.

The *Clonmel Nationalist* (13 September) took it more seriously:

The Government, having, in accord with the fantastic play-acting of the Carsonites, again refused to make any concession to Ireland's national demands, and resorted to the old Castle methods of repression and oppression, has plunged the country into a terrible state, and each turn of the coercion screw only helps to make confusion worse confounded. It is a well recognised rule that force is no remedy, and proof of it is written large on the pages of Irish history ... Ireland did wonders in the war for the freedom of democracy, but today the Irish are the only white people in slavery. England's thanks for Ireland's help in crushing Prussianism in Europe is to lash her with the Prussian whip and put the coercion screw on tighter every day ... England turns a deaf ear to the real voice of Ireland, to the counsel of her own Liberal and Labour organisations, to the insistent advice of the Press and the free governments of the world, to do prompt and generous justice to this country. She pays attention only to the mandates of the Orange Freemason gang, who rule

Dublin Castle … The Government won't apply the only remedy: they muddle along, oblivious of consequences, and allow the Carsonites and coercionists a free hand to do as they like with the country … It is a hopeless confession of failure, a striking example of the bankruptcy of British statesmanship.

The short editorial pieces of the *Galway Observer* (20 September) had a pugnacious anti-government tone, almost indistinguishable from that of Sinn Féin, despite the paper's tradition of cleaving to constitutionalism and the Irish Party. On the police raids on Sinn Féin houses, it wrote, 'We dare say the authorities are quite satisfied with their exploit; it is the English rule in Ireland; they think it is "resolute government". It could never occur to them now as in the past that Irish people look upon it as so much humbug … The government created the Sinn Féiners. They could not stand John Dillon and his followers in the House of Commons so they went on with the tactics that made Sinn Féiners'.

At the end of the year, the *Clonmel Nationalist* (13 December) would sum up the political situation at the end of 1919 in its own one-sided way:

Public and personal liberty, self-determination, and all the other precious principles for which the war was said to be waged, were set at nought and a policy pursued indelibly calculated to sow afresh the seeds of unrest and rebellion. The country was too quiet, too crimeless, to suit the Orange book: excuses had to be made for dragooning and oppressing the people. And the methods of a century ago were therefore callously resorted to … the mailed fist of the Castle was brought to bear with the old brutality and malignant effect all over the country.

On 20 August, the Dáil finally acted to bring its army under tighter control by passing a resolution that all IRA Volunteers should take an oath of allegiance to it. This was not reported on by the provincial press, most likely because it was kept secret from them. For those editors who knew, there was the fear that publicising it would add legitimacy to republican violence and subvert the 'murder gang' narrative of government propaganda, thereby inviting suppression by the authorities. The risk of this increased as the days passed. The *Nenagh Guardian* (27 September) reported that in the previous week, 'no less than 35 Irish papers, including one daily paper, have been suppressed, and the remaining newspapers have either to keep their tongues in their cheeks or court a similar fate. Since the abolition of the Irish Press Censorship … the newspapers of this country are at the mercy of the whim of every Orange Lawyer in Dublin Castle'. It expressed sympathy with sister newspapers, especially the *Midland Tribune,* 'and we are sure that the public will see that no loss in circulation or support is occasioned to the *Tribune* by the action of the self-appointed dictators'.

Fear of suppression may also account for the weak response of the provincial press to the repression itself. Only nine newspapers in the sample commented, four highlighting its futility, three of them in defiance and two in lamentation.

Repression finally reached the level of the national press on 14 December, when the *Freeman's Journal* was suppressed under the Defence of the Realm Act for publication of material alleged to harm recruiting. All copies of the paper for the following day were seized, and the production plant was removed by the military authorities. No issues appeared for the next seven weeks. The paper that had for almost two decades been a steadfast supporter of constitutional politics – though no less critical of British policies for all that – had been in poor financial health since the collapse of support from the defunct Irish Party, and had been bought in October by a local vintner, Martin Fitzgerald, and an English journalist, Robert Hamilton Edwards.[7] The seizure was met with outrage from the provincial press, with thirteen of sixteen commenting papers criticising the government's action while two reported on the debate in the House of Commons triggered by a motion from T.P. O'Connor. The *Westmeath Independent* (20 December), under the heading 'Hands off the Press', wrote that 'The *"Freeman's Journal"* has taken its place in the long list of newspapers suppressed in Ireland during the last few years. Under its new management the *"Freeman"* has adopted a National policy too vigorous to escape the wrath of the powers ruling Ireland at present … justice demands that there should be some justification for the dramatic action taken by Dublin Castle on Monday evening last.' The *Roscommon Herald* (20 December) was sceptical of the motives for the action, reminding readers that one of the new proprietors, Hamilton Edwards, was late of Britain's Northcliffe Press, and speculating that the suppression was a ruse to have the paper pose as a Castle 'martyr' to help it 'fob off some kind of Lloyd George Home Rule on the Irish public'. It forecast that the ban would be withdrawn by the end of the week. The *Kilkenny People* (20 December), already contemptuous of the *Freeman*, also smelled conspiracy and wondered at 'the extraordinary coincidence that Mr Hamilton Edwards, this "thoroughly patriotic Englishman" [as the *Daily Mail* had called him] should have forsaken Fleet St, London, for Townsend St, Dublin. Does he stand by himself, one wonders, or does he in any way represent the Northcliffe interest? As he seems to have graduated on the "stunt" press, is he really trying off one of his stunts in Ireland?' If these last two papers saw grounds to reconsider their insinuations a year later, when Fitzgerald and Edwards were imprisoned in Mountjoy Jail for a month for publishing a report on army brutality, they did not show it.

Less than a week after the *Freeman* incident, on Friday 19 December, the IRA attempted to assassinate Lord French near a gate of the Phoenix Park as he was returning to the Vice-Regal Lodge. Failing to kill the Viceroy, the attackers lost one of their own members. Of twenty-three newspapers in the sample that carried the story, only six condemned the attack or expressed relief at its failure, while seventeen reported it without comment, probably reflecting the unpopularity of French as the author of the repressive measures currently in effect. The *Dundalk Democrat* (27 December) harked back to the Phoenix Park murders of Chief Secretary Lord Frederick Cavendish and Under Secretary Thomas Burke in 1882 for a precedent: 'The Irish people as a mass are not responsible for or in sympathy with this act of criminal madness', but confessed that 'the attack on the Viceroy moves us far less than the murders, during the past year, of a dozen simple, honest

Irish policemen shot down in midnight ambuscades in quiet country places or in city streets for no reason but that they were doing their duty'.

The attack was condemned the following day by the *Irish Independent* as 'an appalling and revolting deed ... deliberate murder of any person is wrong, criminal and absolutely reprehensible, and reflects discredit on the country; but when with malice aforethought, an attempt is made to take the life of one occupying the high official position of Viceroy, the crime may have regrettable consequences here in Ireland and effects outside prejudicial to our reputation'.

On Sunday night, a group of about fifty armed and masked men entered the *Independent* office, held up the staff and proceeded to smash the machinery with sledge hammers and crowbars. A note was left in the editor's room that claimed to give the reason for the raid: 'You have outraged the sensibilities and endeavoured to misrepresent the sympathies and opinions of the Irish people'. In contrast with the official suppression of the *Freeman* a week earlier, this act of attempted suppression merited condemnation from only four of the fifteen papers that covered it, and this in tones of wounded surprise. (The newspaper found alternative printing facilities and was on the streets the following day with a full report of the raid.)[8] The *Roscommon Herald* (27 December) called it an 'outrage', especially since the *Independent* had helped Sinn Féin to win the election. The *Westmeath Independent* (27 December) was similarly shocked:

> *The destruction of the property of the Independent Newspapers is one of the most deplorable incidents which has occurred in this unhappy island of ours for many a long day. It implies that the Freedom of the Press is now no more than an empty shibboleth. On the one hand, the Government of our country, by enactions, suppressions and proclamations have put journalism in chains; on the other, it seems as if the extreme forces of Irish disaffection are working for the same ends ... The 'Independent' has not merited this outrage. It has done good service to the cause of Irish freedom. Alone it stood out against the ineptitude of the Irish Party, and for years it has been the sole organ of those who have the good of the country at heart.*

The Redmondite *Connacht Tribune* (27 December) quoted the *Independent's* denunciation of the deed, but also found 'an ironic touch in the circumstance that the "Irish Independent" did more than any other factor in Ireland to make the path easy for a Sinn Féin triumph. No doubt, in seeking the overthrow of the old Constitutional Party, our contemporary had in view the establishment of an independent party, but it reckoned without the realisation that there was no other constitutional party on the lines it advocated to take the place of that which it exercised so much misdirected zeal to overthrow.'

E. HOME RULE AGAIN

In the autumn of 1919, with the ratification of the last of the Paris peace treaties, the Home Rule Act of 1914 was due to come into effect soon if no action were taken. Since it had never been amended (the promised amending bill not having been enacted) to provide for the exclusion of the unionist counties, the Act conflicted with the British government's pledge not to coerce Ulster and so could not be allowed to come into force. The Cabinet began to consider the way forward in its Irish policy. On 7 October, it appointed a twelve-man committee under the chairmanship of Walter Long, a former leader of the Ulster Unionist Party, with the lord lieutenant, Lord French, and the chief secretary, Ian Macpherson, serving ex-officio, to map a plan of action.[9] On 4 November, the committee reported to the Cabinet that it would recommend neither the repeal nor the postponement of the 1914 Act, but would frame a new bill aimed at solving the Irish Question once and for all. There would be only two limitations: they would rule out any solution that would break up the unity of the British empire and any attempt at 'what has so often failed in the past' – the establishment of a single parliament for all Ireland.[10]

By Christmas the committee had drafted the outline of a new double Home Rule scheme – one that provided for separate Home Rule parliaments for two Irish entities, 'Southern Ireland' and a 'homogeneous north-eastern section' of the island. This was introduced in a Commons statement by Lloyd George on 22 December. The prime minister's speech left the way open to Irish unity by mutual consent: 'We propose to clothe the Irish Legislatures with full constitutional powers, so that they would be able, without reference to the Imperial Parliament, and by identical legislation, to create a single Irish Legislature discharging all or any of the powers not specifically reserved to the Imperial Parliament. It would then rest with the Irish people themselves to determine whether they want union, and how they want union.'

The speech excited comment from twenty-two newspapers, of which twenty-one were critical to the point of outright rejection while one sought to find some positive features. Comments ranged from 'utterly unworkable' (*Longford Leader*) to 'the greatest joke of the season' (*Waterford News*) to 'A Farce of a Scheme' (*Limerick Echo*). The *Roscommon Journal* (13 December) wrote: 'England has become so anxious to give us Home Rule that she hasn't time to discover that we do not want it. Of course there is an explanation of their anxiety to give us self-government. The explanation is one word – America! Woe betide us today if we had not internationalised the Irish Question.' Once again, as in 1917, the partition issue was at centre stage. The *Kilkenny People* (21 December) was not for entertaining any notions of self-determination for 'certain Ulster counties': 'Ireland asks for one Parliament with sovereign power derived from the will of the Irish people to shape the future destinies of the country, untrammeled and uncontrolled by an alien authority. Mr Lloyd George seeks to force on her two so-called legislatures, one for certain Ulster counties and the other for the rest of Ireland, neither of them possessing any real power … such a transparent humbug… a miserable, makeshift measure … a legislative abortion that is really certain to be strangled before its birth as an Act of Parliament.' For the *King's County Independent* (27 December), it was evidence once again that 'there is no genuine desire on the part of the English

Government to deal fairly or justly with the Irish people'. In bold lettering it continued:

> *The Nation is to be split in two, the bleeding of Irish resources and wealth is to continue, and in all matters of National importance, England is to reign supreme! This belated attempt to throw dust in American eyes will serve but to arouse afresh the contempt we have always felt for the would-be Machiavellian and treacherous methods of English politicians ... One thing is sure: Neither Mr Lloyd George nor his Carsonite slave-drivers have ever for one moment thought that the Irish people would entertain the absurd proposals which have been so brazenly advanced as a 'settlement'.*

The *Galway Observer* (27 December) predicted that:

> *Ireland, Nationalist and Sinn Féin, will unite in opposition to the plan now proposed. Two and a half years ago Mr Lloyd George was prepared to offer 'the largest measure of Home Rule' possible in the circumstances of the war. His plan then was the Home Rule Act with six counties excluded, their exclusion to be reviewable every five years. Now he proposes to give legislative validity to the permanent veto of 'Ulster' over effective Home Rule for the rest of Ireland, to emasculate the Home Rule Act, and to retain 15 millions a year of Irish revenue until such time as a Joint Exchequer Board may adjust Irish taxation to Irish capacity ... a political cynic's bad joke at the expense of a nation which he has thrown into chaos.*

The *Wexford People* (27 December) claimed 'the country from end to end is seething with unrest and discontent ... Mr Lloyd George's contribution to restore harmony turns out just as people expected. It will not be accepted in Ireland: its partition proposals, apart from everything else, damn it at once'.

Only the *Tuam Herald* (29 November) had anything positive to say, and that was when it had gleaned a preview of the proposals a month before the official statement. It speculated that the hoped-for plan of settlement would 'provide for two provincial parliaments, one for Southern Ireland and another for the Ulster Province, with a dominant Central Parliament controlling both legislatures'. The paper seemed to assume that the 'central' body would be there from the start rather than come into being only by the joint agreement of the other two. However, it was at least willing to consider a scheme that it called 'an acknowledgement of the difficulty of otherwise dealing with Ulster than by provincial partition'.

During the following eighteen months, the slow progress of this bill, the principles it contained – partition and retention of a British connection – and its implementation would form the unchanging political backdrop to the grim events that provided the newspapers with their daily headlines.

Chapter 7

WAR AND PARTITION, JANUARY 1920–JULY 1921

A. 'MURDER MOST FOUL'

In January 1920, urban council elections, using proportional representation, gave Sinn Féin majorities in nine out of eleven municipalities and in sixty-two of ninety-nine urban councils, including the cities of Dublin, Cork and Limerick, while a Nationalist [former Irish Party]–Sinn Féin coalition won a majority of seats in Londonderry/Derry, giving nationalists control of that city for the first time since 1690. In the local elections in the rest of the country on 12 June, Sinn Féin took control of twenty-eight of the thirty-two county councils and 172 of 206 rural district councils. These local government results were an emphatic endorsement of the general election outcome of December 1918. Throughout the year, the new councils would gradually withdraw their allegiance to the government-sponsored Local Government Board and transfer it to Dáil Éireann as 'the duly elected government of the Irish people'. In May, the unionist *Irish Times* lamented that 'the whole south of Ireland has fallen under the government of Sinn Féin'.[1]

A month-long respite followed the IRA's assassination attempt on the lord lieutenant, but by late January 1920 it had resumed and intensified its campaign of assassination, ambush and attacks on police barracks. Policemen were now being killed at the rate of one every five days; in the two months between 20 January and 20 March, sixteen members of the RIC and (DMP) were shot, twelve fatally, along with a former resident magistrate and banking lawyer, almost equalling the police death toll for the whole of 1919.[2] This attrition, combined with the effects of the boycott of the RIC begun in 1919, the intimidation of police families that peaked during 1920 and the abandonment of many barracks following attacks, induced many members to resign or take early retirement from the force. During May, June and July, 566 men resigned from the RIC, forcing the further closure of smaller barracks in remote regions and leaving large areas of the south and west unpoliced.[3]

The vacuum in policing left the way open for a popular takeover of the justice system, especially in the south and west and in areas of agrarian agitation. In response, the Dáil in August 1919 announced a scheme of national arbitration courts. Even before the Dáil ministry had finally approved the scheme the following summer, local courts were set up in many districts with prominent members of the community acting as judges. Though many of these courts were run by local factions or were Volunteer 'courts martial', the first court set up directly under Dáil authority heard its first case in County Mayo on 17 May 1920. By that date, the police in many areas were reporting that 'Sinn Féin Courts' had 'practically put an end to Quarter Sessions and Petty Sessions'. The *Irish Times* wrote in June that 'the King's writ runs no longer in many parts of the country'. Through the summer and autumn, the new courts gradually acquired recognition as a popularly sanctioned and fairly administered system of justice, even from those hostile to Sinn Féin. The southern Unionist Lord Dunraven admitted to *The Times* that 'an illegal government has become the *de facto* government. Its jurisdiction is recognised. It administers justice promptly and equitably and we are in this curious dilemma that the civil administration of the country is carried on under a system the existence of which the *de jure* government does not and cannot acknowledge, and is carried on very well'.[4]

A symptom of the general disorder in early 1920, one that threatened to overwhelm the new courts system, was the resurgence of agrarian agitation to a level not seen since the Land War of 1882.[5] This agitation took a particularly violent turn, involving the methods if not the personnel of the IRA, in the case of a notable murder in County Galway, that of a civilian, Frank Shawe-Taylor, JP, a land agent and former High Sheriff of the county, who was ambushed and shot dead on 3 March while motoring to Galway Fair.[6] The headlines of the *Connacht Tribune's* report (13 March) told the story of the 'Moorpark Murder' and its aftermath: 'Vigorous Condemnation of the Coshla Outrage/"Foul Inhuman Crime"/Athenry Priests and the Shooting/Protestant Bishop's Reference/... Clergy's Condemnation/Murder Strongly Denounced by the Rev Father Lynch CC' (as a 'cold-blooded, brutal, inhuman and callous crime').

Provincial press and clerical reaction to the political murders was mostly confined, as in the previous year, to the localities of their occurrence. That changed on 20 March with the reprisal murder of Thomas MacCurtain, lord mayor of Cork, a prominent member of Sinn Féin and also the commander of Cork No. 1 IRA Brigade. The murderers were later found by an official inquest to be a group of policemen with blackened faces who forced their way into his home at night. The crime and its circumstances, taking place in front of the victim's wife and child, caused nationwide shock, with eleven of twenty-five commenting papers registering their horror and seven more casting it as part of a government conspiracy; a further seven placed it in the context of the other recent political murders. Several editorials carried the title 'Murder Most Foul' (*Cork Examiner, Meath Chronicle, Limerick Echo*). The *Dundalk Democrat* (27 March) called it 'mysterious and peculiarly horrible'; the *Killarney Echo* (27 March) gave it full news page coverage under the headline 'The Murder Gang'; the *Mayo News* (27 March) called it 'A Foul Murder' that had 'thrilled the country with horror and aroused feelings which will not easily be allayed'. The last paper's editor, P.J. Doris, revealed that he had served time in Reading Jail with MacCurtain, whose word as commandant, he said, 'was law'. Most papers, while publicising the victim's status as Sinn Féin lord mayor, were much more reticent on the question of his position in the IRA.

Two pro-Sinn Féin papers were ambivalent in their responses to the wider implications of the murder. The *Leinster Leader* (27 March) wrote obscurely of the need for 'the restraint of passions and the patient enduring of the trials and tribulations that the country is undergoing. The past week has provided a particularly bloody chapter to contemporary history, and an exhibition of the effects of the attempt to rule a people by force'. The *Midland Tribune* (20 March), in what may have been veiled criticism of the policy of assassination of police, hinted at a broader context for the crime: 'Every morning brings sinister news. Ireland is passing through a period of great trial, and it behoves the people to be thoroughly on their guard, and to give no provocation which may be used against them by those who are opposed to their national aspirations'. The Redmondite *Westmeath Examiner* (27 March) was more forthright in setting the murder against the background of recent events: 'they [the series of recent murders] are clearly a violation of the law of God and an usurpation of the authority of the Almighty, which cannot be justified by any motive, cause or object in view. The most noteworthy of these horrible tragedies was the murder on Friday night of the Lord Mayor of Cork under circumstances of atrocious brutality and cold-blooded callousness.' The *Munster News* (3 April), with no idea that much worse was to come, wrote: 'March 1920 will probably rank as one of the black dates in our history. Never has the land been so harassed by criminals; never have so many isolated tragedies been crowded into a few days; never have life and property and public peace been so completely at the mercy of the enemies of society'.

The *Munster Express* (20 March) had reported on an earlier tragedy in County Kilkenny, the armed attack on Hugginstown RIC Barracks in which a young policeman, Constable Ryan, was killed. The account included a letter from Most Reverend Dr Brownrigg, Bishop of Ossory to the parish priest, deploring the 'sad and distressing' attack by a large crowd of assailants heavily armed in which 'an innocent and inoffensive policeman met with a sudden and violent death while discharging his duty… [at the hands of] misguided young men'. A week later, when most other papers were fully focused on the MacCurtain case, this paper carried no coverage at all, but returned to the Hugginstown Barracks story with a report of the scathing comments of Lord Justice Ronan at the Grand Jury Assizes at Kilkenny - 'an appalling state of things in a civilised country … a gallant, courageous, daring band estimated at from 60 to 200 came to that place with shotguns, slug, hand grenades and bombs, and proceeded to storm and fire into that house and on the woman and her 5 or 6 children, and they murdered one policeman.' The same issue also carried news of the 'gruesome tragedy' of Constable Murtagh, shot dead in Cork on 17 March while attending church.

By contrast, the *Leinster Leader* (27 March), which could see only blood spilled by agents of the government, noted, 'A horror-stricken country had scarcely recovered from the shock of the murder of the Lord Mayor of Cork under circumstances that stamped it with a callousness and cruelty, altogether un-Irish, than the streets of Dublin are stained with the blood of defenceless men and women shot by British soldiers [a reference to the shooting dead of two civilians by soldiers returning to barracks who had come under stone-throwing and gunfire at Portobello Bridge] … But while this is taking place English politicians complacently look on unmoved.' The *Meath Chronicle* (27 March) called the MacCurtain murder 'an abominable crime' but seemed fatalistic in its acceptance of the logic of war: 'we have only to hope, as indeed we do hope and expect, that should the trial come to other homes, as it may, that the same Spartan spirit will prevail, and that the example of the Lady Mayoress of Cork in the simplicity of its nobility will be followed.'

Speculation as to the identity of the perpetrators was short-lived, and most nationalist organs were soon in no doubt that it was the work of enemies of Sinn Féin. The *Kilkenny People* (3 April) lambasted the *Daily Mail* for claiming 'on unimpeachable authority that official inquiries in Ireland have proved beyond doubt that Alderman Thomas MacCurtain, the Sinn Féin Lord Mayor of Cork … was actually the victim of Sinn

Féin vengeance.' The *Irish News* (23 March) in an editorial titled 'A Reign of Terror' wrote, 'We do not know who murdered MacCurtain, nor Constable Murtagh, nor Professor Stockley, nor Constable Scully, nor the ex-soldier Quinlisk nor John Charles Byrne nor many other gruesome and appalling tragedies'. But there must be suspicion, it added, regarding the alacrity of the authorities in getting to the scene of the crime within an hour – was it to remove evidence, as many believed and as T.P. O'Connor asked Chief Secretary Macpherson in the House of Commons?

The *Drogheda Argus* (27 March) drew an anti-unionist political lesson:

> *No matter who is responsible, the lesson to be drawn from the perplexing position is the hopelessness of expecting anything but chaos and worse to come from the present system of government, and especially so long as the supposed 'law and order' is administered by despots at Dublin Castle ... On reading the proceedings of the Coroner's inquiry at the Lord Mayor's death one is dubious ... The country has been deluged in blood, and the responsibility for the importing of arms whereby such outrages were perpetrated must be left at the door of Carson and those who aided and abetted him in his drilling and arming the Ulster Volunteers. Those who did so are now members of the present government. The Irish people, or the majority of them, could not be blamed for showing the Cabinet that this was a game that two could play at.*

The IRA continued to escalate its campaign, its killings in the second quarter of 1920 reaching almost double the toll of the first, and then almost quadrupling again in the third. The number of policemen shot in the second was the same as in the first quarter; the increase was accounted for mostly by a rise in the number of civilians killed, from one to sixteen. This resulted from two causes: the onset of reprisals by the police and army for IRA killings, and the outbreak of sectarian violence on the streets of Londonderry/Derry. In early April, the IRA burned over 300 abandoned RIC barracks in rural areas and almost 100 income tax offices. The 'Black and Tans', recruited in January, had first appeared on the streets in late March. The pattern soon became established of an ambush or assassination of a policeman being followed by the arrival of a lorry load of Black and Tans who proceeded to burn homes and businesses in the nearby town and sometimes fire indiscriminately at the civilian population. One of the first of these reprisals took place in Miltown Malbay, County Clare, on 14 April, when a joint British army–police detachment fired into a crowd gathered to welcome home hunger strikers just released from prison in Dublin, shooting fifteen civilians, three of them fatally.

Violence came to a previously peaceful Tuam, County Galway, on 19 July, when an IRA unit ambushed a police party, killing two RIC men. That night, a squad of police reinforcements rampaged through the town, firing and throwing grenades, and burning the town hall and a drapery business. The *Tuam Herald* (31 July), in an editorial titled 'An Anxious and an Awful Time' summed up the savage realities of daily life: 'Never before in the chequered history of this ever-distracted country did things look so bad, was the prospect so gloomy … as it is at this moment. Day after day, nay hour after hour, the sad tale of murder, lawlessness, disorder and outrage keeps mounting up … The floodgates of disorder seem open and the most appalling crimes are being openly committed. The systematic murder of unfortunate policemen is followed on their part by passionate reprisals and fierce retaliations …' The *Ballina Herald* (12 August), in its weekly column written by the *Tuam Herald's* proprietor, R.J. Kelly KC, a kind of surrogate editorial, commented that, 'Day after day, nay hour after hour, the sad tale of murder, lawlessness, disorder and outrage keeps mounting up until, as the patriotic Bishop of Ross said in that impressive address we printed elsewhere, "the country is on the brink of destruction". The floodgates of disorder seem open and the most appalling crimes are being openly committed … The systematic murder of unfortunate policemen is followed on their part by passionate reprisals and fierce retaliations, of which we had an awful example in the town of Tuam …'

The *Wexford People* (28 August) wrote:

We repeat our denunciation of the taking of human life, whether by military, police or civilians. There cannot be any justification for it. The terrible provocation the people of Ireland have been receiving for a long time, dreadful though it is, does not justify the taking of human life. Nor does the shooting of policemen justify the reprisals that follow, evidently part and parcel of a pre-arranged programme – the wholesale burning of shops, the looting and destruction of property … If they cannot bring culprits to justice they are surely not warranted in wreaking vengeance on innocent householders and businessmen.

B. THE NEW HOME RULE BILL

At the end of March 1920, the House of Commons passed, by 348 votes to ninety-four, the Second Reading of the Government of Ireland Bill, introduced the previous December by Lloyd George to near-universal rejection by Irish nationalists (see Chapter 6). Not only did the bill embody partition, setting up two Home Rule parliaments – one for twenty-six counties, the other for six – but the powers ceded to them were extremely limited. As with previous Home Rule bills, services 'reserved' to Westminster control included matters relating to the Crown, peace or war, defence forces, foreign policy and the judiciary. However, the new bill also reserved, initially at least, the postal services, income tax, transport, agriculture and health, matters which had been devolved under the 1914 Home Rule Act. The condition, and the incentive, for obtaining enlarged powers in these areas lay in the bill's other feature – the all-island Council of Ireland, a body to be set up by mutual agreement between the two devolved parliaments.

The press response was predictable. Republican and Redmondite organs were united in condemnation, with seventeen of eighteen commenting organs dismissing it outright, many labelling it 'The Partition Bill'. The *Meath Chronicle* (20 March) wrote, 'The abortion passed prior to the war, and which will be repealed, should the present Bill become an Act, was a generous and fair attempt at settlement in comparison with the latest measure … All Ireland … have declared against partition … it is not practical politics and can never become a "fait accompli" … a gigantic fraud'. The Redmondite *Westmeath Examiner* (3 April) called it 'Naked Partition … an absolute travesty of Home Rule'. From its similar perspective, the *Drogheda Argus* (3 April) agreed: 'What the country wants is Colonial Home Rule; what the country does not want is being inflicted on it in the shape of a Partition Bill. The Education Bill was a bitter pill which the Irish people were asked to swallow, but the Partition Bill was the limit.' The *Munster News* (3 April) reckoned that the sole reason for bringing in this bill was to repeal the 1914 Home Rule Act at the behest of Carson: 'the Act of 1914 was Asquith's betrayal of solemn pledges; the Act of 1920 is Lloyd George's submission to his master, Carson'.

The *Derry Journal* (24 March) made its own connections between the violence and the political stalemate: 'It is becoming plain the objects of those in high places who pretend to impartially exercise governmental jurisdiction are by deliberately provocative and aggressive acts, on the one hand, and by glaring neglect of their obvious duties on the other – plunging the country not alone into a condition of intense general indignation and insecurity, but into a deep abyss of distraction, desperation and ever-present danger resembling what is recorded of the leaders of the Red armies of Russia.'

C. SECTARIAN VIOLENCE ERUPTS IN ULSTER

The *Derry People* (12 June) in an editorial titled 'Unionism Dead', exulted in the result of the local elections: 'North and South, East and West, the Sinn Féin candidates have swept the field and nowhere has their success been more remarkable than in the Province of Ulster. Henceforward, let us hope, we will hear less of the two-nations theory and less of the demand for the segregation of any part of Ulster from the rest of Ireland.'

It was an old nationalist trope that dated back to the 1880s – the notion that the political aspirations of the Ulster unionist community could be eradicated at a stroke by the result of an election. The blow to the unionist psyche in Derry was severe, and exacerbated the latent sectarian tensions in that city and across the province (if the word sectarian is understood as concerning not purely religious/theological issues but those of cultural/national identity, of which confessional allegiance is the most visible marker).

In early 1914, when armed battalions of the UVF were marching on the streets of Ulster, John Redmond had twice intervened to avert sectarian clashes in the tense atmosphere of Derry, once by asking the local bishop to have a nationalist public meeting called off, the second time to cancel a route march of a Derry unit of the Irish Volunteers. Carson had met Redmond's desire for peace by issuing strict orders to officers of (UVF) units to 'Restrain the hotheads ... Remember we have no quarrel with our nationalist neighbours'.[7] A measure of the deterioration in the situation in six years was that now, in early June 1920, the successors of those Volunteers were not merely marching but intent on extending their armed attacks to majority-unionist districts, as they demonstrated by attacking police barracks in Counties Down and Tyrone and killing a policeman in County Armagh. Although the attacks were incompetently carried out, they ignited an eruption of serious sectarian rioting and gunfire in Derry city over a week in mid-June that led to the deaths of nineteen people (fifteen Catholics and four Protestants).[8] The *Anglo-Celt* (26 June) headlined its report 'Civil War in Derry/Street Battles and Sniping for Six Days'. The *Drogheda Argus* (26 June) drew a connection between the violence and the local election result:

> *The mere thought of having to surrender the Northern Frontier came as a shock to the 'Die Hards', and despite all the wire-pulling of the British Government, which is now recognised as a mere tool and plaything of Sir Edward Carson, the fact remains that the Catholic population is now in the majority in Derry City ... but this grim outstanding fact was too much for the Tory 'true blues'*

to stomach, and consequently they resorted to armed violence to the Catholic population, and they did so in no unmistakeable style … The fact remains, however, that when life and property are in the greatest danger the military are not protecting them.

The *Derry Journal* (2 July) went further in explaining the violence as a government conspiracy: 'The tragedy of Derry is an instance of the infamous endeavours which are being made to divide the Irish people against itself. It was hoped by those who promoted the riots that the whole Province of Ulster would blaze with sectarian war, and the Irish people be so weakened by the holocaust that the British Government could feel certain of retaining its grip upon the nation. The shameful plot has failed.' The British government had believed the Derry riots would inflame sectarian passion in Belfast, but nothing of the kind happened – 'the most hopeful sign we have yet been given that Ulster workers have begun to realise who their real enemies are … [the interests of British Imperialism].'

These hopes, based on notions of Labour solidarity, were not borne out: just a few weeks later, the same paper reported (26 July) a second explosion of sectarian violence in Derry that left an estimated forty people dead, and a new outbreak in Belfast: 'The terrible ordeal of Derry last month descended on Belfast last week with, as in the former case, lamentable results in loss of life, in personal injuries, and in widespread destruction of property.' IRA attacks on the Belfast tax offices (all but one were burned down) brought about the revival of the pre-war UVF. The normal tensions associated with the Twelfth of July holiday in that city boiled over a few days later, after the assassination in Cork of an RIC senior officer and his funeral in his home town, Banbridge, County Down. An angry meeting of Protestant shipyard workers was convened that condemned the IRA penetration of Ulster. In the week after 21 July, there followed the violent and traumatic expulsion from the Harland and Wolff shipyards, and from factories such as the Sirocco engineering works, of some 5,000 Catholic workers and other members of trade unions affiliated to the Irish Labour Party, some of whom were beaten or thrown into the water.[9] Gunfights between members of the UVF and armed nationalists produced a death toll of twenty-two in the city. The *Irish News* (21, 22 June) claimed that the violence was 'begun by mobs acting under "Unionist" inspiration'. Unionist leaders had either lent themselves or lost control, it alleged, and the government had not raised a little finger though it had full wartime resources at its disposal. 'Has Carsonite rule already come into being?' the paper asked. This episode was the start of a two-year cycle of violence that would see at least 450 people killed – over two-thirds of them Catholics – more than 600 houses and business premises destroyed and the sectarian geography of Belfast polarised as never before.

In August, the IRA scored a significant coup in Lisburn, County Antrim by assassinating RIC District Inspector Oswald Swanzy, recently transferred from Cork and one of those named by the coroner's jury as responsible for the murder of Thomas MacCurtain. The killing was followed by the expulsion of almost the entire Catholic population of Lisburn and the destruction of over 300 homes.

D. FRAGILE HOPES FOR PEACE

The *Clare Champion* (14 August) commented on the cycle of murder and reprisal: 'we hope that our people, even under such provocative circumstances, will exhibit disciplined calmness and restraint ... We are represented every day as a people out for murder and bloodshed. Yet this week the nation prostrates itself in prayer – praying for freedom and peace. Has the Government no responsibility in the matter? ... the Government of Ireland is a Government of violence... peace can be restored in a week by giving the people freedom ...'

On 24 August, a conference of moderate nationalists and southern unionists assembled at Dublin's Mansion House to agree on a proposal that might chart a course for peace. Sir Horace Plunkett, who had chaired the 1917–18 Irish Convention, was again in the chair. Plunkett said that the conference was prepared to accept 'nine-tenths of the Sinn Féin demands' in the form of 'full national self-government within the Empire'. The *Irish News* (23 August) wondered if it was 'a ray of hope'. The conference's more immediate concern, however, was to lobby the government and King George to release the Sinn Féin prisoners in Mountjoy Jail who had begun a hunger strike after their arrest on 12 August. The strike was led by Terence MacSwiney, MacCurtain's successor as both Cork IRA commander and Sinn Féin lord mayor of Cork. The British press was almost unanimously in favour of release, the king was sympathetic and the Cabinet was split. However, the tougher views of senior ministers prevailed, the prisoners remained in jail and MacSwiney's hunger strike continued on its fatal course. The *Longford Leader* (11 September) commented, 'We cannot find words to express our horror at this revelation of brutality towards Irishmen now for the first time in this fight revealed.' It prayed that something would avert the tragedy hanging over England and Ireland, or 'such a feeling of indignation will sweep over the whole country as may lead to some dreadful and ever to be deplored outbreak'. The equally moderate *Limerick Leader* (24 September) counselled patience: 'We are living in troubled times when any departure from calm steadfastness would be well calculated to bring about an unparalleled and irretrievable disaster to our country and her people. Those responsible for the present regime of misgovernment in our midst would desire nothing better than to see young Irishmen recklessly throwing themselves in combat against the armed forces that have been let loose amongst us.'

The *Mayo News* (28 August) waxed sceptical on the 'Irish Peace Conference':

The gentlemen who constituted the conference desire peace. Their panacea is apparently Dominion Home Rule with partition, and this scheme is already damned by the great mass of the Irish people ... The peacemakers are wasting their time if they imagine that the Irish people are going to allow themselves to be drawn into any discussion with the British Premier, or the would-be modern Cromwell, [Chief Secretary] Sir Hamar Greenwood … The Egyptian people stood firm in their demand for absolute independence, and have now attained that goal … Ireland, after 700 years' experience of British rule, is not going to be fooled by the suggestions, however honestly put forward, by men who have hitherto strenuously opposed the National will, and now, when that will is nearing the goal of victory, would step in to check its progress or divert its course. The Irish people have spoken.

The *Meath Chronicle* (28 August) also indicated why the prospects of the conference were poor:

[Hamar Greenwood] *may still foster the delusion that he can get rid of the Irish Question by a patent nostrum, which might be named Dominion Home Rule. If he is aware of the situation as it stands; if he appreciates the determination and sincerity of the Irish people, he can only mean one thing when he says he can settle the Irish Question, and that one thing is the total clearance of himself and his army of occupation, his civil power and all the rest of it out of this country, and that in double quick time.*

The *Tuam Herald* (28 August) disagreed. The meeting, in its view motivated by 'high patriotic purpose', had been 'undoubtedly successful. It showed the present, deep strong feeling of the country among all classes and creeds, the passionate longing and desire at any cost to end the present awful and harassing condition of things and bring about peace …'

The *Ballina Herald* and *Tuam Herald*, both with Redmondite legacies that put them at the front of the forces of moderation, might have been expected to lend their support to the peace initiative. Different, however, was the *Roscommon Journal*, a fierce critic of the government and a newspaper unequivocally pro-Sinn Féin since 1917. In a rare departure for such a paper, it published in mid-November (by which time the police death toll had exceeded 100), under the pseudonym 'Justitia', a letter to the editor appealing for an end to the shooting of police officers:

Has not the time now fully arrived … when the attacks on members of the RIC should cease? Is there anyone in the community who is not now convinced of the utter futility of such attacks, apart from all other considerations? The attacks … have now continued for close on two years, in the course of which some hundreds have been killed and wounded. Of recent months these attacks have been followed by reprisals of a terrible nature, not at the hands of the old-time policemen, the subjects of the attacks, but, it is generally believed, at the hands of the new order of policemen … Is it not now time to take stock? We have, then, on the one side, some hundreds of policemen killed and wounded, and some hundreds of police barracks burned. As against this we have had some millions of property burned or destroyed and a staggering burden to be faced in the shape of rates to meet the position forced upon us by the with-drawal of the grants in aid … What has been gained in these last two years of horror that could not have been gained by measures of sanity? I have been a Home Ruler all my life and am most willing and anxious to be in the ranks with my fellow countrymen, but I shall never join a vendetta against the decent men of the RIC to spite Johnny Bull, who does not care a curse how many Irishmen are wiped out in that exhaustive process.

The letter implored the press, priests and all right thinkers to join in a solemn appeal to stop this 'senseless and cruel vendetta'. As endorse-ment, the paper also published the remarks of Justice Wakely at the Roscommon Quarter Sessions in which he condemned the murders of police.

Every line of the Roscommon letter assumed common knowledge of the identity of the organisation responsible for the police killings – the guerrilla army whose members only recently, after eighteen months of killing in the name of the Irish people, had finally taken an oath of allegiance to Dáil Éireann.[10] Uniquely, however, the *Donegal Vindicator* (19 December) insisted:

An irresponsible body, not Sinn Féin, has been engaged in killing policemen, soldiers and others. That is not war, it is barbarism, and we are in a position to state that it is not the Sinn Féin policy. Far from it. These acts have led to an influx of new police and of soldiers from England in tens of thousands. Sinn Féin did not want that ... The new forces have run amok. They slay, burn, and generally play the devil all over the country ... Sane Sinn Féiners are in camps or in jail, the men who should be there are absent.

The appeals for peace negotiations went unheeded by both sides as the autumn brought the intensification of attacks by the IRA and of reprisals from the army and police, now augmented by the 'Black and Tans' and the newly-deployed Auxiliary Division of the RIC, recruited in Britain from among veteran army officers. Each month added fresh high-profile events. On 20 September, an ambush of British soldiers took place in Church St., Dublin, in which three British soldiers were killed and five injured. The same day, the village of Balbriggan in north County Dublin suffered a chain of horrific events. The *Drogheda Argus* (25 September) recorded its 'feelings of horror, loathing, disgust and dismay' at the murder of two policemen, a head constable and a sergeant, in Balbriggan, followed by the reprisal murders of two innocent civilians [suspected to be IRA members], the sacking of the village by Auxiliaries [this was inaccurate: the reprisal was carried out by regular RIC members], damaging or destroying forty-nine homes, and the burning of business houses, including the destruction of one of the town's hosiery factories. 'Those who attacked and shot the two policemen at the Balbriggan public-house in the fracas,' it wrote, 'must share alike with the "Black and Tan" reprisalists the guilt for the terrible devastation and ruin which has been brought by their unworthy and ill-advised and wanton conduct.' The sack of Balbriggan caused a sensation in the British press and made the reprisals policy an urgent topic for debate in parliament. Only two days later, a similar series of events in magnified form took place in County Clare when the IRA succeeded in killing six police officers in an ambush at Rineen, along with a resident magistrate, an action swiftly followed by reprisal attacks on nearby villages that killed five civilians.

The *Carlow Nationalist* (2 October) headed its commentary 'A Momentous Crisis':

The utmost patience and restraint and fortitude are absolutely essential at the present time in Ireland, if our unfortunate country is to come through a crisis unparalleled in the history of two hundred years ... there can be no justification for irresponsible acts of violence. Not only are such acts against the moral precepts of our holy religion, but they are against common sense ... The Irish Nation is marching to victory, and if the Nation be dignified and patient that victory will not be delayed when it pleases Providence to allow it. The violence of an enemy government is no excuse for irresponsible acts of violence on the other side. Young Ireland must be patient.

The *Clare Champion* gave the Balbriggan and Rineen events large-scale coverage, calling the latter 'a desperate affair in west Clare'. In mid-November, what seemed a further reprisal for Rineen was carried out when Auxiliaries arrested four IRA members who were later found shot dead on Killaloe Bridge after, according to the official statement, 'attempting to escape from custody'. These killings spurred that paper (4 December) to plead for a peace agreement and repeat the call a week later: 'It might be difficult to arrive at a permanent settlement, but it should not be so difficult to arrive at a workable settlement which might be given a reasonable trial, and which would in all probability end in permanent peace.' In its 25 December edition it reprinted the pastoral letter of Bishop Cohalan of Cork against violence.

On 25 October, MacSwiney's 74-day hunger strike ended with his death. The protracted reporting of his ordeal and the huge funeral obsequies that followed generated enormous newspaper coverage and a rich propaganda harvest for Sinn Féin. The execution on 1 November of a young IRA member for his part in the Church St. killings kept popular feelings running high. On 21 November came the horror of Bloody Sunday when the IRA assassinated eleven intelligence officers, answered by the indiscriminate reprisal shooting at Croke Park of fifteen civilians later the same day. A week later, a well-prepared IRA ambush at Kilmichael, County Cork, took the lives of seventeen cadet members of the Auxiliary force along with those of three IRA members. This was shortly followed by an ambush in Cork city that killed an Auxiliary, whose colleagues responded by executing two IRA members in their home and, in the biggest reprisal yet seen, by burning down a large section of the commercial centre of the city along with City Hall and Carnegie Library on 12 December. All these events received massive coverage in the British press, making the public aware that intermittent violence had turned into a small war. Martial law had been proclaimed the previous day for the four south-western counties of Cork, Kerry, Limerick and Tipperary, and four more (Clare, Waterford, Kilkenny and Wexford) would be added early in January 1921.[11]

The *Westmeath Examiner* (27 November) wondered if the worst had yet happened; people wanted to believe, it wrote, that the corner had been turned. The *Cork Examiner*, which had carried a reverential 'Requiescat in Pace' editorial on MacSwiney's death, commented (30 November), 'The appalling state of things prevailing in Ireland at the present time is enough to fill peaceful-minded and moderate people with despair. The terrible events that are of daily and nightly occurrence – ambushes, reprisals, burnings and so forth – continue in horror and intensity, life and property are being sacrificed with a prodigality that sets thoughtful men aghast, and terror follows in the devastating trail of blood.'

As in 1919, no united voice came from the Catholic hierarchy in condemnation of the violence, but four senior clerics made public interventions. The most highly publicised of these were the pastoral letter of Cardinal Logue calling on both sides to end the violence and the call of Archbishop Gilmartin of Tuam in late November for the combatants on both sides to observe a 'Truce of God' over the Christmas period. Of the thirty-one papers that responded to the Bloody Sunday events, ten (seven Redmondite and three pro-Sinn Féin, though all seventeen of the Redmondite organs were implicitly in support) took up this call, including the *Sligo Champion* (4 December) and the *Drogheda Argus* (4 December), which wrote: 'Those who ignored the wise words of warning from Cardinal Logue, and the timely intervention of [Arch]

Bishop Gilmartin calling for a Truce of God as peaceful citizens were preparing for Christmas, to repeat the orgy of slaughter and assassination … the unchristian and murderous work of the previous Sunday [are] … the greatest enemies of their country. They are neither Christians nor patriots.' The *Wexford People* (4 December) headlined its editorial 'A Truce of God', writing, 'That the people of Ireland are heartily sick of the present state of affairs is abundantly clear. On all sides level-headed men condemn the condition of murder and anarchy in the country; all right thinkers do so … The vengeful slaughter of the past year is something terrible to contemplate, and we firmly believe it is damaging the cause of Irish Nationality … Almost everyone in Ireland is yearning for a cessation of hostilities.' It quoted the remarks of Roger Sweetman, Sinn Féin TD for North Wexford, that 'the methods of warfare now being deployed are deplorable in their results to our country, both from a material as well as from a moral standpoint'. In January, Archbishop Gilmartin released another pastoral letter in which he mourned for an Ireland 'drenched in tears' and stated that those taking part in ambushes carried 'the guilt of murder'.

Following the mid-December reprisals in Cork, the local bishop, Dr. Cohalan, issued a decree that denounced such reprisals but also warned that 'anyone within the diocese of Cork who organises or takes part in ambushes or murder or attempted murder shall be <u>excommunicated</u>'. At least four newspapers published the decree, while another was critical of the bishop. The *Irish News* (14 December) reported:

The Decree issued by the Bishop of Cork excommunicating from the Catholic Church all participants in ambushes, kidnappings, shootings etc, has given rise to great resentment on the part of the followers of Sinn Féin. A specially sum-moned meeting of the Cork Corporation was held yesterday, at which Mr J.J. Walsh MP [sic] said the Bishop had not uttered a single word of protest against the burnings which had been going on for weeks. Now, after the city had been decimated, he saw no better course than to add insult to injury. The Bishop's utterance would, he said, be used for propaganda purposes to blackmail the

Irish people, to hold them up as evildoers ... Lord Mayor O'Callaghan said it was terrible to think that when part of the city was in ruins, at the termination of a week of unbridled ruffianism, there was no word of condemnation from the Bishop.

Cork Corporation had also rejected a resolution of Sir John Scott welcoming the efforts of the Irish peace conference and offering co-operation to Archbishop Gilmartin, instead adopting a Sinn Féin resolution calling for peace consistent with recognition of Ireland as a sovereign state. Under the headlines 'Murder Is Murder/Striking Letter from Bishop of Cork/All Crime Denounced/His Lordship and the Consequences of False Teachings/The MacCurtain Tragedy', the same paper reported (20 December) that the decree had been read in all Cork churches on the following Sunday. In response, however, *The Kerryman* (18 December) reprinted the two critical speeches and commented, 'We submit that [excommunication] cannot be hurriedly decided by individual bishops, thus presenting contradictory decisions in different dioceses. Nor can such a tremendous moral and political problem be decided upon without reference to those who, politically and nationally, have a full mandate to represent the Irish people.'

A fourth clerical intervention came from Bishop Finegan of Kilmore after the shooting of two policemen in County Cavan. The *Anglo-Celt* (25 December) reported the bishop's denunciation of the murder of Constable Shannon and the wounding of Sergeant Morahan: 'Up to now the Diocese of Kilmore has been free from political murders and reprisals. On the night of Friday last the life of a police constable was taken in the village of Swanlinbar, and from there his blood, like that of Abel, cries to Heaven for vengeance on his murderers ... We do not know that Ireland has ever had a blacker Christmas.'

As with *The Kerryman* and the *Mayo News*, other papers could be found that refused to join in the general hand-wringing: the *Midland Tribune* (18 December), in an editorial titled 'Stand Fast!', insisted: 'All wish for peace, but there must be no back-down in the National demand for full self-determination … There will be no secret negotiations with British Ministers. If further coercion comes the people will bear it. The National spirit will not be broken.'

As the year 1920 closed, the *Drogheda Argus* (25 December) summed up the situation:

> *The country is seething with rebellion; murder is rampant; raids and burnings of cities are things of common occurrence; and outrages and burglaries are universal. The jails are filled with untried and suspected prisoners; hold-ups are nightly incidents; unemployment is universal; the cost of living has gone beyond the margin of human decency; and the last load, and perhaps the bitterest gall which Ireland has been called upon to swallow – and that, too, under the guise of a measure of Home Rule – the Partition Act – has been placed on the Statute Book, thus repealing and annulling what once shaped like a measure of Self-Government – the Act of 1914 … The nation has been rent in twain … Hell has been let loose in Ireland … When the Partition Act comes into force, as it will in Ulster in a few months, the plight of Catholic Ulster can easily be imagined.*

The clerical appeals for peace, along with the impending legislation for two Irish parliaments and the accompanying need for elections to both bodies, placed conciliation once again, for a time, on the agenda. Joe Devlin, MP for Belfast Falls and one of the Irish Party's few survivors of December 1918, found an intermediary in the Irish-born Archbishop Clune of Perth, who shuttled between Arthur Griffith and Lloyd George during December with outline proposals for a truce. The prime minister, though open to the idea of negotiations, was adamant that the IRA must surrender its arms as a precondition, and Clune was unable to shift him from this position. As Townshend comments, 'neither side was yet really under enough pressure from events or its own public opinion to compromise its objectives'. The peace approaches came to nothing for the moment. Instead, Lloyd George relied on the estimate of senior military officers that, if martial law were applied to the whole country, the 'terror could be broken' sufficiently within four months to allow free elections to take place. On that basis the latter were set for May 1921.[12]

213

The *Mayo News* (22 January) under the title 'Peace Talk Humbug' gave its opinion of the peace contacts: 'This willingness [of Lloyd George for peace] is, however, conditional, and the conditions give us the key to the Premier's difficulties and the sources of his inspiration. Mr Lloyd George knows he cannot negotiate a peace in Ireland because he, himself, is not in a position to deliver the goods. We might have peace in Ireland if we accepted the Partition Bill and submitted to the restrictions on National liberties which Sir Edward Carson would impose. We know what that means.'

E. THE BELFAST BOYCOTT

Spontaneous boycotts of Ulster firms began in early 1920 in Galway and Mayo in response to the threat of partition embodied in the Government of Ireland Bill. In response to the outbreak of sectarian violence in Belfast in July (called a 'pogrom' by nationalists since they were disproportionately the victims), a representative of nationalist members of Belfast Corporation presented a memorial to the Dáil urging a commercial boycott of the Belfast distributing trades as the only way to stop the 'war of extermination' being waged against nationalists. Leading members of the Dáil were sceptical or even hostile to the idea, regarding it either as unworkable or as likely to reinforce partition. Arthur Griffith worried about it being tantamount to a declaration of war on one part of the nation's territory, and urged instead that it be made illegal for any employer to impose a discriminatory test on an employee. However, responding to continuing pressure, the Dáil mandated its Department of Local Government to enforce a boycott of banks and insurance companies headquartered in Belfast. The sanction soon surpassed this limit, and by September local elected bodies all over the country had passed boycott resolutions against goods both distributed and manufactured by firms in Belfast and several other Ulster towns. These boycotts were often enforced by local units of the IRA.[13]

In view of its widespread operation across nationalist Ireland in 1920–21, it seems surprising that the boycott received relatively little editorial support from the provincial press. Only four papers in this sample took up the theme. The *Kerryman* (26 February 1921) framed it as vengeance for partition:

> *Now that the appointed day for the coming into existence of Carson's mock Parliament for North-East Ulster is approaching, those bigots who have so consistently and so zealously supported its creation, with a view to destroying Ireland's solidarity and rendering nugatory Ireland's long drawn out, ago-nised struggle for the realisation of her national aspirations, are beginning to perceive that the fruition of their parliamentary achievement may be dire results which they never counted on. The economic boycott of Belfast, which has taken place as a reprisal for the anti-Catholic pogrom perpetrated in that city last year, gives an indication of what might be done if it were taken up on a national scale.*

In the view of the *Connaught Telegraph* (14 May), 'the Government will still find that the people of Ireland will never accept partition. Ulster may have her Parliament in full operation, but she will soon feel the baneful effects of being cut off from her best customers, as, no doubt, the economic boycott will be rigid and relentless.' The boycott call also received support from the *Limerick Leader* (19 January: 'Teaching Bigots a Lesson') and later from the *Donegal Vindicator* (15 July: 'Boycott of Carsonia by Ireland Will Strangle Belfast'). The *Kerryman* returned to the theme (26 March) with a somewhat different interpretation of the boycott, linking it with the Dáil's initiation of an intensive campaign for the development of Irish industries with 'the progressive exclusion of certain articles of British manufacture … until the British war of aggression ceased'. It was 'instituted as a reply to the introduction of political and religious tests as a condition of industrial employment in Belfast and started on a peaceable basis, has recently been prosecuted forcibly and with astonishing thoroughness. The last report to the Dáil on the Belfast boycott stated that it has made great progress all over the country, and that the stoppage of Belfast goods is rapidly becoming absolute …'

Following the ratification of the Anglo-Irish Treaty and in the context of the tentative negotiations conducted between Collins and Craig for a working north–south relationship, the Belfast boycott would increasingly be seen as counter-productive and was abandoned in early 1922.

F. THE TWO PARLIAMENTS ELECTION

The new Home Rule Act, nicknamed from the start 'the Partition Act' by nationalist newspapers, had received the royal assent just before Christmas 1920. Of the seventeen papers that commented, this time ten dismissed it out of hand while seven articulated a more measured criticism. The overwhelming negativity that had attended every stage of the bill's slow progress through parliament now attached itself to the prospect of the elections. In the early months of 1921, against the background of ever-heavier casualties on both sides, fifteen of twenty-five commenting papers laid the blame for the violence on government repression, while eleven blamed the political stalemate on the plan for what the *Tuam Herald* called the 'unnatural division of Ireland.

The *Wexford People* (1 January) saw 'Little Hope' as it sang a dirge for the lost constitutional movement:

> *Carson and his friends will not agree to the majority being given what they have so long yearned for … There would be still no agitation in Ireland but the constitutional agitation were it not that poor Mr Redmond was let down, and the greatest act of treachery ever perpetrated on this country by the passage of the Home Rule Act for a certain object, and placing it on the Statute Book though it was never intended to come into operation. It was this colossal act of deception at the instance of Carson and his friends that brought about the recrudescence of the physical force movement which had been banished from this country.*

The *Dundalk Democrat* (29 January) reacted with Redmondite wasp-ishness to the re-appearance in Ireland of Éamon de Valera, who had returned from a two-year publicity and fundraising tour of the United States in December and launched a 'manifesto to the Irish People' in mid-January. It wrote:

> *It is couched in romantic language calculated to inspire Mr De Valera's friends, but it contains no word that can reconcile any thinking Irishman to the conditions brought about in the first instance by the movement of which Mr De Valera is the titular head. It recapitulates the sufferings – or some of them – which Ireland has had to endure during the past two years. We in Ireland know what these sufferings are, much better than Mr De Valera, who has spent almost the whole of the two years in America. It was only the distant echoes of Ireland's troubles that affected the calm of the Waldorf Astoria ... The unhappy people of this unhappy land have known for these two distressful years what it means to live in daily and nightly terror ...victims of some incident of the foredoomed and hopeless appeal to armed force against an overwhelming power ... That is what this fight, of which Mr De Valera speaks in lofty and poetic language, means to the people at home in Ireland.*

The *Leinster Leader* (29 January), clearly aiming to address a Liberal British readership, rejected the urgings by British ministers that the Irish should 'eschew all countenance of violence' and return to con-stitutional means of remedy. Delivering a long recital of Irish political events since 1909, it added, 'Martial Law and Partition have today supplanted Home Rule and Conscription as the [dual policy] remedy for Irish Republicanism, and it is likely to be as effective ... The most impartial and detached mind ... cannot in justice convict the people of Ireland of rejecting constitutional methods without good and sufficient reason. Besides it is a fallacy to say that they have abandoned such methods. It could be more accurate to say that they have returned to that more robust and pure patriotic allegiance that swayed the men of '48 and '67.'

Despite the calls in many newspapers to ignore or boycott the approaching general elections in protest at the 'Partition Act', a call endorsed by Irish Party leader John Dillon, the Sinn Féin leadership weighed up the pros and cons of participation. The *Connaught Telegraph* (14 May) explained the issues:

> *There are 104 county, sixteen borough and 8 University constituencies in Southern Ireland, and, as each candidate must lodge £150, it means that £19,200 must be provided out of the National Fund, and though practically all put forward will be returned unopposed, none of the money will be returned unless the members take their seats in parliament. In Ulster there are fifty-two members, and this means a further draw of £7,800 on the National Fund, and, as the intention of the Sinn Féin candidates, if elected, is to ignore the Parliament, this sum will also be lost ... it is a fortunate circumstance there will be no contests in the Southern area, almost the whole of which is under military dominance. What the outcome of the elections will be we do not know. It is evident the present intention of the Government is to set up two Parliaments, but it is likewise the intention of Nationalist Ireland to make the one for the South unworkable, and, if possible, also that for Ulster ...*

Swayed by the huge propaganda potential for the party, and despite the contradiction between rejection of the Act's legitimacy and the effective acceptance of its machinery, Sinn Féin decided to nominate candidates for both of the new parliaments. In the 'Southern Parliament' area, no candidates were fielded against Sinn Féin in any of the 128 seats except the four Dublin University seats which were effectively conceded to unionists. The *Connaught Telegraph* (7 May) published de Valera's manifesto for the general election, calling for all nationalists to vote for Sinn Féin candidates only. The document sought voters' endorsement of the 'principle of Irish independence', 'the right [of Ireland] to rule itself', 'the right of the people of this nation to determine freely for themselves how they shall be governed', 'an association of nations based upon self-determination', 'Ireland undivided' – but made no mention of a 'republic'.

The *Mayo News* commented (14 May), 'The elections for the Partition Parliaments are proceeding and Irish voters can strike a blow more effective than fifty ambushes by seeing to it that ... every constituency in what is called Southern Ireland ... returns as its representative a supporter of Mr Éamon De Valera and his policy. That is the road to peace ...' Most newspaper comment refused to take the elections seriously. 'On With The Farce!' wrote the *Leinster Leader* (14 May); 'Tragi-comedy in Ireland ... a pantaloon farce' was the verdict of the *Munster News* (14 May).

The result gave 124 of 128 seats to Sinn Féin in the southern area but only six of fifty-two seats in the northern area (against thirty-six unionists, with two seats won by Labour). The *Carlow Nationalist* (21 May) commented:

> There was only one point of view before the minds of the Irish people. None with any scintilla of nationality wanted the Partition Act, which is intended to kill the spirit of Irish nationality. It was indeed strange that the vast majority of Unionists in these parts of Ireland, as evidenced by the result of the elections, are opposed to any partition, or indeed any scheme of national self-government that would not be a distinct improvement on existing systems in the country. Southern Unionists had not the least notion of sending forward candidates, although they may not be in sympathy with Republicanism.

The *Kilkenny People* (21 May) claimed that the result proved how 'absolutely detested' was the very idea of partition; every section of southern public opinion had demonstrated its 'supreme contempt' for the government's programme. As for the future, the *Connaught Telegraph* (21 May) reckoned 'it is doubtful if the Northern Parliament will be a success. Ulster, boycotted by the rest of Ireland, will ... soon find that a woeful mistake was made. As the Southern Parliament cannot now function, what will happen? We are promised Crown Colony Government, but that will take us no further; and now that Nationalist Ireland has again spoken, through the medium of an election, the Cabinet cannot any longer shirk its duty. The unanimity of the people of the South on the question of partition has impressed the people and press of England, except the Cabinet.'

G. ULSTER GETS HOME RULE

Given the universal scorn heaped by nationalist Ireland on the government of Ireland legislation over the previous eighteen months, the response of the nationalist press to its first material product was predictably negative when King George opened the Northern Ireland parliament at Stormont Castle outside Belfast on 22 June.

Of twenty-five newspapers that referred to the event in some form, six were scathing of the new assembly or of partition in general, another eight voiced more measured criticism while two carried objective reports without comment, including the *Sligo Champion*, which printed the full text of the king's speech. Others allowed the Catholic bishops to speak for them. Many papers published in full or in part the annual Maynooth synod statement of the Catholic hierarchy, described by the *Waterford News* as 'the most important manifesto ever issued by the Irish Bishops'. Its remark that 'in defiance of Ireland, a Government has been given to one section of the people, remarkable at all times for intolerance' was quoted approvingly by at least six of the papers. A few others confined themselves to the familiar abuse or ridicule of Ulster unionists or criticised the king's speech for seeming to ignore the situation of sectarian conflict obtaining at that moment in Belfast. Ten papers ignored the event altogether.

'The little tinpot Parliament of Ulster – the Imperial county council of the Orange Compound,' mocked the *Clonmel Nationalist* (25 June). According to the *Leinster Leader* (25 June), it would be 'impossible to imagine that the travesty which has just been enacted in North-East Ulster could result in anything only making confusion worse confounded'. It was 'the posturing of puppets in Carsonia … the folly of the foolish faction of North-East Ulster … the narrow and bigoted population which thrives and fattens on such bigoted and archaic sentiments'. The *Meath Chronicle* (25 June) judged the king's speech to be 'merely a series of platitudinous phrases, which in existing circumstances mean nothing' and claimed that 'the very event itself … was an outrage on the Irish people and the Irish Nation … an attempt to decapitate the country [with] a toy parliament'. These responses were at the extreme end of the spectrum.

The Redmondite *Longford Leader* (19 February) had already seen the irony of 'Carson's Parliament' but allowed itself to indulge a pipe-dream:

As a result of the working of this moribund pigmy Parliament which he [Carson] has induced the anti-Home Rulers to accept we look to a very quick change of feeling towards a genuine settlement of the Irish Question from that partitioned province. To begin with, these people must realise that they who had sworn a covenant never to have Home Rule have been the first to have it. This is for them a very peculiar bitter irony indeed. By offering them a puny, powerless Parliament and inducing them to accept it, Mr Lloyd George has cleverly broken down their one and only safeguard against Home Rule. This must in a short time force itself on the dullest of the herd. Secondly, when it is in operation for some short time and they see how powerless they will be they will be driven not by the opinions of the Nationalists but by their own experience to realise that their one and only hope lies in joining their fellow countrymen for a real genuine measure of Home Rule … We look forward with confidence to seeing a demand for such a Parliament not coming from Nationalist Ireland but from the Unionist Parliament … so that we are confident it will yet be found that the man who really got Home Rule for Ireland was the very man who raised hell in Ireland to prevent it.

The most pertinent, if one-sided, points were made by the more moderate Ulster papers. The *Derry Journal* (24 June) wrote that peace had reigned 'for a few hours in Belfast on Wednesday while King George and his Consort remained in that city. The pogrom municipality in an ecstasy of loyalist fervour temporarily effaced its customary notorious leanings to riots, rapine and bloodshed, whereby many hundreds of its Catholic residents have been made victims of the most outrageous anti-Christian conduct, and it assumed for a brief spell a show of good behaviour'. However, the king:

> *might as well have been furnished with a passage for reading from Hans Andersen's Fairy Tales, and the excerpt … would, for the most part, have as much relevance to existing facts. Early in his Speech King George used these words: 'I am confident that the important matters entrusted to the control and guidance of the Northern Ireland Parliament will be managed with wisdom and moderation, and fairness and due regard to every faith and interest …'* [This] *must be a confidence of a very childlike character indeed. How the 'management' of the recent Belfast elections must have laughed in their sleeves at hearing mention of 'moderation and fairness'.*

The paper went on to allege that 'every form of electoral illegality was pressed into service' to secure 'such a majority as would make their position continuously "safe for Orangeism and Ascendancy"'.

The *Irish News* (23 June) claimed that '… Mr Lloyd George's hand is visible in every sentence [of the Speech]. The first half is composed of vague professions signifying nothing. At the beginning of the second half, the people of this country are reminded of that "full partnership in the United Kingdom and the religious freedom Ireland has long enjoyed". We know what that "full partnership in the United Kingdom" has brought to our land and nation. And what malevolent sprite within the Cabinet concocted that phrase about "religious freedom" for use within a quarter of a mile of the Belfast shipyards?'

H. PEACE HOPES REVIVE

From March onwards, peace feelers were being extended again, even as the killing intensified further on both sides – deaths of Crown forces personnel and IRA Volunteers in the first quarter of 1921 both increased by almost half again over those of the last quarter of 1920. The reprisals policy was coming under increasing public criticism in Britain while King George made his disapproval of the policy known privately to the Cabinet (it would be officially abandoned on 3 June). In April, the withdrawal of Lord French, a chief symbol of military coercion, and his replacement as lord lieutenant by Viscount Fitz-Alan, a Catholic, were interpreted as conciliatory gestures. As the casualty rate peaked in the spring and early summer (casualties for the second quarter would not exceed those of the first), misgivings and demoralisation within the IRA at its shortages of weapons and its failure to extend its war significantly beyond the south-western counties was matched within the Crown forces by a conviction that they were slowly gaining the upper hand.[14] Large-scale military confrontations like the Kilmichael and Crossbarry ambushes of the previous winter remained exceptional events due to increased British army activity, and the majority of actions still consisted of sniping and assassinations of policemen.

The republicans were still coming under fire from Catholic clergymen for these killings. The *Limerick Leader* (20 May) published the words of Bishop Hackett of Waterford 'on the present crisis': '… they were at present going through a great crisis in the history of Ireland, but that crisis need not terrify them. The cause that was just, and the cause which had God's blessing upon it was bound to conquer … if they strove to secure that liberty without bringing upon themselves God's anger, they need not fear … On the other hand, they should remember that sin would not bring a blessing on them and crime would not foster the cause of liberty. They lived in times when exasperation was carried to extreme.' The shooting of a constable at Letterkenny provoked Bishop O'Donnell of Raphoe to condemnation, as reported by the same paper (23 May) under the headline 'Revenge No Remedy': 'An evil deed has been perpetrated in our midst that brings sorrow to us all. Until yesterday this district was free from bloodshed … [it is] particularly revolting to every Catholic feeling … I trust, the relations between the people and the various forces will not be embittered by this deplorable deed … I earnestly hope no idea of vengeance will be entertained. Vengeance belongs to the Lord.'

The *Midland Tribune* (28 May) felt compelled, evidently by the power of local public opinion, to correct a report it had earlier published on a policeman's funeral. Under the headline 'The late Constable Dunne's Funeral/A Regretted Error in *Tribune* Report', it wrote, 'Our attention has been called to a statement in our issue of last week with reference to the funeral of the late Constable Dunne, a victim of the Kinnitty ambush, that "the number of civilians attending was not large". We much regret the publication of this statement, as the number of civilians attending was large and representative of the people of Birr, by whom the late Constable Dunne was much respected.'

Driven by pressure from de Valera to 'deliver a smashing blow' to the British administration, the IRA staged an unprecedentedly large operation in the centre of Dublin city on 25 May by burning the iconic neoclassical Custom House with its mass of civic and historic records. Of more than 120 men who took part, six were killed in a shoot-out with Auxiliaries while more than eighty were captured, a figure that rose to over 100 with follow-up arrests. The *Southern Star* (4 June) tried to distract from the Pyrrhic victory by republishing an apologia from Sinn Féin's *Irish Bulletin*: 'We, in common with the rest of the Nation regret the destruction of historic buildings. But the lives of 4,000,000 people are a more sacred charge than any architectural masterpiece ... The destruction was an unavoidable military necessity.'

The *Clare Champion* (21 May) wondered if settlement talks would follow the result of the elections – would Lloyd George and de Valera meet? The *Waterford News* (24 June) claimed that Lloyd George was 'climbing down' and asserted that a truce would come soon. After the opening of the Northern Ireland parliament by the king in Belfast, the prime minister on 24 June sent invitations to de Valera 'as the chosen leader of the great majority in Southern Ireland' and to James Craig, the Northern Ireland premier, to meet with him in London to 'explore to the utmost the possibility of a settlement'. Before responding, de Valera issued his own invitation to Craig and to some prominent southern unionists including Lord Midleton to come to Dublin to discuss the answer to be given to the British. Craig declined the invitation but Midleton and his colleagues met with de Valera at the Mansion House where, after two days' discussion, Midleton agreed to convey truce proposals from the Dáil Cabinet to Lloyd George. He returned to Dublin on 8 July with the prime minister's agreement to a truce. In the meantime the South African General Jan Smuts had arrived in Dublin as an intermediary and was told by the Sinn Féin leaders that they had decided to refuse Lloyd George's invitation because of Ulster's non-involvement. Smuts successfully persuaded them to accept the olive branch or risk losing the support of public opinion.

The announcement of the truce, to take effect on 9 July, was greeted with anxious enthusiasm by the general population. The dominant tone of press commentary was one of relief and joy at the news, as expressed by nineteen (59 per cent) of the thirty-two papers that commented. A further eleven (34 per cent) papers were more phlegmatic or cautious as to the durability of the agreement, while two were pessimistic about its prospects. The 'general rejoicing reflects the mind and heart of the country,' wrote the *Carlow Nationalist* a week after the start of the truce (16 July). 'The scenes of rejoicing in Dublin will convince any who doubts' (*Dundalk Democrat*, 16 July); 'the country yearns for peace' (*Cork Examiner*, 8 July). The *Longford Leader* (16 July) welcomed the 'peace festivity' in which all creeds and classes had joined. The *Derry People* (16 July) claimed that the people of Ireland were demonstrating their 'utmost satisfaction' at the peace – all except for the 'Orange die-hard element'. The *Galway Observer* (16 July) wrote that the people of Galway were 'greatly relieved' but knew that a fight still lay ahead. The *Mayo News* (16 July) cautioned against anticipating a certain road to peace, given the 'slick methods' of the British. The *Munster News* (13 July) argued that self-control was the need of the hour, while the *Limerick Echo* (12 July) reminded readers that 'every individual is the custodian of the Nation's honour' in ensuring against violations of the peace.

Press commentary for the 1919-21 period is summarised in Chart 6.

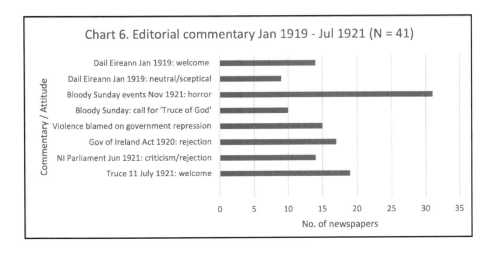

Chapter 8

TRUCE, TREATY AND CIVIL WAR, JULY 1921–MAY 1923

A. THE TREATY AND RATIFICATION

The opening of substantive talks between Sinn Féin and British representatives in London on 11 October occasioned less comment, and less again of the optimistic kind, than had the truce. Of twenty-one newspapers that commented, six were confidently optimistic while thirteen expressed caution and two were pessimistic. Redmondite papers were among the cheerleaders: the *Westmeath Examiner* (15 October) called the conference a 'momentous gathering' of the representatives of the two nations and wrote that 'Ireland passionately wants success'; the *Cork Examiner* (10 October) was happy that 'the keenest intellects on the two sides' were engaged in the quest for a settlement. The *Tuam Herald* (8 October) felt that, though the task would not be easy, the 'temper of the English people' was now 'creditable and satisfactory' and favoured a settlement.

The pro-Sinn Féin *Meath Chronicle* (16 October) however, had 'scant hope' and nourished the 'deepest suspicion of Lloyd George and the British Cabinet'. The *Kilkenny People* (16 July) extolled de Valera's 'splendid statesmanlike qualities', a judgment it would have cause to re-examine in the following year. The *Dundalk Democrat* (15 October), on the other hand, found ominous the wording of the Sinn Féin leader's recent statement, published by several newspapers, that peace would be secured by the 'stern determination of a close-knit nation steeled to the acceptance of death rather than the abandonment of its rightful liberty … Were the prospect of further horrors or further sacrifices to cause her to quail or falter for a moment all would be lost … the slightest lowering of the nation's morale [now] would be fatal …' It wondered what his motive could be in issuing such a 'resounding manifesto on the eve of a conference in which representatives of the British and Irish Nations are to seek a means of reconciling Ireland's national aspirations with Britain's claim as enunciated by Mr Lloyd George' – a reference to the prime minister's reported insistence that he would negotiate with the Sinn Féin delegates on the basis of Ireland's remaining a member of the British empire and not of its recognition as a republic. Meanwhile the *Donegal Vindicator* (7 October) reckoned that the prospects for peace depended on the will of international Jewish bankers. It worked an antisemitic conspiratorial theme into its response to two *Daily Mail* stories that anticipated a settlement, one reporting that an order had been placed for 1,000 uniforms for the IRA's Dublin Brigade for the day it would come out as an official force on parade, the other concerning new investment in Dublin's shopping district:

> *The Jew holds the purse strings of the earth today, he orders or stops war to suit his purpose. He has done so for hundreds of years and at this moment he is the power not only behind the throne but upon it … Also members of the ONE RACE* [sic] *which has an unerring financial instinct have begun to make investments in Grafton Street, Dublin's chief shopping centre, in preparation for the era of peace, which THEY FORESEE, AND HAVE, PERHAPS, TO SOME EXTENT DECREED'* … *The Jewish Banker decrees peace with Ireland, and if he has spoken peace it will be no matter at what cost.*

The signing and publication of the text of the Anglo-Irish Treaty on 6 December elicited a higher rate of newspaper comment than any event of the previous three years. Most editors seemed to know immediately where they stood. Of thirty-four papers that commented, twenty-three expressed unadulterated rejoicing, eight were willing to accept it despite admitted flaws (including its failure to remove partition) and only three hedged their response. The *Munster News* (7 December) under the heading 'Peace At Last!' hailed the Treaty: 'The delight with which the news from London was received may be more easily imagined than described ... The terms of settlement ... embody all the essentials of liberty. The very name 'Irish Free State' is exhilarating. It opens up a vista of great promise for a nation no longer under foreign domination'. The *Clonmel Nationalist* (10 December) declared 'We have won our liberty!' and called it a 'settlement of epoch-making importance'. The *Carlow Nationalist* (10 December) paid tribute to the 'noble body of young Irishmen' who had made the outcome possible, but added soberly, 'Ireland becomes a Free State in the British Commonwealth of Nations. Great Britain officially acknowledges the nationhood of Ireland within that ... We have always been conscious of nationhood, and we still believe in the final destiny of our country, complete independence. However, we must face hard facts. The Irish envoys, given full powers, have undoubtedly made the best bargain they possibly could ... There is now "Peace with Honour"'. The *Drogheda Argus* (10 December) framed the theme of the Commonwealth in a positive light: 'Allegiance alone could never bind together the Commonwealth of Nations which has been mis-named the British Empire. Such an institution can only exist as a league of free nations, independent, self-respecting, and respecting each other and working together for one common cause, the cause of progress, peace and civilisation. The Imperial idea is exploded in the twentieth century ... They [the Dominions] have long outgrown that status, and they are now voluntary members of a big Commonwealth'. Both of these papers, and others, used the term 'Commonwealth' in place of the actual wording in the Treaty clause: 'the community of nations known as the British Empire'.

The *Mayo News* (10 December) described the Treaty as 'a victory of sacrifice. It is the fruit of the holocaust of young lives sacrificed in the

Cause of Irish liberty … The Treaty of Peace is the crowning victory of the Sinn Féin Movement, an example which must light the paths of other small nations in their struggles for freedom'. The *Southern Star* (10 December) voiced its reservations on the Ulster issue: although 'not ideally perfect', the Treaty 'commands respect and challenges obedience … The solution of the Ulster problem may not be wholly satisfactory, but the Orangemen are Mammon-worshippers and are sometimes wise in their generation. They have no more to expect from Westminster'. The *Derry Journal* (9 December), on the other hand, thought that the Treaty 'obliterates Partition', an assessment true only in the sense that it had closed down much discussion of partition as an issue. The *Donegal Vindicator* (9 December) deluded itself that the 'Ulster puzzle' would now take care of itself: 'Belfast, it is reported, is not averse to the terms. There is indeed little room to doubt that it will throw in its lot with the rest of Ireland. Its little Parliament is costing more than a big one; the frown of Ireland has damaged its commercial standing and its merchants know full well that in the Free State there will be an industrial activity like to, but far, far greater than that which stirred the land when last, in College Green, Irishmen made laws for Ireland.'

As these first reactions to the Treaty were going to press, Éamon de Valera came out against its terms in a statement addressed to the Irish people. Three papers responded with prevarication. The *Waterford News* (9 December) published the various statements but declared that it would make no editorial comment for the present; the *Donegal Vindicator* (9 December) was ambivalent ('Our harvest has come … we pluck the fruit … But Éamon de Valera has spoken… we must be calm & full of trust') as was the *Roscommon Herald* (10 December): 'In theory de Valera is right – but …'

De Valera's statement did not prevent a majority of the Sinn Féin Cabinet voting to recommend it to the Dáil, though it divided that body into two camps. The daily *Cork Examiner* (10 December) was mildly anxious at the divergence of opinion: 'The Manifesto issued to the Irish people by Mr De Valera and the statement of Mr Arthur Griffith simultaneously published, have naturally been the subject of much concern to all classes in this country, and the enemies of Ireland will seek to find in their differences of opinion evidence of disunion and possibilities of rupture. We do not take a gloomy view of the situation as it has now developed, though we confess to complete surprise at Mr De Valera's attitude regarding the Peace Treaty … in view of the worldwide chorus of approval that has welcomed the Peace Treaty, which the Irish delegates after months of incessant labour and magnificent effort have succeeded in formulating, it is to be regretted that its reception by the Dáil Éireann Cabinet has not been unanimous.' The *Southern Star* (17 December) was sanguine: 'Bitter experience has steeled the nation against disunion. *There will be no split.* There may be sharp differences of opinion, but as President De Valera has said, and as Mr Michael Collins has repeated, there will be no bitterness and no recriminations.'

The *Mayo News* (17 December) wrote that Ireland would 'accept the decision of An Dáil on the issue of acceptance or rejection of the Treaty of Downing Street … While the Treaty is a very substantial step, and may possibly materially advance the interests of the country, it is not free from defects, but we, in common with the people of Ireland, generally, have every confidence that the Irish plenipotentiaries weighed its every clause carefully in the light of all the facts available.' The *Tuam Herald* (17 December) worried: 'We write before the fateful and ultimate decision of Dáil Éireann is given on the most important issue ever presented to a popular body of representatives. Upon their wisdom the future of Ireland depends. If they agree to accept the Treaty which their plenipotentiaries signed on their behalf the country can go on its way to assured peace and prosperity. If they reject the proffered terms there will be nothing before the people but confusion and internecine warfare.'

As the Treaty debates proceeded, at least eight newspapers in all parts of the country carried coverage of local public meetings of county councils, other elected bodies and farmers' associations. The *Derry People* (7 January) carried a particularly wide-ranging coverage of meetings of public bodies and regional Sinn Féin organisations all over the north-west, all of them practically unanimous in demanding ratification of the Treaty. The *Cork Examiner* (29 December) commented that 'the spontaneous expression of opinion that is recorded from various parts of Ireland in favour of the ratification of the Peace Treaty' drove home the lesson that it must be ratified : 'We do not anticipate that any member of the Dáil will place their individual opinions against the concentrated judgment of the majority of the Irish people'. In similar vein, the *Clonmel Nationalist* (7 January), citing the 'unanimous call to An Dáil' of Tipperary's county and urban councils and farmers, wrote: 'The country hungers for peace and, realising that an honourable peace and a glorious future for the country has been secured by the terms of the Treaty, ardently desires ratification … Ireland has won nine-tenths of her demands, her future lies in her own hands, and she has the power to develop her national life on the widest possible lines without outside hindrance. A tremendous victory has been wrested from an all-powerful nation under the most trying difficulties.' Perhaps surprisingly for a newspaper with such uncompromisingly republican credentials, the *Mayo News* (7 January), writing before the vote was known, noted:

> *It is doubtful if ten per cent of the people of Ireland have any desire to have Republican rule … We do not understand the mentality of those who profess keen scruples about the sacredness of oaths* [a subject much in play in the Treaty debates], *but who, having been elected to represent the people, declare their contempt for the wishes of their constituents. The first duty of a representative is to voice the feelings of his constituents. If the members of An Dáil do so Ireland will hail their decision with joy and relief. If they ignore the will of the people, then they may be justly accused of violating a pledge more sacred and more binding than any form of oath which can well be conceived.'*

Commenting on another prominent topic in the debates, de Valera's counter-proposal for a 'Treaty of Association' with the Commonwealth (the so-called Document No. 2), the *Kilkenny People* (7 January) claimed that 'many people fail to discern any substantial difference' as it did not propose to set up an independent republic nor get rid of Ireland's liability for public debt as fixed in the Treaty, and there was to be no coercion of Ulster. 'There are, in fact,' it wrote sardonically, 'far more ingenuous people in this country than we gave the country credit for. What did they think Messrs Collins and Griffith were sent to Downing St for, and what did they expect them to bring back? An Irish Republic in one hand and the corpse of the British Empire in the other? They could hardly bring back one without the other.' The *Sligo Champion* (7 January) added its voice, calling 'political insanity' the 'contemptible quibbles' over Document No. 2. The *Connacht Tribune* (7 January) claimed that about half of the elected TDs were obstructing the will of the people regarding the Treaty. The *Carlow Nationalist* (7 January) foresaw a 'crisis unparalleled' and urged the Treaty's acceptance as a 'stepping stone' to greater freedom. The *Tuam Herald* (7 January) called on the people to understand the seriousness of the situation: the real choice was between the Free State and chaos.

After nine days of acrimonious public debate, the Dáil on 7 January 1922 voted by sixty-four to fifty-seven to 'ratify' the Treaty (legally, it was merely approved, and could not be ratified until a new elected parliament had come into being). De Valera resigned as president of Dáil Éireann, and the Provisional Government was set up with Michael Collins as chairman, to be subject to the Dáil. Press comment on the news of the ratification appeared mostly the following weekend and did not differ significantly from that expressed on the Treaty's publication, with twenty-seven of thirty-two papers supporting it and five neutral or ambivalent. The *Cork Examiner* (9 January) wrote that the result would be received with gratitude and relief, and reckoned that popular support for the Treaty was probably about 90 per cent. The *Longford Leader* (14 January) congratulated Griffith and Collins on their 'wonderful victory': 'We earnestly hope that the anger of debate and the heat and anxieties of the whole Session will not be further remembered. The decisions that have been made were made in the best interests of the country. They are not, in any sense, related to mere personalities. It is not that Griffith has triumphed over De Valera but that the substance has been grasped and the shadow rejected.' The *Kilkenny People* (14 January) commented that 'the Irish Free State, which is about to come into being, does not give everything that Irishmen would like to get. It gives a good deal of what Irishmen have for generations been vainly striving to get. Why should we not make the most of it and work it for what it is worth?' The paper, itself a past pioneer in extreme political rhetoric, lamented the drift towards an "acute crisis" in a country "deluged with oratory". For the *Southern Star* (14 January), the very possibility of a split was 'unthinkable'. The *Limerick Leader* (9 January) vented its relief that the Treaty was safe but was sad at the division among old comrades.

Of the papers initially sceptical of the Treaty, none directly opposed its ratification. The *Waterford News* (13 January) tried to argue that there was a 'fundamental unity of sentiment' between the followers of Griffith and de Valera. The *Roscommon Herald* (7, 14 January) was haunted by the 'hideous possibility of another Split' [a reference to the nine-year Parnell split of the 1890s], carrying a front-page cartoon of a monstrous Lloyd George figure rejoicing in a split among Irishmen. The *Donegal Vindicator* (20 January), writing as the handover of power and the evacuation of British troops were imminent, wrote that 'the Bastille has fallen' and 'Silence is Golden'.

Following on the Treaty's 'ratification', the transfer of authority, with all that entailed – the disbandment of the RIC and the commissioning of a new police force, the evacuation of the British army and its replacement by a national army – would, even under ideal conditions, have involved the risk of a temporary power vacuum. The Provisional Government wished to put the issue of the Treaty to the people as soon as possible, but agreed to a request from the anti-Treatyites to defer a general election for six months to allow the people to consider it. Until the election could be held, legal ambiguities persisted as to the relationship between the Provisional Government and the Dáil, and between both and the British government. For some weeks, two parallel governments existed – the Provisional Government under Collins and the Dáil under Griffith.[1] Overarching this was the bigger disagreement on the meaning and acceptability of the Treaty and the powerful opposition to its implementation, which greatly worsened the crisis of authority. For the Provisional Government and supporters of the Treaty in general, the Volunteers of the IRA must be subordinate to the elected Dáil. For the anti-Treatyite leaders, the supreme focus of loyalty of the armed force must be the 'Republic', the virtual entity declared at Easter 1916. An attempt by senior anti-Treaty IRA officers to call an IRA convention with the aim of setting up the Volunteers as 'the Army of the Irish Republic under an executive appointed by the convention' was proscribed by the government on 15 March on the grounds that 'any effort to set up another body [than the Dáil] in control [of the Army] would be tantamount to an attempt to establish a Military Dictatorship'. The convention, however, went ahead on 26 March but without participation by pro-Treaty officers.[2]

B. VIOLENCE IN ULSTER

A meeting between Collins and Northern Ireland premier James Craig took place on 21 January. Although Collins was able to declare an end to the South's boycott, no agreement was reached that might have quelled the autonomous actions of local IRA units in Ulster, where the truce had not been observed. In early February, forty-two leading loyalists were abducted in County Tyrone, held as hostages and taken across the border to Clones. In a gunfight at Clones station on 11 February, an IRA officer and four Ulster special constables were killed. This bloodshed set off a chain reaction of sectarian atrocities, culminating on 24 March in the massacre of an entire Catholic family, the McMahons, by gunmen who broke into their home in Belfast, an incident that shocked opinion in the two islands. In the ten weeks from 10 February to 21 April, 127 Catholics were killed and some 300 injured in Belfast.[3] Over the full two years of conflict between July 1920 and July 1922, approximately 500 people were killed in Belfast. Catholics, who made up about a quarter of the city's population, accounted for 56 per cent of the deaths while Protestants accounted for 39 per cent, a 4:1 preponderance of Catholic victims in per capita terms.[4]

Twenty-three newspapers were moved to comment on the violence, the vast majority confining themselves helplessly to deploring it. Four indulged in anti-Orange invective, two alleged British connivance and two hinted that the South should intervene. For the *Galway Observer* (15 April), the 'murderous pogrom' was part of a plan to smash the Treaty. It was 'Orangeism gone mad' (*Carlow Nationalist*, 25 March), 'War on Catholics and Nationalists' following the British game of 'divide and conquer' (*Midland Tribune*, 25 March), 'A Reign of Terror' – the Orange mobs were worse than South Sea cannibals (*Nenagh Guardian*, 25 March). The *Connaught Telegraph* (25 March) thought that the boycott should not have been lifted. An undercurrent of sectarian tension was evident in some of the papers, though it never spread beyond scattered localised expressions. The anti-Treaty *Waterford News* (24 March) wrote that the Treaty controversy should be dropped, as a coalition government was 'absolutely essential' to deal with the Belfast savagery. In two other editorials the paper went much further, casting suspicion on and making veiled threats against local Protestants for their alleged silence on the Belfast violence. On 13 January, it wrote, '… And what about the so-called Southern Unionists who never, as a body of Irishmen, protested publicly against the murder and pillage of our fellow Catholics in the North-East? Do they, or do they not, experience a sense of humiliation and shame? They prate now about their allegiance to the Free State, the heads of which, a few months ago, these same Unionists, North and South, were describing as leaders of a Murder Gang. We are suspicious of these sudden somersaulting repentances.' On 21 April, it warned: 'The Southern Unionist has good cause for anxiety for it is pretty certain that if the murder and plunder of Catholics in Belfast cannot be stopped, and if the destruction of their property is part of the programme, it will very soon be impossible to restrain the Catholic population of the Ireland which is outside the jurisdiction of Sir James Craig and his murderous associates, British and Irish'.

On 15 April, the *Roscommon Journal* published a letter, called by the paper 'A Timely Protest', from Roscommon Protestants condemning the violence perpetrated against Belfast Catholics. This does not seem, however, to have saved Protestants in neighbouring counties from intimidation. The *Connacht Tribune* on 10 June carried a news article headlined 'Weekend of Terror/Protestants' Trying Ordeal', detailing shootings and robberies by armed masked men at the houses of several disbanded policemen and a Protestant family in the Mayo–Sligo area, undertaken for the purpose of forcing them out of the district. In Cork, intimidation was of a different order of magnitude. The *Cork Examiner* reported over four days (27 to 30 April) on a spate of murders of a total of thirteen Protestant men in the area of Bandon-Dunmanway, west County Cork, by local anti-Treaty IRA members. The killings were condemned by the Dáil cabinet, Cork Corporation and the Catholic bishop of Cork, Dr. Cohalan, who referred to the context of the anti-Catholic violence in Northern Ireland. The perpetrators were never brought to justice and, although even the anti-Treaty West Cork IRA commandant, Tom Hales, condemned the actions, controversy has persisted into the 21st century about the motivation – whether sectarian, vendetta or political – of the killers.[5]

C. THE CRISIS OF AUTHORITY

The *Offaly Independent* (4 February) (the old *King's County Independent* under its new title, now reappearing for the first time in 15 months following its suppression by the British authorities in November 1920) registered its unease at the signs of growing disunity in the country: 'A very deep debt of gratitude is due to President Griffith, Deputy De Valera and Deputy Collins for their magnificent services but let us not allow our esteem and admiration to turn us into mere hero-worshippers, blindly following and unhesitatingly supporting the one or the other … Is there any necessity, any reason for the disunion and acrimony which day by day is steadily growing more apparent?' The *Sligo Champion* (18 February) in an editorial titled 'Government versus Anarchy' warned:

The cause of Irish peace is suffering sadly by happenings in Ireland, the bitter dissensions in Southern Ireland being as much responsible as the terrible happenings in the North … It is folly to attempt to hide the fact that there is a strong movement to prevent the Provisional Government from functioning, and a not inconsiderable body of extremists who would be misguided enough to attempt to overthrow the Provisional Government by force of arms. It is all very deplorable … Occurrences such as the dreadful affair in Clones are only to be expected in areas where the atmosphere is tense with political and religious prejudice, but a sinister defiance of all law and order in evidenced in the raids in Sligo this week, where raiders robbed the Bank of Ireland and the Provincial Bank of thousands of pounds and got [away] scot free in broad daylight. Such acts as the Sligo bank robberies are typical of many throughout Ireland during the past years.

A Sinn Féin Ard-Fheis (general conference) held during February maintained a semblance of unity in the party. Internal evidence suggests that the party was overwhelmingly pro-Treaty at this stage.[6] Later that month, however, the tensions generated by dual loyalties in the military wing were highlighted in Limerick, where two opposing IRA factions comprising 700 pro-Treatyites and 800 anti-Treatyites disputed control over the military barracks being evacuated by British troops. Open conflict was narrowly averted at the last minute, but similar stand-offs would soon occur in other parts of the country, notably in Athlone. In mid-March, de Valera, who had said during the December debates, 'There is a constitutional way of settling those differences of ours; in God's name let us not depart from it', embarked on a speaking tour of Munster towns in the name of his new organisation, Cumann na Poblachta ('Association of the Republic'). His message to his followers was uncompromising. In

Dungarvan, he said that future Volunteers, if they wished to achieve the goals fought for over the past four years, 'would have to complete it, not over the bodies of foreign soldiers, but over the dead bodies of their own countrymen. They would have to wade through Irish blood, through the blood of the soldiers of the Irish Government and through, perhaps, the blood of some of the members of the government in order to get Irish freedom.' De Valera used identical language in successive speeches in Carrick-on-Suir, Thurles and Killarney. (He later denied that he had used such language.)[7] The *Sligo Champion* (25 March) was horrified by such 'wild words'; the *Wexford People* (25 March) found them 'astounding'. The *Offaly Independent* (25 March) was equally aghast:

> *By the tactics he* [de Valera] *employs to destroy the Treaty won for Ireland by the Irish Plenipotentiaries, Mr De Valera is fast losing all the esteem and affection in which he was once held by the plain people of this country. To the regret and amazement of countless thousands of his former followers, he has, at several successive meetings addressed by him within the last week, made use of language of so seemingly a reckless character that it calls forth an instant and earnest protest … 'only by civil war' … 'over the dead bodies' … 'wade through Irish blood'… THESE ARE TERRIBLE STATEMENTS TO COME FROM A MAN HOLDING THE RESPONSIBLE POSITION THAT MR DE VALERA HOLDS. The most charitable thing that can be said for him is that, for the moment at any rate, he is in a very bad temper, because he knows in his heart of hearts that the people of this country want the Treaty and mean to have it.*

The *Drogheda Argus* (25 March) believed the coming election would resolve the tensions and was inclined to take incitements to civil war with a 'grain of salt'. The *Waterford News* (24 March), however, defended de Valera against his critics. The latter had challenged Griffith and Collins to stand on the same platform and let the people decide between them and de Valera:

*The liberal and broad-minded attitude of Eamonn De Valera' was not recip-
rocated and the Irish people 'will look with curiosity for some response ... A
question arises, as the rival platform rises[?] ... Why is a General Election
being held before the new Government is established in Dublin? There was
no General Election prior to the setting up of the 'Northern' Parliament ...
England herself is not commanded to get ready for a General Election ... The
Dáil has already ratified ... If this is so, why does England dictate that there
is to be a 'Treaty' General Election in Ireland, whilst there is to be none in
England? The ratification of the Dáil should be all that Ireland should be
asked to contribute, just as all that England contributes is ratification by her
Parliament.*

On 6 April, an IRA group staged a midnight raid on the Dublin premises
of the *Freeman's Journal* and wrecked its machinery. The *Cork Examiner*
had reported on 25 March that seizure and burnings of consignment
parcels of the *Freeman* had occurred every day that week at Limerick
Junction. The *Clonmel Nationalist* had suffered a similar shutdown in
February on the orders of the local IRA chief, Seamus Robinson. Both
papers were attacked because of their support for the Treaty. The latter
commented (29 March) on similar occurrences in the south: 'Sunday's
disturbing incidents in Waterford and Dungarvan show the extremes to
which the Anti-Treaty Party goes in the effort to stampede the country
... The Pro-Treaty Party is placing the Treaty and the new Irish constitution before the electorate, to be decided on by them as the sovereign
authority, the ultimate court of appeal, and it seems to be totally unfair
for any minority party to interfere with that legitimate and democratic
course of action and by force to try and prevent the free expression of
opinion by the people on a matter in which they alone are the supreme
authority.' The IRA attacks on the *Freeman* and the *Nationalist* were
but incidents in a wider pattern of increasing lawlessness, both civil and
political. Old scores from the pre-truce period were still being settled,
and shootings of policemen continued. Between the truce and the ratification of the Treaty, six members of the RIC had been shot dead; five
more such killings took place in February, rising to twelve in March, six

in April and twelve again in May. Some were killed in Ulster counties where truce conditions scarcely prevailed; some while attempting to prevent robberies or arrest suspects; several were men recently disbanded or retired from the force. In addition, there were the murders in late April, already mentioned, of thirteen west Cork Protestant men by local anti-Treaty IRA members.[8]

The *Tuam Herald* (15 April) lamented the:

> *many manifestations of disorder and lawlessness that are breaking out in parts of this country and the growing disregard of authority and the sanctity of the law of property and liberty that are taking place in our midst. The unfortunate disunion in the ranks of the people's leaders is the occasion if not the cause of these unfortunate occurrences. Public liberty, the ordinary freedom to speak one's opinions, is being interfered with with alarming impunity and with frequency by organised bodies of armed men attempting to carry out a systematic plan of terrorism and obstruction, a policy and a programme of action which if persisted in would reduce society to a condition of chaos and absolute anarchy.*

The *Derry People* (15 April) noted that 'for months past incidents of a most disquieting character have been a daily occurrence. A continuance of this state of things can only result in chaos and anarchy … Every sane-minded person will admit that it is time adequate measures were taken for the protection of life and property, and that the elementary rights of citizenship were safeguarded. The people in the South and West … will not submit to a new form of militarist tactics introduced by sections of their own countrymen acting without authority, and by armed individuals.' The *Clonmel Nationalist* (19 April), in an editorial titled 'Denying Popular Rights', detailed the type of activity that obstructed the right of individuals and of the people as a whole to speak, campaign and decide freely on matters of national importance, great and small. This, it asserted, and not the Treaty per se, was the overriding issue:

Notwithstanding the Ard-Fheis pact, and the appeals of the Irish leaders, free election activities are denied in many parts of the country. Here in Clonmel the IRA and their friends have been actively engaged in propaganda for some time, and are not interfered with, but on two occasions when the pro-Treaty party put up leaflets they were torn down, pro-Treatyites were searched, and their houses raided. A member of our staff who was with the pro-Treaty leaflet posters was held up and searched in the streets, and was subsequently arrested and kept in custody in the military barracks, where he was questioned about the possession of arms ... [his trade union protested vigorously that the arrest was 'an outrage on the liberty of the subject which could not be tolerated in any self-respecting community'] ... *His continued incarceration has caused much indignation in the town. The incidents we have referred to are surely sorry examples of the kind of liberty we are 'enjoying' in Ireland just at present ... It is particularly exasperating in a district like this, where the overwhelming mass of the people are in favour of the Treaty and the Free State, and are only awaiting the elections to ratify both with a huge majority.*

Early in April, the leaders of the two sides agreed to a request by the archbishop and lord mayor of Dublin to meet in conference. The *Dundalk Democrat* (15 April) welcomed the announcement of another peace conference to 'find a basis of understanding', noting, 'The situation was growing desperate. Only by the strenuous intervention of the clergy was a conflict averted in Athlone between two sections of IRA. A fight for the possession of an old police barrack in Tullow was reported on Tuesday ... Furthermore the approach of Easter led to sundry speculations on the part of people who seem to expect a rising on every successive Easter Monday as the most fitting way of commemorating the day.' The paper did not hold out much hope of an accommodation; the only way forward was to agree to let the people decide. The *Sligo Champion* (15 April) hailed the conference, as well as statements by the Irish Labour Party and the bishops of Tuam and Killaloe: 'That the overwhelming majority of the people are utterly tired of present conditions and crave for peace is amply evidenced by the strongly worded manifesto issued by the

National Executive of the Irish Labour Party.' The *Carlow Nationalist* wrote on 15 April: 'During the last few weeks there have been many regrettable incidents in Ireland … but we are glad to say that there is now a probability as we forecasted last week of a rapprochement between the two parties which should never be sundered … What we do want is a spirit of independent compromise; that spirit manifested at the Ard-Fheis.' The *Clare Champion* (15 April) adopted a similarly neutral stance, though it published alongside the editorial Bishop Fogarty's sermon of the previous Sunday at Ennis, which trenchantly criticised 'a military junta, who, without sanction or authority from the people, had disowned all Government in the country except their own armed will, and who seem to claim a right to suppress freedom of speech, to suppress and smash up such of the national Press as they disapprove of.' Did this juxtaposition carry a hint that the anodyne editorial voice was adopted under intimidation from local anti-Treatyites?

In any case, these newspapers were premature in their hopes for rapprochement. The previous day, Good Friday 14 April, in an action too late for that week's editions, a 200-strong anti-Treatyite military force under the command of Rory O'Connor had set about re-enacting history by commandeering both the Christian festival of Easter and a major public building in Dublin, this time by occupying the Four Courts building, the chief bastion of law in Ireland. The *Meath Chronicle* (22 April) represented the neutralist view when it commented a week later, at a time when there was still no news of the outcome of the peace conference:

We cannot believe that either Éamon de Valera or Arthur Griffith will leave an avenue unexplored in the endeavour to save our country from the dangers which beset it … Can either suggest that their irrevocable determination is sufficient cause for Irishmen to take up arms against each other; shoot, destroy and devastate; brother shoot brother; Irishmen destroy Irish property; Irish soldiers destroy Irish soil? Will Arthur Griffith or Éamon De Valera stand behind that proposition? … Are we not entitled to expect something more from these men? ... We put it to Mr De Valera and Mr Roderick O'Connor; to Mr Griffith and Mr Collins, that, while they suffered, while they fought, while they endured, the people suffered and the people endured. We will not question their right as a united body to ask the people, if necessary, to face the English tyrant, but we do question their right to ask the people to suffer or endure the horrors of civil war. They have no right to ask the people to do that, the people who stood nobly by them against England. The people have borne a lot; it were well that the leaders now in conference should understand that there are things they will not bear: they will not bear civil war ...

Most ministers were clear in their understanding that the Four Courts occupation represented an open challenge to the authority of the Provisional Government. However, Collins held back from open confrontation. As he did so, he came under increasing pressure from Churchill and the British Cabinet to act, increasing the tension. The expressions of concern noted above came from a wide range of newspapers spanning the political spectrum. Some were former Redmondite, others pro-Sinn Féin; some had staunchly supported the military campaign in the recent war and were willing to renew it should the fighting resume, others were more pacifist in sentiment. Some were more ideologically committed to the goal of the republic than others. All were, for the moment, united in dread of what increasingly looked like looming civil war. The *Southern Star* (15 April) was in fear of 'the awful dangers and dread possibilities of a situation towards which this country seems to be drifting. The mass of the people – hopeless, helpless, bewildered, dismayed – looks on with grief and apprehension. The present state of affairs, unless checked and controlled, may develop into internecine strife, ruinous anarchy and utter chaos.' In the deteriorating situation, the *Dundalk Democrat* (20 May) was impatient for the election: 'It is clear that until the people have declared their will in a general election the country cannot hope for a strong and resolute government, and until we have strong and resolute government we cannot look for peace, tranquility or order.'

D. THE GENERAL ELECTION

On 19 May, President Griffith asked the Dáil to declare an election in the twenty-six counties, to be held on 16 June, saying:

> *'the people of Ireland have been for the last six months kept in a state of suspense, kept in a state of being muzzled, kept in a state of being denied the fundamental right of the people of any country to decide whether they will or will not have a measure that affects their lives, that affects their property, and that affects their destinies... They have suffered for six months under an insolent denial of their right to say whether they, the sovereign people of Ireland, will accept or reject that Treaty. They must suffer no longer, so far as we are concerned.'*

Speaking for the anti-Treatyites, Cathal Brugha opposed the election, pointing to serious deficiencies in the electoral register and objecting to the failure to call the election for all thirty-two counties and the consequent disenfranchisement of the people of the six Ulster counties.

The following day, Collins and de Valera, in an effort to avoid a bitter electoral contest, agreed on a seven-point pact under which all Sinn Féin candidates for the election, pro- and anti-Treaty alike, would be nominated to a united Sinn Féin 'panel', each side nominating as many candidates as it currently had TDs. The right of other interests and parties to contest the election was acknowledged, but the pact was an attempt to maintain the fiction that the Treaty was an issue subordinate to the need to maintain national unity as embodied in the 'national movement' of Sinn Féin.[9]

During the election campaign, the two wings of the pact refrained from attacking each other and concentrated their fire mainly on the candidates of the Farmers' Party, the Irish Labour Party and other 'independents'. The *Connaught Telegraph* (10 June) hoped that 'new blood will be introduced into an assembly that so far has not covered itself with any glory, in fact has brought our country to the verge of ruin, and the danger is not yet over … we believe that the electors are not under the slightest obligation to the members who strove to wreck the Treaty, and it would have cleared the air a good deal if there was an end put to their activities'. The following week, with the results not yet in, the paper castigated both Sinn Féin factions and the pact:

> Those who have almost lost us the Treaty, and one side is as bad as the other, have chloroformed the voters. We are having a general election of a sort. So far the sitting members only have been returned for the constituencies where no contests took place, and where contests have been produced both parties in the Dáil are united in destroying the chances of the independent candidates … [Voters'] opinions are set at nought by those who have sickened the country with talk since the Treaty was brought home, and who decided that they would remain in office whether the voters liked it or not. It is a piece of brazen effrontery that will not be without its evil effects. Some people seem to think that the Dáil was set up specially to enable them air their eloquence and fool the country … The country is sick of this humbug … To say that the Dáil reflects the opinion of the voters is a lie …

The result gave ninety-four of the 128 available seats to the Sinn Féin panel, thirty-four of them without contest where no non-panellists had been nominated, and sixty of the ninety it had to contest. Within the panel, the pro-Treatyites won forty-one seats and had seven defeated candidates as against the anti-Treatyites who won nineteen seats and had twenty-two defeated candidates. A notable feature of the result was the success of the Irish Labour Party's campaign: the party had seventeen of its eighteen candidates elected and it might have won more seats had it fielded more candidates. Labour candidates won more than the total vote of the anti-Treatyites and not far off double the votes per candidate of all the Sinn Féin panellists. In summary, pro-Treaty Sinn Féin won 38.48 per cent, anti-Treaty Sinn Féin 21.26 per cent, the Irish Labour Party 21.33 per cent, the Farmers' Party 7.84 per cent and independents 10.59 per cent of the vote. Assuming all of the non-panellists were willing to work the Treaty (non-panel voters gave twice as many transfers to pro-Treaty as to anti-Treaty candidates), this gave an aggregate pro-Treaty vote of more than 78 per cent and ninety-two pro-Treatyite seats out of 128. Had anti-Treaty candidates not automatically taken seventeen of the uncontested thirty-four seats, their proportion of seats would have been lower than the 28 per cent they won.

Of thirty-one papers that commented on the election result, twenty-three (74 per cent) accepted it gladly as the verdict of the people on the Treaty, despite the features of the election that had tended to mask the real issue. Another six were evasive or carried no comment. Some of these, pro-Treaty organs from whom approval of the election result might have been expected, such as the *Limerick Leader* or the Waterford *Munster Express*, may have wished to avoid comment for fear of antagonising the strong anti-Treatyite elements in their localities. The *Irish News* (26 June) urged that the new government must assert its authority in all parts of the twenty-six counties or else face chaos and ruin. The *Cork Examiner* (20 June) wrote that 'the Third Dáil is duly authorized to express the will of the people and to implement majority rule'. The *Kilkenny People* (24 June) interpreted the outcome as 'The Nation's Clear, Strong Voice'; the *Dundalk Democrat* (24 June) called it an 'unmistakeable pronouncement of the people for the Treaty'. For the *Offaly Independent* (24 June), the popular verdict was never in doubt; the *Westmeath Examiner* (24 June) urged the anti-Treatyites to 'bow to the well-known will of the people'. The *Midland Tribune* (24 June) wrote of the result, 'To the impartial observer this has been clear for months past. The fact is now made absolute to everyone. Had the elections all been fully contested we believe that the victory of the pro-Treaty party would have been even more decisive …' The poor showing of the Anti-Treaty Party was 'due solely to the fact that they were in opposition to the people's will on the Treaty'. The *Connaught Telegraph* (24 June) claimed that, had the election been a free one:

a dozen Anti-Treaty candidates would not have been returned… The people were not free to choose whom they might, nor were those who would seek their suffrage free from the perils of intimidation and of personal violence. Yet, in spite of all the circumstances which combined to silence the complete expression of the people's views the electors and their candidates have shown that the voice of the people will not be drowned. The remarkable success of the Labour and Independent candidates is not so much a victory for the class interests they represented as for the interest of the nation as a whole. In so far as they might the Irish people have shown that they approve of the Peace Pact between Ireland and Great Britain.

Dissenting, or at least eccentric, opinions came from the *Roscommon Herald* (24 June), which reflected that the outcome showed 'the ingratitude of the voters to the fighting men', and from the *Donegal Vindicator* (23 June), which asserted that 'The people have bowed the knee to English domination. The "democratic" constitution which vests in the English King the power to veto Irish laws was before them as they voted. Someday we, or our children's children, will wipe out the record.' The *Waterford News* (30 June) claimed that 'We have lived to see the rotten Dublin daily press stampeding the Irish people to the same cry: "Down with De Valera! Don't let the IRA dictate to Irish voters! Beware of a military dictatorship!"'

E. CIVIL WAR

Just before the election, events had seemed to be tending inexorably in the direction of civil war. The course of the election campaign itself, with its unique arrangements, had bizarrely hidden this tendency behind a façade of 'unity'. The election result, and the decisive mandate it gave to the Provisional Government, as well as other events, soon restored a sense of reality.

Even before the result was announced, the anti-Treaty IRA, at its third convention, was debating, amid a temporary split on the issue, immediate resumption of the war against the British.[10] Meanwhile, pressure from Churchill and the British government on the Provisional Government to end the chaotic state of affairs in Ireland increased in intensity. When Field-Marshal Sir Henry Wilson, former military adviser to the Northern Ireland government, was assassinated in London by anti-Treaty IRA men on 22 June, the pressure became irresistible. Lloyd George privately warned Collins that the 'ambiguous position' of the IRA and the 'open rebellion' persisting at the Four Courts could no longer be ignored and that His Majesty's Government 'cannot consent to a continuance of this state of things'. On 26 June in the House of Commons, Churchill threatened that if the Four Courts rebellion were not brought to a speedy end, 'we shall regard the Treaty as having been formally violated'. The British military drew up plans to attack the Four Courts, but these were not activated as talks had now begun between Griffith and the National Army and British military authorities on the supply of the equipment needed by the Provisional Government to eject the rebels from the Four Courts. On 27 June, the trigger was supplied by the arrest of an anti-Treaty officer while carrying out a raid in Dublin, followed by the arrest by the republicans of a Treatyite officer and his detention in the Four Courts. An ultimatum to the rebel garrison early on 28 June to vacate the Four Courts building having been ignored, the National Army began shelling the building using four eighteen-pounder field guns supplied by the British. Other detachments amounting to about 500 rebels barricaded themselves into a hotel and other buildings on the north-eastern side of O'Connell St. Two days later, the Four Courts rebels' munitions store close to the Public Records Office was hit by a shell and exploded, causing a fire that destroyed the vast store of centuries-old archival records housed there. The 130 survivors of the garrison surrendered that afternoon. It took several days more to take the O'Connell St. positions. By 5 July the Dublin battle, and the first phase of the Civil War, was over, with casualties amounting to at least fifteen deaths on the rebel side, at least thirty on the government side and possibly more than 250 civilian deaths.

Of the twenty-seven newspapers that commented on the outbreak of armed conflict, at least ten expressed sorrow or horror at the fratricidal strife. Nine were insistent that the central issue was that of authority, four were evasive on the issue and another four were clearly constrained in their commentary by military censorship or isolation in anti-Treatyite-dominated areas. The *Sligo Champion* (1 July) wrote that 'the 'ominous cloud' had burst, defying the incorrigible optimists. The *Tipperary Star* (1 July) called it a 'hideous tragedy', but qualified this by stating that the sovereign will of the people had been impeded. The *Derry Journal* (5 July) called it a 'sad and sanguinary struggle', while the *Derry People* (24 June) said it was futile to appeal to de Valera to accept the people's verdict. The *Kilkenny People* (1 July) headlined its editorial 'Ireland's Crown of Sorrow' while the *Meath Chronicle* (1 July) lamented the fact that Irishmen had fired upon Irishmen and begged anti-Treatyites to realise that the country had decided against them and 'bow to the inevitable'. The *Leinster Leader* (24 June, 1 July) had avoided comment on the general election result by concentrating on details of the new Free State constitution, and it now adopted the same approach to the Civil War. Similarly, the *Carlow Nationalist* (1 July) had avoided acknowledgement of the pro-Treaty election victory and now preferred a recitation of ancient historical grievances to facing up to the emerging conflict. The *Dundalk Democrat* (8 July) described the scene: 'The Four Courts is a heap of smoking ruin, and, in its ashes lie, lost for ever, the priceless records filed therein. O'Connell St. from the Pillar to the Rotunda, is almost wholly gone, as completely as the lower half of that fine street was after the 1916 Rebellion'. Some fifty innocent civilians were dead, mostly by snipers' bullets; material losses were estimated at £2-4 million in 'the fight begun by Mr Rory O'Connor and joined in later by De Valera and other leading lights'.

At the opposite end of the spectrum of opinion was the *Waterford News* (30 June), which saw the fighting as the outcome of a British plot against Irish freedom: 'that Plot has never failed to cause the effusion of blood in Ireland in every generation for the past 750 years. Dublin is once more the scene of this blood-pollution … The present blood effusion may be styled the Churchill Plot'. Had de Valera's warnings of last March (not threats, it added, 'as the rotten Dublin daily press distorted his words') been heeded 'the present bloodshed would have been averted, and a strong Coalition Gov would by this have restored stable conditions to Ireland. But Ireland listened to England's voice …' The *Donegal Vindicator* (30 June) was shocked at the use of heavy artillery against what the Provisional Government called 'lawlessness': 'we confess Michael Collins' way would not be our way'. The paper offered its own alternative, which would be to surround the building with military, do nothing and allow nobody in or out until the garrison opened fire, or wait for hunger and boredom to take effect; then 'we would have the consciousness of having beaten "lawlessness" and had our hands clear of Irish blood. Spectacular effect may be a grand thing but we prefer methods that smack less of Britain. Nobody can argue that there was any hurry in clearing out the Four Courts … Let those who can do so justify the use of big guns against Irishmen. We cannot.'

As the fighting spread in all directions outside Dublin, some newspapers found their operations hampered by the wartime conditions. The pro-Treaty *Connaught Telegraph* (8 July) announced to its readers that 'owing to the dislocation of the railway and telegraphic facilities, we are unable to supply news at first hand, and that given in our columns this week has been supplied officially by the [anti-Treaty] IRA, Castlebar. In short, all news relating to the present unfortunate hostilities is turned out under the supervision of Headquarters, 4th Western Division IRA, Castlebar.' Its news pages duly appeared under the headline 'Irish Conflict/To Uphold the Republic'. The following week, its editorial carried further, if mild, evidence of censorship by the anti-Treaty side: '… There is another predominant factor, which we admit candidly, and that is: that while Mayo is held completely by Republican forces there is no terror. The men who compose that force, while acting politically contrary to the will of the majority of the people, are worthy of admiration. We, while maintaining our adherence to the principle of the Free State … look on in admiration of those men and their methods …' (With the capture of Westport and Castlebar at the end of July, this pressure on the paper was lifted.) The *Cork Examiner*, published in the anti-Treaty-ite-held southern capital, carried no editorials on the war during July; the editor instead notified readers that the paper was under IRA censorship. This situation continued until Provisional Government troops captured Cork on 10 August. With Limerick city in republican hands until the last week of July, the pro-Treaty *Limerick Leader* suspended publication for two weeks that month rather than submit to the other side's military censorship. The paper urged republicans (31 July) to 'bow to the will of the people and the rule of the majority'. On 11 August, after the anti-Treatyite forces had been forced to withdraw, the paper had to announce another suspension due to the collapse of advertising revenue, a step also taken by the city's three other newspapers; both it and the *Limerick Echo* reappeared in mid-October. The *Waterford News* did not need pressure from anti-Treaty forces to express support for their cause: on 7 July its editorial was titled 'Today's Republican Bulletin'. The following month, after the city had been taken by Provisional Government forces, it had reason to complain of military censorship from the government side. The same city's *Munster Express,* which carried news but no comment on the general election or the outbreak of the Civil War, suddenly sprang to life on 26 August, following the shooting dead in the city of Lieut.-Commdt. Eamonn O'Brien of the National Army, by publishing the local bishop's 'grave admonition to the people', which denounced the claim that the army, or part of it, could declare its independence of all civil authority. Anyone who set himself up against his bishop's teaching was 'not fit to receive Absolution'.

The sudden deaths, ten days apart in August, of the two leading figures in the Provisional Government, Arthur Griffith, president of the Dáil, and Michael Collins, commander-in-chief of the National Army, caused shock and consternation across the country. Griffith's death of a stroke on 12 August evoked nationwide grief. The killing of Collins in an ambush by anti-Treatyite forces in west Cork on 22 August compounded the sense of national calamity. Thirty-one newspapers of the sample reacted with predictable grief and anguish to the news of their deaths. The *Cork Examiner* (14 August) paid tribute to Griffith's 'perfectly balanced mind'; the *Derry People* (26 August) called his death 'an incalculable loss to Ireland'. The *Kilkenny People* (19 August) wrote of Griffith's 'ceaseless energy and incessant toil, guided by an almost superhuman gift of foresight, which directed the country to the position it now holds'. The *Meath Chronicle* (26 August) wrote of Griffith and Collins as an 'ideal team' and called their deaths 'a stunning blow upon the Irish Nation'; the *Southern Star* (26 August) lamented that 'woe and pain, pain and woe are our lot'; the *Connaught Telegraph* wrote of 'Ireland's Double Tragedy' while the *Sligo Champion* (26 August) headed its editorial 'A National Calamity'. The *Roscommon Journal* (26 August) wrote that Collins had been admired by all and had been 'a Republican in spirit'. For the *Derry Journal* (25 August) the loss of Collins was 'too poignant for tears'.

By mid-August in Munster, and mid-September in Connacht, the war had ceased to be a conventional one fought for the possession of towns and, on the anti-Treatyite side, had become a guerrilla campaign increasingly confined to areas of difficult terrain and the more remote rural parts of the south and west, though isolated units could strike any-where. The death of Collins had an embittering effect on the conflict, ensuring that, where opposing forces had previously been reluctant to fire on each other, the war became an even more vicious re-enactment of the anti-British violence of recent years: ambush met with reprisal killing, assassination with counter-assassination. The insurgents faced the (mainly passive) hostility of most of the population as well as the opposition of the Catholic clergy. In mid-October, the Catholic hierar-chy, which had opposed anti-Treatyite actions since the April occupation of the Four Courts, met at Maynooth and issued a blistering pastoral letter condemning their continued campaign. The letter labelled the

'Irregular insurrection' as 'a section of the community ... [who had] chosen to attack their own country as if she were a foreign power'. What they called a war was 'morally only a system of murder and assassination of the national forces', characterised by 'cruelty, robbery, falsehood and crime'. The pastoral received the endorsement of twenty newspapers, most of them reprinting it in full, while another two published it without comment. The *Southern Star* (14 October) highlighted in its news page a key passage: 'The guerrilla war now carried on by Irregulars is without moral sanction and therefore the killing of National soldiers in the course of it is murder before God'. The *Tuam Herald* (21 October) called it 'momentously important ... the united voice of the Church and Nation'. The *Sligo Champion* (14 October) called it a 'forceful denunciation of Irregular actions and a statement of citizens' duties'. The *Clonmel Nationalist* (14 October) supported its condemnation of the 'revolt against the legitimate government'. The *Wexford People* (14 October) called on the 'misguided people wreaking havoc' to 'heed the Bishops' warning on the moral law'. The *Drogheda Argus* (14 October) reckoned that forty per cent of Irregular fighters were 'victims of a perverted sense of honour'. Only the *Donegal Vindicator* (14 October) differed from the mainstream, writing that the Provisional Government must now meet the republican leaders to discuss peace.

It was about this time that the government's director of communications, Piaras Béaslaí, issued instructions to the newspapers as to the terminology they were expected to use in relation to the conflict. Henceforth, government troops were to be referred to as the 'National Army' or the 'Irish Army'. Anti-Treatyites were to be termed 'Irregulars' and not 'Republicans', 'IRA' or 'troops', and the ranks of their officers were not to be published. Papers were not to publish letters regarding the treatment of Irregular prisoners.

A week before the bishops' pastoral, the government had announced a 'full amnesty and pardon' for all anti-Treatyites already 'in insurrection and rebellion against the State' who surrendered their weapons and munitions on or before 15 October. On that date, the government's new emergency legislation, the Public Safety Act, was to come into effect, setting up military courts that could impose the death penalty for the possession of arms. In a combination of government carrot and ecclesiastical stick, many of the papers published this amnesty offer, signed by the new Dáil president, William Cosgrave, alongside the bishops' pastoral.

On 11 November, the British-born Erskine Childers, former Home Ruler and gun-runner for the Irish Volunteers in 1914, now chief propagandist for the anti-Treatyites, was arrested in Wicklow in possession of a pistol (ironically, a gift given to him by Collins). Under the new legislation, he was executed by firing squad on 24 November. In the meantime, at least seven anti-Treatyite prisoners had been executed for the same offence. In retaliation for the executions, the 'Irregular' chief of staff, Liam Lynch, issued his 'Orders of Frightfulness' on 30 November, identifying fourteen categories of people to be shot on sight, including members of the Dáil and Senate who had voted for the Public Safety Act, hostile newspaper editors and judges. The first fruits of this new policy came on 7 December, when two pro-Treaty TDs, Sean Hales and Pádraic Ó Máille, were shot on a Dublin street, Hales dying in the incident. The *Cork Examiner* reacted the next day, under the title 'Quo Vadimus?', with an implied call for further draconian measures: 'Yesterday's Dublin tragedy should set the Irish people seriously thinking whether the country is not only drifting but driving headlong. If members of the Dáil are to be shot because they do their duty as elected representatives of the Nation, we may bid farewell to ordered government and the last vestige of civilisation in Ireland. The country will be reduced to a state of anarchy, from which it will be impossible for Republican or Free Stater to rescue it.' The government's response was swift: the following day, four of the imprisoned leaders of the former Four Courts garrison were summarily executed by firing squad. Since they had been captured in July before the passing of the emergency legislation, this act was one of highly questionable legality; some ministers did not try to defend it on any grounds other than as simple counter-terrorism.[11] Two days later, the house of Sean McGarry TD was burned down by anti-Treatyites, his seven-year-old son dying in the blaze.

These weeks of executions, from that of Childers to those of the Four Courts prisoners, evoked mixed reactions in the press. Of thirty-one papers that commented on the general state of the country at this time, only eight expressed support or accepted the need for the executions, while seven protested or implied opposition, and another five confined themselves to lamentation. Ten found it easier to ignore them altogether, while one called for peace talks. For the *Dundalk Democrat* (25 November), the Childers execution was the 'flavour of grim reality' needed to show that the government was 'in grim earnest'. The *Offaly Independent* (30 December) also expressed support, affirming that 'the people's will shall prevail'. The *Derry Journal* (11 December) wrote that 'many will deplore and condemn executions without trial' but defended them on the grounds of 'military necessity'. For the *Irish News* (8 December), the restoration of order was 'the national need of the hour'. On the other side, the *Southern Star* (16 December) condemned the assassination of Hales and 'no less strongly' the executions of the Four Courts four. For the *Meath Chronicle* (9, 16 December) all these events were 'shocking developments' but the executions were 'no remedy'. The *Midland Tribune* (2 December) was 'against executions, and we do not consider this to be the best policy to pursue. We are also against ambushes, the taking of people from their homes at night, the breaking up of railways and the general destruction of property. Despite arguments about the Pact we consider the Government the legitimate Government elected by the majority of the Irish people'. The *Waterford News* (1, 15 December) did not comment but published an account of Childers' death titled 'How He Died' and later the last messages of two of the Four Courts prisoners. The *Kilkenny People* (9 December) grieved that 'the nation is bleeding to death' as though there were 'a curse on the country'.

Before the Hales murder and subsequent executions, one of the most trenchant comments came from the *Clonmel Nationalist* (29 November):

Ireland is passing through an agonising time, and the people's patience is being severely tried. The fiendish work of wreckage and destruction goes on, the De Valeraites are still 'wading through blood' to the will-o'-the-wisp objective, and now a vendetta of vengeance is being openly preached … relentless warfare is carried on against the people and their duly and properly constituted Parliament and Government, and unscrupulous methods are adopted to reduce the country to ruin and desolation, and prevent the operation of normal law and ordered conditions. The will and wishes of the citizens are flouted, morality and religion are thrown to the winds, and an armed and reckless minority who will not listen to reason or commonsense, ravage the land and seek to turn it into a regular inferno. It is an appalling situation to contemplate … The present deplorable state of affairs, with all its attendant miseries, hardships and huge losses, will continue until the Irish Government asserts its authority in right earnest, puts an end to the agonising deadlock … It is time to end it all … The very life of the nation is at stake.

The *Carlow Nationalist* (16 December) wrote prophetically, 'We are living through a terrible period of turmoil, misery and bloodshed, the effects of which must outlast the generation, even two or three generations, unless they come to an end immediately'. On 16 December, the *Galway Observer's* news page headlines summed up the reality of the Civil War: 'New Terror/Work of Incendiaries/Houses of Senator, Dáil Member and Government Officials Attacked/Many Night Fires in Dublin/Narrow Escape of Sleeping Children' (16 December).

F. THE ADVENT OF THE FREE STATE

Against this background of daily violence, the legal ramifications of the Treaty were worked out. On 25 October, the Third Dáil (elected in June) adopted the Constitution of the Irish Free State, framed according to the terms of the Treaty. On 5 December, the Irish Free State Constitution Act received the royal assent; under its terms the constitution came into effect the following day. The Free State was now established by law as a parliamentary system of government under a form of constitutional monarchy; the Provisional Government was replaced by an executive council headed by William Cosgrave. In a strange turn of the wheel of history, the former constitutional nationalist turned *bête noire* of Redmond's Irish Party and Sinn Féin sympathiser, Timothy Healy, was appointed to the post of governor general, the representative of the king who would replace the lord lieutenant.[12] Also under the terms of the Act, the parliament of Northern Ireland, theoretically part of the Free State from the beginning, was given the power to opt out of it within one month. Prime Minister Craig and his colleagues wasted no time in doing so, and on 7 December King George received and assented to the petition of the Stormont assembly that it be exempted from the powers of the Free State.

Of twenty-five newspapers that commented on these events, fifteen hailed the historic nature of the occasion, though many found their celebration of the event overshadowed by the gloom of civil war. The *Connacht Tribune* (16 December) spoke for these when it wrote that there would be jubilation if conditions were different. Apart from this reality, the issue that marred the occasion for some was that of partition. However, for an issue that had been, more than any other, the source of the turmoil of the previous six years, that had fuelled a deeper and more enduring public rage than had the executions of 1916, had destroyed the Irish Party and, as recently as 1921, had hardened nationalist opinion against any acceptance of the Government of Ireland Act, the reaction was remarkably low-key. In part, this may have reflected a desire not to give ammunition to the anti-Treatyites. It seemed that reality had been accepted and the rage had turned into a cold huff. Only five papers mentioned partition as a shortcoming of an otherwise satisfactory settlement, and their comments were mostly mild. The *Sligo Champion* (2 December) was dispassionate about the implications: 'It is a foregone conclusion that the Six-County Parliament will contract out, and the Consequential Provisions Bill deals mainly with the conditions which must arise in these circumstances. The effect of the measure will be to treat the Six-County area as part and parcel of Great Britain. A Customs barrier will, therefore, be necessary, and a land frontier will be established for the purpose of regulating the import and export of goods ...' The still nostalgically Redmondite *Westmeath Examiner* (9 December) reflected that, for the difference between Home Rule and the Free State, an appalling price had been paid. On partition, it was more hopeful: 'Were it not for two serious drawbacks there would be reason today to rejoice in Ireland. One is the exclusion of six counties from the jurisdiction of the Free State. All true Irishmen, north and south, will hope that this exclusion is only temporary and will be of short duration. The second arises from the strife and demoralisation which exist among our people.' The paper forlornly hoped that those currently in opposition 'may now be convinced of the reality of the Treaty and of the position in which Ireland stands as mistress in her own house ... [and] lay down their arms and unite with their fellow countrymen'. The *Clonmel Nationalist* (9 December) was even prepared to consider the merits of conciliation above coercion where Ulster was concerned. In an editorial titled 'Our Own Again!' it wrote:

> At long last foreign domination has been thrown off ... her people are in undisputed possession of those rights and privileges which are the proud heritage of freely governed, independent countries. Ireland has now taken her ancient place amongst the nations, her destinies are in her own hands, her Government is wholly Irish from the Governor General down ... True, we have partition, but that question is settling itself by the cold logic of facts and events, and it is quite obvious to all observers that self-determination and self-interest, too, will eventually heal the breach in the north and bring all the counties into the national fold. All seem to agree that where coercion might fail reason and commonsense must in good time solve the problem of the north ... the trend of things [is] *towards a reapproachment* [sic].

Only the *Mayo News* (16 December) flagged 'The Evil of Partition', writing that the government must find a way of dealing with it.

As to the future, the *Irish News* (8 December) wrote soberly that, 'The feuds and bitternesses, dissensions and distrusts that have resulted in hideous quarrels and that have been deliberately fomented and nurtured with hellish ingenuity from outside Ireland for three centuries, up to the passing year, cannot be dispelled within twelve months, or twice, or thrice, that period unless circumstances and conditions thoroughly favourable to the cessation of strife and the triumph of common sense arise in the North-East and throughout the rest of the common country'. Regarding the hopes invested by many nationalists that the Boundary Commission clause of the Treaty could dramatically reduce the territory of Northern Ireland, the paper commented on Craig's speech in the 'opt-out' debate:

> In Sir James Craig's 'deliberate opinion' – fortified, he said, by the views of lawyers – the portion of the Treaty which dealt with the (Boundary) Commission was 'ultra vires' – beyond the power of the British Government to enforce ... Sir James Craig's attitude is constitutionally unsustainable ... he should remember that there is a very narrow boundary line between stubbornness and mere stupidity ... It is not stubbornness on one side or rigid insistence on legal rights on the other that can help to bridge the chasm of Partition. The Northern and Free State Parliaments and Governments must give practical effect to the conciliatory sentiments expressed on both sides of the present 'Boundary'. If these sentiments are sincere indications of good spirits on both sides, they can be translated into deeds. One quarrel begets another. The way to peace can be found if the quest for it is seriously pursued.

G. THE END OF THE CIVIL WAR

The Civil War continued into the early months of 1923, with anti-Treaty military activity increasingly confined to guerrilla actions in the remoter areas of the south and west and isolated actions throughout the country aimed at destruction of infrastructure and arson attacks on the homes of unionist landowners, pro-Treaty members of the Dáil and prominent Free State supporters (in all, 192 such homes were burned). Official executions of republican prisoners continued into the new year until early February, when they were suspended by the Free State government. However, as the fighting continued, 'unofficial' executions were running at about twice the official level; by the end of the war, the toll would reach seventy-seven official and about 150 unofficial executions. During March, the conflict, in Kerry in particular, became even more vicious. The use of landmines to ambush Free State soldiers was answered by several incidents of counter-atrocity in north Kerry in which selected republican prisoners were executed by being tied to landmines. The government's tight control of war news ensured that these incidents were not reported in the local papers although widely known in the localities.

With senior anti-Treatyites, including de Valera, wishing to abandon the war as hopeless, the army executive met during March in a remote Munster valley, where it was decided by a single vote to continue the campaign. However, the capture of the anti-Treaty TD for north Kerry, Austin Stack, and above all the death in action on 10 April of the chief of staff, Liam Lynch, whose vote had been decisive for continuance, were sufficiently demoralising to remove the remaining obstacles to a peace move.

In an open letter to the government, de Valera outlined his terms for a cessation. These included two conditions that could not be accepted by the government: the abrogation of the oath of allegiance to the Free State constitution to be taken by all members of the Dáil, and the placing of armaments in dumps under 'Irregular' control. President (the Free State title of the prime minister) Cosgrave indicated the government's rejection but made no counter-proposals. There the matter rested on 12 May when the apparent 'breakdown in negotiations' was reported in the newspapers. The *Connaught Telegraph* reported baldly under the heading 'Irish War News': 'The reply of the Government to Mr De Valera's proclamation, ordering a "cease fire" after noon on Monday week, was a rigid silence and the execution of two anti-Treatyites 48 hours after.' Altogether, fifteen newspapers reported or commented on the news, although only five carried detailed commentary on the two sticking points. Though there was disappointment at the breakdown, most papers assumed that the mere existence of peace overtures must mean that a formal cessation could not be long delayed.

Among those who supported the government's position on the sticking points were the *Drogheda Argus* (19 May) and the *Connaught Telegraph* (12 May), which wrote, 'Now that this armed revolt against established Government has been crushed out, the opinion of law-abiding people is that all firearms be collected.' The *Midland Tribune* (12 May) wrote that the oath was an integral part of the Treaty, and could not be abrogated or ignored without abrogating the Treaty: 'For ourselves, we think that, sooner or later, this oath will be either modified or abolished … It can only be done by a united demand from a united people … The oath question can well go for decision to the people at the election.' Much more critical commentary came from the *Galway Observer* (12 May): 'Our view of Mr De Valera and his peace proposals is quite justified. He means to carry on all the time, but the means he has adopted to deceive the people is anything but honourable'. It based this assessment on an intercepted letter written in prison by Irregular leader Ernie O'Malley, who had said that the 'military position is splendid' and looked forward to a resumption of hostilities. From this, the paper drew the conclusion that de Valera had made his peace proposals knowing the government could not accept them: 'That is to say, he is only trying to humbug us'. At the opposite pole of sympathy, the *Meath Chronicle* (19 May) expressed 'profound regret' at the breakdown but thought it premature to abandon hope of a settlement. It credited de Valera's manifesto with being 'sincerely devised to bring to a period the disastrous civil war … Mr De Valera is accused, perhaps rightly … of being a weaver of words. Does it not seem as if some of his opponents are wedded to a shibboleth, that any move of this gentleman must necessarily be insincere and dishonest?' Regarding the issue of the oath, it recognised that it was 'impossible for a certain type of republican to accept it without outraging his conscience' but sought for a way to square the circle: 'Is there any way by which it [the oath] could be, if not abrogated, at least so arranged that it could be taken by the most determined opponent of Royalty? The only way would seem to be by the consent of England as a contracting party to the Treaty. Would England consent to the abrogation of the oath if representations were made to her? We have very little belief in England's goodwill to this country, but if there was goodwill …' But even this republican-friendly paper was with the government on the second matter of the dumping of arms: 'There can be only one Government in this country, and accordingly the functioning Government must have control of the arms.'

Most of the twenty-four newspapers that commented in some way on the winding down of the war did not wait for the formal announcement of the end of hostilities at the end of May to express their sense of relief and their hopes for a better future. The *Derry Journal* wrote (18 May), 'Everyone is hoping that the last has been seen of that turbulence and terrorism, which in many districts developed into sheer lust of destruction … The danger of such a calamity is passing. People are settling down to business with a stronger sense of independence and security than they have experienced for generations'. 'The revolt against popular Government in Ireland has practically collapsed,' wrote the *Clonmel Nationalist* (19 May). 'The stern words of the Bishop of Waterford in his address to the people of Clonmel should have a powerful influence in many directions and especially in impelling those who had looted property to restore same as quickly as possible.' The *Wexford People* (19 May) saw a 'Brighter Outlook': 'A general air of settling down to the ordinary routine of business is noticeable … Peace was never more needed.' The *Westmeath Examiner* (26 May) took the success of the Royal Dublin Society Spring Show as a barometer of 'returning stability'. The *Sligo Champion* (26 May) thought that the re-opening of the Great Southern and Western Railway line to Sligo 'indicates a rapid return to normal conditions and is a hopeful augury for the future'. Finally, on 29 May, the *Cork Examiner* carried the headlines 'End of War/Orders of Irregular Chiefs/Arms to be Laid Aside' and, on 30 May, 'To Cease Fire/Order of 24 May to be completed by 28 May.'

Two broad strands of editorial opinion were now evident in the news-papers. On one side was a group of eight organs that were not yet willing to let the disruptors of the nation's peace escape responsibility. Several of this group quoted words from a recent sermon of Bishop Fogarty of Killaloe that 'the past year was one of the most disgraceful, sorrowful and shameful Ireland has ever experienced … [there had been] more destruction carried out by Irishmen within the past few years than could be laid to the charge of England in 50 years'. The *Wexford People* (12 May) believed that the country was relieved at the end of

> *the foolish but criminal conduct that has been devastating the land … It is distressing in the extreme to think that Irishmen celebrated the coming of their country's freedom by this huge sacrifice of the lives and property of fellow-Irish-men … these misguided young men, who certainly were led into certain channels of thought by hearing extravagant speeches and views during their most impressionable years … [there] could be no objection under any circum-stances to any section striving for a Republic or any other form of Government … if they believed they could achieve it by reasonable and constitutional means. But to employ the same drastic and terrible methods against their own Government and their own fellow countrymen that they employed against an alien Government some time before – methods the morality of which everyone is far from agreeing – was indefensible and reprehensible, no matter from what standpoint it is viewed.*

The Redmondite *Westmeath Examiner* preached its own sermon that was not about to let Bishop Fogarty, 'a supporter of the policy that dethroned the old Constitutional movement', off the hook either: 'The inevitable outcome of the election of 1918 was a resort to force. All who assisted in bringing about its result are responsible for the consequences that ensued.' Many had foreseen these consequences during the election, others had been too short-sighted; some were 'carried away by idealism with little foundation, others by antagonism towards those [the Irish Party] who had elevated the country to a position little short of economic and political independence.'

The *Drogheda Argus* (3 June) mocked the tone of de Valera's final message to his 'Soldiers of Liberty, Legion of the Rearguard', with its 'high-sounding language, the comic opera style of eulogy in which he speaks of his misguided followers and their disastrous war on public life and property'. The *Kilkenny People* (2 June) wrote that de Valera had 'confessed the failure of his disastrously costly effort to subvert democratic rule in this country and to substitute for it the domination of an armed minority. The effort has failed, but the cost to the country has been enormous. Priceless lives have been lost and millions' worth of property, public and private, has been ruthlessly destroyed. By a perverse system of logic which seeks to prove too much this is all supposed to have been done in the sacred name of Liberty!' The bitterest comment came from the *Tuam Herald* (2 June): 'Defeated, discredited and vanquished in his unholy war, Mr De Valera has at long last admitted his defeat and acknowledged his grave and serious error which plunged the country into as terrible a condition as ever inflicted a land. If he had the sense and judgment to take this step only twelve months ago he would have saved many hundreds of valuable lives among his own followers as well as among his countrymen and spared his country the moral waste and ruin he can never make good. He caused Ireland to lose some one hundred millions of its money, and now at the bitter, bloody end he admits his mistake.'

On the other side was a group of about twelve papers that, while deploring the strife of the past eleven months, were glad that de Valera and his anti-Treatyite colleagues had come to 'see sense' and were anxious to put the past behind them and move forward to the national task of reconstruction. The *Nenagh Guardian* (2 June), in an editorial titled 'Peace – and the Future', opined: 'Fighting has almost entirely ceased, and we may now look forward to more settled conditions in the political and social life of the country. The great need, henceforth, is hard, unremitting work to repair the losses of the past. We must become strong industrially and commercially ... stringent economy must be applied to the finances and administration of the nation ... It is still within our power to Gaelicise every nerve and every institution within the Free State, and unless we relentlessly pursue our efforts to that end all the sacrifices of the past will be in vain.' For the *Carlow Nationalist* (2 June), while all deeply deplored the fratricidal strife and wanton destruction of property of the last year, there was 'no use talking of the past ... the first thing wanted now is national unity'. The paper took its cue from the 'words of wisdom' and 'message of conciliation' of a recent speech of Minister of Home Affairs Kevin O'Higgins (whose elderly father had been murdered at his home by republicans a few months earlier): 'if those who had been opposed to them would now become a political party within the nation to press any claim they might have, then the country would quickly forget what had happened.' The *Southern Star* (9 June) exulted that 'the supremacy of the people has been vindicated. Every right-minded citizen is rejoicing at the restoration of law and order, which is being effected far more quickly than was expected ... the country is slowly and steadily returning to normality.'

For the small number of papers sympathetic to the anti-Treatyite side, full-throated support for 'Irregular' actions and criticism of the government's war policies were inhibited by the military censorship. Commentary from this quarter was thus inevitably subdued. The opinion of the *Meath Chronicle* on de Valera's peace proposals has already been described. The *Waterford News* (25 May) limited itself to publishing an Associated Press report on the end of the hostilities, quoting extensively from de Valera's statement, which it viewed as a guideline on 'how to provide a basis for peaceful political action'. The *Mayo News* (2 June) simply reprinted the text of the latter's message to the 'Rearguard'.

For many years after the end of the Civil War, little effort was made on either side to make a reliable count of the casualties of the conflict.

Such research has been undertaken only in the past two decades. The best current (as of 2022) estimate is of between 1,500 and 1,700 deaths for the period January 1922 to November 1924, comprising 800-900 National Army, at least 426 IRA and 300-400 civilian deaths. Numbers wounded are assumed to be a multiple of this figure but are much harder to determine.[13]

Despite the national trauma of four years of death and destruction, in facing the challenges that lay ahead, the *Connacht Tribune* (26 May) probably spoke for a practically unanimous body of opinion when it took comfort from the words of Bishop Cohalan of Cork that 'the history of the past ten months has proved that Irishmen can rule themselves, and gives ground for hoping for a bright and prosperous future for the country … heartening words … helpful to those on whom the task, difficult in all truth, has been thrust of maintaining ordered government and the reign of law in the country.'

Press commentary for the late 1921-23 period is summarised in Chart 7.

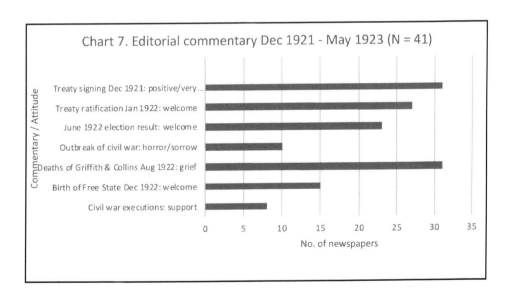

Chapter 9

CONCLUSIONS

The evidence presented in the foregoing chapters documents a dramatic shift in political allegiance in a significant number of provincial newspapers between late 1916 and the watershed event of the revolutionary period, the general election of December 1918. An analysis of editorial commentary relating to this shift can reveal those political issues that were uppermost in the concerns of the writers and, by extension, in the minds of their readers.

In terms of the evolution of their political allegiances through the period, the forty-two newspapers studied may be divided into three groups. The first is a group of seventeen which maintained loyalty to the Irish Party and its leadership (Redmond until his death in March 1918, Dillon from then until December 1918) throughout the period. The second is a group of fifteen which supported the Party at the time of the 1916 rebellion but by late 1918 had deserted it, either, as in the case of twelve, to support the policies of Sinn Féin, or, in the case of three, to adopt a neutral stance as between the Irish Party and Sinn Féin. Of the remaining ten, four had been either latently or overtly hostile to the Party at the beginning and were predictably in the Sinn Féin camp by the end; four had begun as neutral or apolitical but had embraced Sinn Féin by the end; and two maintained an uncommitted editorial stance throughout the period.

To summarise, as shown in Table 2, in the short space of two years from late 1916 to late 1918, support for the Irish Party and the constitutional policy fell from 76 per cent to 40 per cent of the newspaper sample, while hostility to the Party and support for Sinn Féin rose from 10 per cent to 48 per cent of the papers. The number of uncommitted newspapers did not change appreciably (14 per cent to 12 per cent).

These proportions of near-equality of newspaper support for the two main political groups at the time of the 1918 election do not support the notion – one that has prevailed for many decades – of a complete rout of constitutional nationalism in the wake of the Easter rebellion. However, comparing them with the results of the election, they fail to predict the share of the popular vote won by Sinn Féin (just over twice its rival's vote – 48 per cent against the Party's 23 per cent). The disparity may be explained in terms of the tendency of newspaper editors and proprietors to belong to the traditional nationalist establishment, to view politics conservatively and to be more reluctant to abandon the constitutional approach than the newly enfranchised electorate as a whole.

What were the political issues that brought about this extraordinary shift in loyalties? Turning to the issues that galvanised newspaper opinion, it is clear that, in early 1914, the Ulster issue, first intruded as an obstacle to the Home Rule Bill's progress in 1912 and now taking the form of a proposal for temporary partition, was foremost (see Chapter 2). The unenthusiastic reception of the March 1914 proposal of temporary partition by a large majority (78 per cent) of the papers was confirmed by the overwhelmingly hostile response (95 per cent) to the announcement in July of the Buckingham Palace Conference. Most of the papers commenting took exception to the fact that the conference was taking place at all, interpreting it (correctly) as an attempt to extract a further concession on partition from nationalist Ireland, and indignantly dismissed the talk of civil war as a unionist political ploy.

Redmond was saved from a serious backlash only by his intransigence and the consequent breakdown of the conference. Any questioning as to why he and Dillon had allowed themselves to become involved in the conference was averted by the breathtaking succession of events that followed. The outbreak of the Great War within little more than a week, the pro-British stance adopted by Redmond, the sharp oscillation in nationalist sentiment following the deaths at Bachelor's Walk, the proposal that the Volunteers might defend the coasts of the island, the seven-week preoccupation with the placing of the Home Rule Act on the Statute Book and the subsequent recruiting call for nationalists to enlist in the British forces all seemed to lend the future a great deal more fluidity than theretofore imagined.

Nevertheless, amid the celebrations of the royal assent, something under a third of the papers were restrained in their jubilation by worries about the promised amending bill and Asquith's pledge that the coercion of Ulster was 'unthinkable'. That the issue was still there in 1915, though in abeyance, is clear from the response in May to the formation of the coalition government, when half of the thirty papers that commented expressed misgivings regarding the implications for Home Rule of the return of Unionist ministers to the Cabinet (see Chapter 3). The partition issue was not always mentioned explicitly, but it was evident that the concern was that either the Home Rule Act might be postponed indefinitely or the pressure for a strong amending bill would become stronger as the implementation of the Act drew nearer. The partition issue thus had the potential to cause serious trouble for the Irish Party long before it actually did so. These considerations form the indispensable context for what would happen in 1916.

Before assessing the after-effects of the rebellion on public sentiment relating to Home Rule and the Irish Party, it is worth recapitulating the issues that did not cause serious trouble for the Party. The agitation against war taxation that took place in the early months of 1916 may be taken as a lightning-rod for the wider discontents that circulated in nationalist society relating to the prolongation of the war and the continued postponement of Home Rule. Chapter 3 demonstrates that, of nineteen newspapers that expressed a view, a mere seven, most of them already in the small anti-Party camp, took up the campaign with any vigour and only one directly attacked the Party's handling of the issue. Even after the rebellion (see Chapter 4), although unease at the future of Home Rule remained, criticism of the finances of the Home Rule

Act was confined to six papers (despite the sustained crusade of the *Irish Independent* on this topic), while thirty-two papers expressed confidence in the Act and looked forward to its implementation, and twenty-seven expressed confidence in the Party and its leadership.

Neither did the rebellion have negative direct consequences for the Irish Party. John Dillon's ambivalent speech in the House of Commons on 12 May steadied the nerves of those Party supporters who otherwise might have inclined to an abandonment of sympathy with constitutional methods. Despite the century-long dominance of the narrative, originated by the IRB Supreme Council member and Sinn Féin propagandist P.S. O'Hegarty, of a 'revulsion of feeling' in the country caused by the executions of the rebellion's leaders that brought about the radical change in sentiment that led to the fall of the Irish Party,[1] press criticism of the executions and martial law was relatively muted and confined to fourteen papers, less than half the number (29) that condemned the rebellion itself. Of the few papers that expressed anger, only one hinted at a withdrawal of its support for the Party.

The revulsion of feeling that did occur arose later from the recrudescence of the issue that had been most prominent in nationalist politics before the war and had not gone away. The publication in June 1916 of Lloyd George's plan for immediate implementation of the Home Rule Act accompanied by provisional partition of a six-county Ulster bloc, a substantial advance for Ulster unionists on the temporary partition scheme of 1914, aroused an unparalleled degree of engagement, both in extent and in intensity, with all but one of the papers in the sample commenting negatively on it and 44 per cent of those refusing to entertain it in any form, temporary or permanent. The sensitivity of the issue and its potential to damage the Party were underlined by the vehemently rejectionist attitude of the Ulster nationalist papers, reflecting that of the powerful Ulster Catholic bishops, and, at a nationwide level, the relentless anti-partition campaign waged by the hugely influential *Irish Independent*.

Notwithstanding the fact that a couple of hitherto loyal newspapers were already prepared to reconsider their support for the Party should the 'dismemberment' deal go ahead, the real damage to the Party occurred in the wake of Redmond's repudiation of the plan. When blame was being apportioned for the breakdown, it was difficult to know in some cases whether it was for the fact that Home Rule had not been delivered or for the partition measure contained in the deal; seven (19 per cent) of thirty-seven papers that had fiercely rejected the latter also castigated the British government for its betrayal of the deal. In any case, fifteen papers, amounting to a significant 38 per cent of the commenting papers, were prepared to lay some or all of the blame on Redmond's entire participation in the Lloyd George initiative. A smaller group, comprising previously loyal titles and newly emboldened long-term critics of the Party, took their cue from the *Irish Independent* in denouncing the Party and calling for the heads of its leaders.

This was the key moment in the beginning of the Party's decline. From now on, it would face a phenomenon it had never experienced since its reunification in 1900 – a large and growing body of nationalist opinion that had written off its capacity to achieve nationalist aspirations. The results were evident in the consecutive by-election losses in 1917 and the defection of more hitherto loyal newspapers.

The partition issue was at its most potent between the autumn of 1916 and the summer of 1917. The collapse of the deal of summer 1916 had removed the vague sense of benign possibility that had persisted around the question of Ulster and the amending bill since September 1914 – a vagueness encapsulated in Redmond's aspirational talk of a new united Irish identity being forged in the heat of a common struggle at the Front. Now that implementation of the Act had come to the top of the practical agenda, matters were returned to where they had stood on the eve of the war and immediately after the breakdown of the Buckingham Palace talks, that is to say, to the status of nationalist–unionist deadlock. The Irish Party was seen to have failed to deliver the only Home Rule worth having, Home Rule for the whole island.

The failure, embodied in the defeat of T.P. O'Connor's House of Commons 'self-determination' motion of March 1917 (the humiliation would be repeated in the Party's last hurrah, the self-determination motion of November 1918) was evident to its own members and supporters, leading to their utter demoralisation. The late Conor Cruise O'Brien wrote of his own Home Rule family: 'It was not so much the loss of the counties themselves … The source of the anguish was the impact on us inside the Catholic and nationalist community … of the tragic and unexpected flaw that had suddenly revealed itself in the whole Home Rule project – and at the very moment of its seeming triumph.'[2]

A constitutional policy that had manifestly failed stood little chance against the simplistic certainties of Sinn Féin. The Irish Party's resolute anti-conscription stance during the crisis of 1918 failed to prevent further droves of its supporters from going over to Sinn Féin. However, after the landslide victory of Éamon de Valera in East Clare in July 1917, the status of the partition issue changed again. It had served its purpose in discrediting the Irish Party, and a triumphant Sinn Féin was now burdened with the difficult responsibility for accomplishing what the Party had failed to do. With Sinn Féin in the driving seat, partition was buried under the catch-cries of 'independence' and 'the Republic' and very little was heard of the Ulster issue from that side in the 1918 election campaign. Many voters would have been hard put to tell the practical difference between the powers of self-government promised by the Home Rule Act and those to be conferred by Sinn Féin's 'independence'. It is hard not to view the campaigning platform of the latter as a displacement issue designed, consciously or otherwise, to draw attention away from the intractable complexities of the Ulster issue. Time would show that Sinn Féin would be no more successful with the partition issue than had the Irish Party – but that was all in the future.

As the election results came in during December, John Dillon seemed at first to believe the election would return a small bloc of 20-25 Irish Party MPs. But he reckoned without the almost complete collapse of morale within the Party – the effect of the combined failure of the two parliamentary 'self-determination' debates of 1917 and 1918 and of the

Irish convention to deliver all-Ireland Home Rule by constitutional means, all of them the consequences of the Ulster issue.

The post-election scene of early 1919 was ushered in by the convening of the first Dáil Éireann, accompanied by the first outbreak of political violence. The victors of the election had a substantial majority of nationalist opinion behind its declared policies of seeking a place at the Paris Peace Conference and implementing its mandate for independence. This body of opinion was reflected in the half of the provincial press that gave its backing to Sinn Féin. With a couple of exceptions, the former Redmondite press (the 40 per cent of the sample that had campaigned for the Irish Party in the election) accepted the election result with good grace, however sceptical it might be regarding the chances of the victorious party obtaining a hearing in Paris, or, even more implausibly, winning recognition of a republic.

The early stages of the campaign of killings of policemen and other agents of the Crown evoked disparate responses from the two sections of the press (see Chapter 6). The shooting of the two RIC men at Soloheadbeg in January 1919 was condemned by one neutral and one pro-Sinn Féin paper, both of them from the immediate county, as well as by two Redmondite papers from further away. The murder two months later of Resident Magistrate Milling in Westport received condemnation from eleven papers, nine of them Redmondite and two pro-Sinn Féin organs, one of the latter denying that the murder could have anything to do with that organisation. The clearest division on the question of violence occurred over the publication of clerical condemnation in the wake of killings. By the autumn, with the death toll of police mounting, at least four newspapers, three of them Redmondite, one neutral, had published denunciations by clergymen and by elected local government bodies. This brought its own reaction from the pro-Sinn Féin camp, four of whose papers trenchantly criticised the clerics in question and insisted that the blame for all violent incidents lay with the British government and its failure to address the political stalemate. The most newsworthy violent event of 1919 was the attempted assassination of Lord French in December, an action that received much news coverage but elicited condemnation from only six newspapers, all of them Redmondite.

The killing in March 1920 of the lord mayor of Cork, Sinn Féin activist and leader of one of Cork's IRA brigades, Thomas MacCurtain, in his home at night by masked assailants widely suspected to be members of the RIC, brought the two sections of the press together in forthright condemnation, though the Redmondite organs were more disposed to place the murder against the background of the assassination campaign being waged against the police, while the pro-Sinn Féin papers saw it as a further provocation by a repressive government or counselled a stoic expectation of such deeds as the price of resistance to its policies. The onset of the British reprisals policy that followed the MacCurtain murder had the effect of silencing the denunciations of specific IRA actions by the Redmondite papers and turning their protests into a generalised hand-wringing at the dreadful conditions to which the country was reduced.

A small number of Redmondite organs voiced support for the August peace conference chaired by Sir Horace Plunkett and campaigned (along with much of the British press) for the release from prison of the hunger-striking Terence MacSwiney, MacCurtain's successor. Their voices were drowned out by an equally small number of pro-Sinn Féin editorials that wanted no truck with solutions that proposed dominion Home Rule with partition.

After the situation had worsened further by November 1920, all of the Redmondite papers implicitly, and at least seven explicitly, took up the Tuam Archbishop Gilmartin's call for a Christmas 'Truce of God'. It was notable that the call also received support from three pro-Sinn Féin papers, including the *Roscommon Journal*, which, uniquely among its peers, had earlier given prominent coverage to a letter appealing for an end to the campaign of shootings of policemen, this 'senseless and cruel vendetta'. Two Redmondite and two pro-Sinn Féin organs reprinted Cork Bishop Cohalan's pastoral letter threatening excommunication on anyone taking part in murderous actions, to be met with an editorial counter-blast from *The Kerryman* and a reminder from an allied paper that 'All wish for peace, but there must be no back-down in the National demand for full self-determination'.

Whatever the differences among the provincial papers on the morality or utility of IRA violence, there was near-complete unanimity on the British government's attempt to break the political deadlock launched at the end of 1919. At every stage of the progress through parliament of the fourth Home Rule Bill (officially, the Government of Ireland Bill), the united response of the newspapers was outrage, contempt and derision. Part of this was directed at the government's severe and unrealistic curtailing of the powers devolved in the 1914 Home Rule Act, beyond whose provisions even Redmondite demands had long ago moved. However, the fact that the bill's most common shorthand designation was 'The Partition Bill' explained everything as to the chief grounds of its rejection – its proposal to create two parliaments in a divided island. Evidently the partition issue was still as potent in the country as it had been in 1916–17 when it had destroyed the Irish Party. In addition, the commonly held view that it was a malign device of the British government 'intended to kill the spirit of Irish nationality', as the *Carlow Nationalist* wrote in May 1921, showed that there had been no increase in understanding of the Ulster unionist outlook in the meantime. The mass signing of the Solemn League and Covenant in 1912 by half a million Ulster men and women might never have happened, and the halting attempts at conciliation embodied in the temporary partition plan of 1914 were a distant memory. Comment was instead dominated by the venting of indignation and anger at the machinations of a government acting always at the 'behest' of the small gang of Tory conspirators led by the nose by the demonic Carson, the most hated name in nationalist Ireland. The peak of enlightenment attained by the press was encapsulated in some of the editorials of the *Tuam Herald* which, while condemning 'the unnatural division of Ireland', acknowledged that Ulster represented a difficult problem to be dealt with and tried to keep its language within the bounds of civil and conciliatory discourse.

It was thus no surprise that the provincial press, in line with the Dublin papers, should greet the opening of the Northern Ireland Parliament in June 1921 with the traditional weapons of venom and derision that had always compensated for nationalist impotence in its attempts to influence Ulster unionist sentiment. To this was added an unfair attempt to paint the unionist community as a whole as responsible for the rioting and the attacks on Catholics, an indictment that mocked the high-minded sentiments expressed by the king and unionist dignitaries at the opening ceremonies.

The Devlin–Clune peace moves of late 1920 had foundered apparently on Lloyd George's insistence that the IRA surrender its arms, but in reality because, according to Charles Townshend, 'neither side was yet really under enough pressure from events or its own public opinion to compromise its objectives'. Between midwinter and midsummer 1921, this situation changed. By June, the pressure of British public opinion had forced the government to abandon its reprisals policy, and this was matched by the pressure of events on the IRA as its capacity to carry the fight to its enemy was seen to have peaked. As for the state of nationalist public opinion, its overwhelming demand for an end to the violence was amply demonstrated by the predominant sentiments of joy and relief with which the newspapers greeted the news of the July truce, and the absence of any significant editorial voices calling for a prolongation of the campaign. The setting up of the Northern Ireland parliament also freed Lloyd George to come to terms with Sinn Féin from a stronger position than before, since the nationalist side, in negotiating any settlement, would now have to deal, not with an easily decried 'Carson gang' but with the *fait accompli* of a democratically elected statutory body representing unionists, one that would be given the legal power to opt out of any all-Ireland institutions that might be established.

The most notable feature of press coverage during the eleven-month period from the truce to the general election of June 1922 was the birth of a new consensus. Papers that had carried the residues of the Irish Party–Sinn Féin controversies into the years after 1918, differing on questions such as attitudes to political violence and Sinn Féin strategy, were now at one on the big political issues of the day. Levels of enthusiastic editorial support rose from nineteen of thirty-two papers (59 per cent) in the case of the truce to twenty-three of thirty-four (68 per cent) for the signing of the Treaty and again to twenty-seven of thirty-two (84 per cent) for the Dáil's ratification of the Treaty. The Redmondite papers in particular took to the Treaty terms with gusto, probably because they closely resembled the dominion Home Rule platform on which they had campaigned in the 1918 general election. Many of the pro-Sinn Féin papers supporting the Treaty, by contrast, found themselves having to backtrack considerably on stances they had recently adopted. For example, the *Meath Chronicle*, in repudiating the August 1920 peace conference, had lashed Ireland's last chief secretary, Hamar Greenwood, for fostering 'the delusion that he can get rid of the Irish Question by a patent nostrum, which might be named Dominion Home Rule'. Likewise, the *Mayo News* had observed of the sponsors of the same conference that 'their panacea is apparently Dominion Home Rule with partition, and this scheme is already damned by the great mass of the Irish people'. With the name Free State substituted and some other symbolic differences, the new settlement was essentially the same as that against which they had held out a year previously. Criticism of the exclusion of the Ulster counties was remarkably muted, considering how explosive the partition issue had been in the recent past, but not all the papers were as clear-eyed as the *Sligo Champion* in taking it for granted that the 'Six County Parliament' would exercise its right to contract out of the Free State with the consequential need for a customs barrier and a land frontier. Most could only turn to hope or self-deception for consolation. It was left to the veteran Redmondite P.J. Hayden, in his *Westmeath Examiner*, to ruminate on whether it had all been worth the price paid in lives and destruction.

Redmondite and Sinn Féin papers were on the same side in deploring the situation of lawlessness that prevailed in the first half of 1922; in their shock at the inflammatory March speeches of de Valera, the increasing military assertiveness of the anti-Treaty IRA and the attacks on newspapers such as the *Clonmel Nationalist*; and in their common dread of the forces that were driving Irishmen towards fratricidal strife. The consensus that had pertained to the Treaty now extended to the results of the June general election, with twenty-three of thirty-one papers (74 per cent) welcoming the assertion of the people's will on the Treaty (at least four other papers chose not to comment though their support for it was not in doubt), while even those that were lukewarm admitted that popular support was overwhelming.

The press consensus persisted through the early stages of the Civil War, with the complication that some papers in anti-Treatyite-held areas were forced to publish republican propaganda. That consensus broke down over the drastic measures introduced by the Provisional Government after the expiry of its amnesty offer to 'Irregular' combatants in mid-October. The executions, first of Erskine Childers, then of other 'Irregular' prisoners under the Public Safety Act, followed by the shooting of the four leaders of the Four Courts garrison in reprisal for the shooting of two TDs, received the support of only eight of thirty-one (26 per cent) commenting papers, with seven against. The objectors were all among the pro-Sinn Féin wing; Redmondite papers were either supportive or stayed quiet.

By the date of the official establishment of the Irish Free State in December 1922, the nationalist provincial press had come full circle. Starting from a near-consensus in support of the demand for all-Ireland Home Rule, it had been split into two camps by the intractable and fissiparous issue of partition, only to end in a new near-consensus in support of an implemented enhanced dominion version of Home Rule coupled with a grudging acceptance of and acquiescence in partition. The consensus would appear to fracture again in later years as elections brought to power a new party committed to rolling back the terms of the Treaty. But insofar as it related to the determination to bring this about by strictly constitutional methods, it became an unbreakable consensus, one that has now lasted a century.

NOTES

Introduction

1   John Horgan, 'Reporting 1916 in the North of Ireland: a study in the political equivalent of the Doppler effect' (November 2015), Newspaper & Periodical History Forum of Ireland, Eighth Annual Conference, Univ. College Dublin, 13 & 14 November 2015: 'Reporting Revolution: What the Papers said'. doras.dcu. ie/21611/2/NPHSI_Conference_Presentation_2015.pdf

Chapter 1

1   Larkin, F. "A great daily organ",: the *Freeman's Journal*, 1763–1924', in *History Ireland*, May-June 2006, vol. 14.

2   Meleady, D. *Redmond the Parnellite* (Cork, 2008)

3   Callanan, F. *Timothy Michael Healy* (Cork, 1996)

4   Larkin, F. "A great daily organ", 2006

5   Freud, S. *Civilization and Its Discontents* (1929–30).

6   Bingham, A., 'Monitoring the popular press: An historical perspective', *History and Policy*, May 2005.

7   Foster, R. 'How Ireland was robbed of Hugh Lane's great art collection,' *The Guardian*, 30 May 2015.

Chapter 2

1   Meleady, D. *John Redmond: the National Leader* (Dublin 2014)

Chapter 4

1   Ó Drisceoil, D. '"Sledge hammers and blue pencils": Censorship, suppression and the Irish regional press, 1916–23', *The Irish Regional Press, 1892–2018: Revival, Revolution and Republic*, eds. I. Kenneally and J.T. O'Donnell, pp.141-155.

2   *Ibid.*, p.144.

Chapter 5

1   Doughan, C. 'A supplementary nationalism: the emergence of the Irish provincial press before independence', *The Irish Regional Press, 1892–2018: Revival, Revolution and Republic*, eds I. Kenneally and J.T. O'Donnell 2018, p.112.

Chapter 6

1   Townshend, C., *The Republic: The Fight for Irish Independence, 1918–1923* (London: Penguin, 2013), pp.86-7.

2   Healy, J., 'The three Joes and the Westport murder', *Mayo News*, https://www.mayonews.ie/comment-opinion/down-memory-lane/28878-the-three-joes-and-the-westport-murder.

3   Townshend, C., *The Republic* (London: Penguin), p.97.

4   Up to 6,500 Belgian civilians were killed by German forces in the first three months of the Great War (August–November 1914), compared with 200 Irish civilians killed by all sides in the twenty-six counties that became the Free State in the three years 1919–21, and none at all killed at the time this comment was made in September 1919.

5   'Sean T. O'Ceallaigh and George Gavan Duffy to Georges Clemenceau Paris', 3 June 1919, Document No. 14 NAI DFA ES Paris 1919, Documents in Irish Foreign Policy.

6   Townshend, C., *The Republic* (London: Penguin), pp.100-01.

7   Larkin, F. 'The slow death of the *Freeman's Journal*', guest post, https://www.markholan.org/archives/6957.

8   Bielenberg, K., '"If you are wise, you will forget my face" – IRA gunman told Independent editor' *Irish Independent*, 21 December 2019.

9   Fanning, R. *Fatal Path: British Government and Irish Revolution 1910–1922* (London: Faber & Faber, 2013), pp.202-4.

10 *Ibid.*, p.206.

Chapter 7

1   Townshend, C., *The Republic: The Fight for Irish Independence, 1918–1923* (London: Penguin, 2013), pp.121-3.

2   The last-named victim was Alan Bell, a banking lawyer engaged on behalf of Dublin Castle in the investigation of concealed bank deposits containing the Republican Loan Funds, which was being managed by Michael Collins. His assassination having been ordered by Collins, Bell was dragged off a tram in Dublin city centre and shot dead on the street. *Ibid.*, p.192.

3   *Ibid.*, pp.115, 137; Charles Townshend, *The British Campaign in Ireland 1919–21* (Oxford: Oxford University Press, 1975), pp.92-7.

4   Townshend, C., *The Republic: The Fight for Irish Independence, 1918–1923* (London: Penguin, 2013), pp. 124-130.

5   Campbell, F. and O'Shiel, K, 'The last land war? Kevin O'Shiel's memoir of the Irish Revolution (1916–21)', *Archivium Hibernicum*, vol. 57, pp.155-200. The agitation affected many counties of the north and south midlands.

6   There was grim irony in the fact that the victim was a close relative of Capt. John Shawe-Taylor who had played a pivotal role in bringing together the land conference of 1902 of tenant and landlord representatives, which paved the way for the hugely successful Wyndham Land Purchase Act of 1903. The act would raise the proportion of land purchased by tenants from 18 per cent to 61 per cent by 1915. Campbell,

F. *Land and Revolution: Nationalist Politics in the West of Ireland, 1891–1921* (Oxford: Oxford University Press, 2005), pp.90-91.

7   Meleady, D. *John Redmond: The National Leader* (Dublin: Irish Academic Press, 2014), pp.274, 291 n.114.

8   Townshend, C., *The Republic: The Fight for Irish Independence, 1918–1923* (London: Penguin, 2013), pp.173-4.

9   *Ibid.*, pp.174-6.

10 See Chapter 7, note 1.

11 Townshend, C., *The Republic: The Fight for Irish Independence, 1918–1923* (London: Penguin, 2013), pp. 217-8.

12 *Ibid.*, pp.223-4

13 *Ibid.*, pp.176-9.

14 *Ibid.*, pp.273-88, 301-05

Chapter 8

1   Townshend, C., *The Republic: The Fight for Irish Independence, 1918–1923* (London: Penguin, 2013), pp.384-86.

2   *Ibid.*, pp.389-92.

3   *Ibid.*, p.381.

4   Cunningham, C. *The Social Geography of Violence During the Belfast Troubles, 1920–22* (Manchester: CRESC, University of Manchester, 2013).

5   Hart, H. *The IRA and its Enemies: Violence and Community in Cork, 1916–1923* (Oxford: Oxford University Press, 1998).

6   Pyne, P. 'The third Sinn Féin party: 1923–26', in *Economic and Social Review*, vol.1, no. 1, pp.29-50.

7   Dáil Éireann Debate, 19 May 1922, https://www.oireachtas.ie/en/debates/debate/dail/1922-05-19/4/.

8   National Police Officers Roll of Honour: https://www.policerollofhonour.org.uk/forces/ireland_to_1922/; Townshend, C., *The Republic: The Fight for Irish Independence, 1918–1923* (London: Penguin, 2013), pp.370-74.

9   Gallagher, M. 'The Pact General Election of 1922', in *Irish Historical Studies*, vol. 21, no. 84, pp.404-21.

10 Townshend, C., *The Republic: The Fight for Irish Independence, 1918–1923* (London: Penguin, 2013), pp.403-4.

11 *Ibid.*, p.442.

12 See *Dundalk Democrat*, 9 Dec 1922, for a superb editorial account of Healy's political career.

13 'Report on talk, 'Establishing the Free State in conflict', archived 20 July 2018; 22 June 2015; National Graves Association, *The Last Post*, (Dublin: National Graves Association, 1985), pp.130-154; Dorney, J. *The Civil War in Kildare* (Dublin, 2011).

Chapter 9

1   O'Hegarty, P.S. *The Victory of Sinn Fein: How It Won It, and How It Used It* (Dublin: University College Dublin, 1924).

2   Conor Cruise O'Brien, *Memoir: My Life and Themes* (Dublin, 1998), p. 7.

INDEX

INDEX OF NEWSPAPERS